HJJ STEFAN LAMBERT WORKING HARD LOWRIDER BIKE LOWRIDER BIKE PART LOWRIDER BIKE FROM
BY MY 1ST BABY HEAVY CHEVY MERCEDES BENZ NEXT INTERIOR PICS YOU LIKE MY CHOICE READY TO
IGGLE WIGGLE KIDO HAH SO FRESH AND SO CLEAN CLEAN BIANCA WARE CAR 13 BANK SCARFACE 100
TIME TO GO CARS TRUCKS CARS HONDAS 2007 300 22 THE CUTLASS WELO SUCH A SHOW OFF CHEVY
TROY FACET PHOTOGRAPHY HIT ME BACK DIS IS MY GATOR CHEVY IMPALA HER NAME IS TJ N A GATOR
O BLUE CHOPPER THIS IS AN AWESOME CAR TURBO BU   MAINE CAMION
WHAT 63 IMPALA LOWRIDER JOHANA HIS RANFLA 1963 IMPALA   MY LIL LOW LOW
3X7 CHEVY CHEVROLET INTAKE INTERIOR 1963 IMPALA 4   YUKON MY LOW
DREAMCARS XTERRA LOWRIDER MUSTANG ROLLIN ON T   EFAN LAMBERT
TANG WWW OGOGOG COM TRUCK XTREME IMAGE RIDE B   ST BABY HEAVY
ON BLUEBERRY HILL REACHING THE PEAK TO SUCCESS   BOMB DIGGLE WIGGLE KIDO HAH
DIS R MY GIRLS 66 CHEVY N 04 TOYOTA TACOMA DIS R MY GIRLS LEGENDARY TIME TO GO CARS TRUCKS
EL PUMPS DAYTONS TV CHROME DV LOW SIEMPRE FIRME NISSAN 370Z TROY FACET PHOTOGRAPHY HIT
1 CAPRICE CLASSIC AFTER THE CAR WASH MOTO LOWRIDER BLUE MOTO BLUE CHOPPER THIS IS AN
2 S 94 CHEVY JUICED ME AND MY 95 LOVEINIT LA MEXICAN MAFIA HATERS WHAT 63 IMPALA LOWRIDER
TLASS SUPREME 13X7 LOWRIDER OLDS CUTLASS SUPREME LOWRIDER 13X7 CHEVY CHEVROLET INTAKE
INE ESPANOLA NM MY 94 CHEVY ON 22 WILL HONDA G35 SNOWED IN DREAMCARS XTERRA LOWRIDER
DER BIKE PART LOWRIDER BIKE FROM WWW TOPLOWRIDER 2007 MUSTANG WWW OGOGOG COM TRUCK
PICS YOU LIKE MY CHOICE READY TO HIT SWITCHES PUTTIN THE BAGS ON BLUEBERRY HILL REACHING
CA WARE CAR 13 BANK SCARFACE 100 GLODEN MI OTRA S10 MY BF RID3 DIS R MY GIRLS 66 CHEVY N 04
S WELO SUCH A SHOW OFF CHEVY CAPRICE WAGON HYDRAULICS 3 WHEEL PUMPS DAYTONS TV CHROME
A HER NAME IS TJ N A GATOR CHEVY CAPRICE AIR RIDE SHAVED 1991 CAPRICE CLASSIC AFTER THE CAR
DE AND JAZMAINE CAMION SKITTLES SKITTLES CAR MI DONK W 22 S 94 CHEVY JUICED ME AND MY 95
MY ART WORK MY LIL LOW LOW THE BOSS 516 SUPERMARIO OLDS CUTLASS SUPREME 13X7 LOWRIDER
P BONESBLACKYUKON MY LOW LOW 1963 LOW RIDER MY NISSAN SKYLINE ESPANOLA NM MY 94 CHEVY
Y RIDE HJJ STEFAN LAMBERT WORKING HARD LOWRIDER BIKE LOWRIDER BIKE PART LOWRIDER BIKE
MY BABY MY 1ST BABY HEAVY CHEVY MERCEDES BENZ NEXT INTERIOR PICS YOU LIKE MY CHOICE READY
MB DIGGLE WIGGLE KIDO HAH SO FRESH AND SO CLEAN CLEAN BIANCA WARE CAR 13 BANK SCARFACE
RY TIME TO GO CARS TRUCKS CARS HONDAS 2007 300 22 THE CUTLASS WELO SUCH A SHOW OFF CHEVY
TROY FACET PHOTOGRAPHY HIT ME BACK DIS IS MY GATOR CHEVY IMPALA HER NAME IS TJ N A GATOR
O BLUE CHOPPER THIS IS AN AWESOME CAR TURBO BUICK REGAL HOMICIDE AND JAZMAINE CAMION
WHAT 63 IMPALA LOWRIDER JOHANA HIS RANFLA 1963 IMPALA MY CAR MY ART WORK MY LIL LOW LOW
3X7 CHEVY CHEVROLET INTAKE INTERIOR 1963 IMPALA 4 DOOR HARDTOP BONESBLACKYUKON MY LOW
DREAMCARS XTERRA LOWRIDER MUSTANG ROLLIN ON TRUES VOGEES MY RIDE HJJ STEFAN LAMBERT
TANG WWW OGOGOG COM TRUCK XTREME IMAGE RIDE BIG MY 2ND BABY MY BABY MY 1ST BABY HEAVY
ON BLUEBERRY HILL REACHING THE PEAK TO SUCCESS SITTING LOW BOMB DIGGLE WIGGLE KIDO HAH
DIS R MY GIRLS 66 CHEVY N 04 TOYOTA TACOMA DIS R MY GIRLS LEGENDARY TIME TO GO CARS TRUCKS
EL PUMPS DAYTONS TV CHROME DV LOW SIEMPRE FIRME NISSAN 370Z TROY FACET PHOTOGRAPHY HIT
1 CAPRICE CLASSIC AFTER THE CAR WASH MOTO LOWRIDER BLUE MOTO BLUE CHOPPER THIS IS AN
2 S 94 CHEVY JUICED ME AND MY 95 LOVEINIT LA MEXICAN MAFIA HATERS WHAT 63 IMPALA LOWRIDER
TLASS SUPREME 13X7 LOWRIDER OLDS CUTLASS SUPREME LOWRIDER 13X7 CHEVY CHEVROLET INTAKE
INE ESPANOLA NM MY 94 CHEVY ON 22 WILL HONDA G35 SNOWED IN DREAMCARS XTERRA LOWRIDER
DER BIKE PART LOWRIDER BIKE FROM WWW TOPLOWRIDER 2007 MUSTANG WWW OGOGOG COM TRUCK
PICS YOU LIKE MY CHOICE READY TO HIT SWITCHES PUTTIN THE BAGS ON BLUEBERRY HILL REACHING
CA WARE CAR 13 BANK SCARFACE 100 GLODEN MI OTRA S10 MY BF RID3 DIS R MY GIRLS 66 CHEVY N 04
S WELO SUCH A SHOW OFF CHEVY CAPRICE WAGON HYDRAULICS 3 WHEEL PUMPS DAYTONS TV CHROME
A HER NAME IS TJ N A GATOR CHEVY CAPRICE AIR RIDE SHAVED 1991 CAPRICE CLASSIC AFTER THE CAR
DE AND JAZMAINE CAMION SKITTLES SKITTLES CAR MI DONK W 22 S 94 CHEVY JUICED ME AND MY 95
MY ART WORK MY LIL LOW LOW THE BOSS 516 SUPERMARIO OLDS CUTLASS SUPREME 13X7 LOWRIDER
P BONESBLACKYUKON MY LOW LOW 1963 LOW RIDER MY NISSAN SKYLINE ESPANOLA NM MY 94 CHEVY
Y RIDE HJJ STEFAN LAMBERT WORKING HARD LOWRIDER BIKE LOWRIDER BIKE PART LOWRIDER BIKE
MY BABY MY 1ST BABY HEAVY CHEVY MERCEDES BENZ NEXT INTERIOR PICS YOU LIKE MY CHOICE READY
MB DIGGLE WIGGLE KIDO HAH SO FRESH AND SO CLEAN CLEAN BIANCA WARE CAR 13 BANK SCARFACE
RY TIME TO GO CARS TRUCKS CARS HONDAS 2007 300 22 THE CUTLASS WELO SUCH A SHOW OFF CHEVY
TROY FACET PHOTOGRAPHY HIT ME BACK DIS IS MY GATOR CHEVY IMPALA HER NAME IS TJ N A GATOR
O BLUE CHOPPER THIS IS AN AWESOME CAR TURBO BUICK REGAL HOMICIDE AND JAZMAINE CAMION
WHAT 63 IMPALA LOWRIDER JOHANA HIS RANFLA 1963 IMPALA MY CAR MY ART WORK MY LIL LOW LOW
3X7 CHEVY CHEVROLET INTAKE INTERIOR 1963 IMPALA 4 DOOR HARDTOP BONESBLACKYUKON MY LOW
DREAMCARS XTERRA LOWRIDER MUSTANG ROLLIN ON TRUES VOGEES MY RIDE HJJ STEFAN LAMBERT

THE CAR IN 2035:
MOBILITY PLANNING FOR
THE NEAR FUTURE

Edited by Kati Rubinyi

Publisher
**THE CIVIC PROJECTS
FOUNDATION**, Los Angeles

Distribution
ActarD
Barcelona - New York
www.actar-d.com
Roca i Batlle 2
08023 Barcelona, Spain
T +34 93 417 49 93
F +34 93 418 67 07
salesbarcelona@actar.com

151 Grand Street, 5th floor
New York, NY 10013, USA
T +1 212 966 2207
F +1 212 966 2214
salesnewyork@actar.com

ISBN 978-84-15391-26-5

Printed in China by
PERMANENT PRINTING LTD.

A Civic Project

Editor
KATI RUBINYI

Design
COLLEEN CORCORAN
TIFFANIE TRAN

Photography (unless otherwise noted)
MONICA NOUWENS

Copy Editing
ELIZABETH PULSINELLI
ERIN JOHNSON

Contributors
Marco Anderson
Alan Dobbins
Steve Finnegan
Jeremy Gilbert-Rolfe
Christopher Gray
Terry A. Hayes
Simon Henley
Mark Hoffman
John Chris Jones
Jeremy Klop
Sang-eun Lee
Steve Mazor
Shannon S. McDonald
Eric Noble
Simon Pastucha
Mohammad Poorsartep
Kati Rubinyi
Tom Smiley
John Stutsman
Doug Suisman
Bill Surber
John Thackara
Bill Trimble
Geoffrey Wardle
Michael Webb

Cover image by Sang-eun Lee.

to the leaders of tomorrow

FOREWORD

Michael Webb

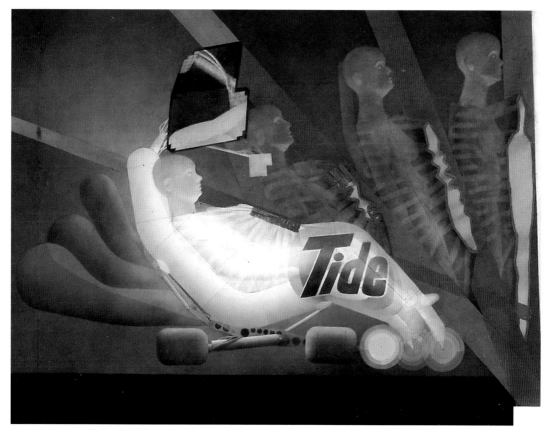

Cushicle, by Michael Webb, 1966.

When an object in common use is super-seded by a more technologically advanced version of itself, we tend to assign the newcomer a name descriptive only of the way it differs from the old, i.e., what it isn't rather than what it is; a name descriptive not of the characteristics it possesses but of those it lacks. When the horseless carriage started proliferating on the streets of London, a Royal Commission was formed from 1904 to 1906 to examine its likely impact. The report produced was sanguine: benefits would include a reduction in the amount of horse manure in the streets with concomitantly fewer flies. Of course, the carriage would never be used for traveling between cities because, well, obviously, there were no roads worth speaking of for it to travel on.

Silly old Royal Commissioners! Consider, though, the impossibility of accurately predicting the future. The likely impact on the study subject of a vast number of variables, tangible and intangible, must be taken into account. How, for example, in 1906, could the commission members have reasonably assumed that nations would be prepared to pave over a goodly chunk of their land surface so as to promote journeys between population centers? How could they have predicted that in the future the power unit of the vehicle would be equivalent to as many as three hundred and twenty-seven horses, rather than the two with which they were familiar? Likewise, today, wouldn't we need to ask how our automotive future might be affected by such tangible considerations as the likelihood of a decision to take global warming seriously, or by the intangibles of fashion or desire, above all desire? For example, why would buyers want to drive a pickup truck almost half of whose length they rarely used? And yet predicting the future market for their products is an essential part of any company's ability to compete. The future is fickle. So they set about not predicting it but creating it. As we have been often told, that's what advertising is. Now your decision to buy that truck is about guts and glory[1]—not about buying a truck with a useless rear half.

And that is roughly the approach the editor of this book and its contributors have taken. They have wisely avoided soothsaying. Instead, the future some of them depict is an idealized present, a future constructed out of images of the present; a present where innovation is embraced unquestioningly by an enlightened public ready to open their hearts and wallets; a present free of killjoys who get in the way and prevent nice things happening; and a present where a project's often quite evident shortcomings seem not to interfere with its smooth functioning. Claiming 2035 as the year in which these wonders will come to pass implies recognition that a twenty-five year time lag exists between the idea and its implementation.

Dating from 1966, the Cushicle project (air cushion vehicle), is more a rumination on the various skins that enclose us than a worthy proposal for future domesticity. The project might best be explained by asking you to imagine a person sitting inside his car inside his garage. He is thus insulated, made an island of, by three concentric skins: the first of wool, cotton, or polyester (his suit of clothes), the second of pressed steel (car) and the third of wood and tile (garage). Now, if he was on his way to a costume party as a mediaeval knight wearing a suit of armor, and if the garage itself was a very untypical metal box, then it might be claimed that the essential difference between the three skins concerns the volume of air enclosed by each, and that the one can meld into the other. In the painting, the room skin is deflated to enclose the bald occupant reclining in her *chaise longue*. The attachment of an air cushion vehicle allows her to whizz around. The deflated room skin, aka suit, has lips that can pull tight or be loosened. As she rises up into the vertical, the lips part. Were another with parting lips to be present, and standing before her, the two suits would become one.

Conversations in the neighborhood greasy spoon among us Archigrammers began to concern buildings as constantly moving and shifting objects. Most buildings were interesting during construction but once completed they just sat around doing nothing. Their static skins revealed nothing of the ever-changing daily lives of their occupants. Video games, with their ever-shifting imagery and, most crucially, the control the user could exercise over that imagery, pointed the way. Out of all this came the Cushicle.

[1] "Guts and glory" is a quote from the 10-grit sandpaper voiceover in an ad for the Dodge Ram 1500 pickup truck.

INTRODUCTION

Kati Rubinyi

THE CAR IN SOUTHERN CALIFORNIA'S FUTURE

With good reason we can assume that our need for mobility in Southern California will only increase and that cars, the most common mode of transportation, are here to stay. It will be difficult, if not impossible, for people in this region to afford to be less mobile, at least in the near future of 2035. Historically, cars did not create the mobility dependence of Southern California, but rather reinforced the interdependence of its far-flung human and natural resources. Even in the earliest days of American settlements in the region, people routinely traveled twenty miles to access raw lumber for construction, or moved agricultural and mining products sixty miles or more. Anaheim, Long Beach, Riverside, San Bernardino, and Los Angeles carried on brisk trade long before there were freeways. The heavy reliance on mobility was characteristic of Southern California from the beginning and continues to offer a huge range of options for people, including opportunities for work and cultural activities. Mobility is one of the factors that turned Southern California into an international mecca for creative activity.

We predict that by 2035, vehicles of a greater variety of sizes, shapes, and degree of automation will comingle on the streets of Southern California. Our decision-making infrastructure should take this challenge as an opportunity to become a facilitator, instead of a barrier, for experimentation in car design, and to positively influence an industry that, even in the recent past, has been notoriously unadaptable and slow to change. Our physical infrastructure, in turn, needs to become responsive to the mobility and urban design implication of various modes and new types of cars.

If transportation and planning professionals considered vehicles and their use from multiple points of view, and at multiple scales, it would smooth the path toward new and improved approaches to vehicle design. We are at an exciting juncture in which to approach the car, streets, and policy more creatively, armed with what we've learned in the three decades since the first oil crisis. We can design and plan our policies and physical environment to accommodate multiple modes of transit, including bicycles and pedestrians, while acknowledging the continuing importance of individual automobile travel in our region's future.

Despite new imperatives for environmental sustainability, our world continues to be shaped by the legacy of the car utopia Futurama.[1] There is broad consensus among the authors of this book that since we've come this far down the path of car-dependence, our streets, cities and region can only benefit from quicker acceptance of technological and design advances in cars. We just need to overcome the obstacles to progress. However, the technological and design improvements will not take place in a vacuum. A study by one author indicates that both the vehicle mix on the roads and any improvements and technological enhancements to streets will strongly reflect economic disparity between neighborhoods. Advances in cars and roadways will not be shared equally.

One question that recurs throughout is how will we cope with the increased variety of both modes and cars, given a physical infrastructure that will remain largely the same as what we have now? What kinds of adaptations will be required of the users of roads, given a crazy mix of sizes and speeds of vehicles, especially since demographics indicate that a great many more of the drivers and pedestrians will be elderly?

At the writing of this book, we can observe the public commons in parts of Southern California deteriorating to levels typically found in the developing world. Luckily, examples abound in the great and even the not-so-great cities of the world of how to create beautiful, uplifting public spaces, great shopping streets, great walking streets, extraordinary bike lanes, and ingenious solutions for how to deal with cars, including where to park them. It's not as if excellence in urban design and planning hasn't been achieved; we don't have to reinvent the wheel. But we have chosen to de-value and underfund our public commons, and although more money would certainly help, it's just a part of the problem. Beneath our physical infrastructure is an underlying decision-making infrastructure in which different kinds of knowledge production (architecture, design, planning, and art, to name a few) assume their roles in hierarchies of professional expertise. These relationships helped establish and now perpetuate the conventions for how our cities are planned, designed and maintained—and it's time for them to be reconfigured. Multiple physical scales in the city should be addressed together, with different types of knowledge-production working collaboratively. We need more flexible relationships, not only between professional roles but also between the usual sequences of steps in a project, in order to achieve synergy between scales of operation. The new hybrid approach has to be efficient, adaptable, project-driven, and implementation-centric. Like design, it will require leaps of faith because it's understood that you don't know the outcome when you start. It also requires open-mindedness and a willingness to experiment and create new sources for funding, sharing ideas across disciplines, and collaborating outside of hierarchies. A rethinking of cars, their roadway infrastructure, and their public policy apparatus is a good subject with which to begin moving this larger project forward.

HOW THINGS WORK

Beyond some basic assumptions that we can all agree on, the authors' versions of 2035 are notably contradictory. I think this reflects the gaps between design and planning, between planning and engineering, between local and regional planning, between social sciences and design, and between design and art. The gaps seem more like chasms most of the time, and anyone familiar with one way of thinking is confronted by an alien landscape when faced with the other.

This book grew out of a discussion group set up for dialogue between domain experts with radically different methodologies for apprehending, predicting, and shaping the future. The result is a fragmentary picture that provides vivid insight into what, in our region, will likely be the same as today, and what is probably going to be different. The contributors come to the subject at hand from a number of non-coplanar directions based on years of experience and professional practice. These practices bring with them beliefs based on evidence about *how things work* (how decisions are made, how money flows, who calls the shots, etc.). These beliefs will, in themselves, have agency in creating the future. But we also know in actuality that things work in an infinite number of ways. Engaging problems from multiple points of view, at multiple scales, and by new arrangements of disciplinary expertise requires rearranging how things work. Admittedly, these kinds of ideas are not new. They were put forward with great eloquence and originality in 1970, in *Design Methods*, by John Chris Jones, the contributor of the last chapter of this book.

IMAGE VERSUS DATASCAPE

The photographs in the book are as important in presenting an idea about the future as the written content. The photographs are not illustrations but rather statements about the present that reflect the future. Moreover, the photographs are generative: the image will create the future. Similarly, the aesthetic and material expressions of our cars, and how we experience them, will determine their future. Throughout the book, the image makes its presence felt, both on its own and in dialogue with another concept, the *datascape*.

The datascape is a full-scale map of the world made of data-points.[2] Many of the authors in this volume anticipate the progress of computation towards this ultimate dream of quantitative research. Every point and movement in space and time will have a corresponding data representation that can be used to enhance efficiency, precision, prediction and customization. This plays out in a number of ways. Networks of sensors will guide our autonomous vehicles safely through our cities in a ballet of optimal traffic flow and real-time control. Transportation planning will benefit from a much finer-grained accuracy of modeling and prediction for the performance capability of cars, roads, and even complex networks of modes of travel. Planners, designers, and developers will be able to generate more realistic visualizations and make more precise assumptions to aid in decision making—financial and otherwise. Current trends suggest that individually tailored revenue collection for infrastructure costs will be one very likely outcome of having a full-scale map of the world. As time goes on and the datascape becomes denser and more pervasive, the image will remain as consequential as it's always been.

THE OTHER FUTURISM

Futurism has two different meanings. One refers to Futurism, the Italian art movement of the early twentieth century that glorified speed, motion, youth, violence, and modernization. The other is the humanistic/empiricist analysis of possible, probable, or preferred futures. Despite sharing a name, the two definitions have little to do with each other except that they are both, in radically different ways, concerned with the future. The historical art movement—which I'll call dirty Futurism—caused a proliferation of

radically new forms in every artistic medium, but was undeniably fascistic, brutal, and dark. This stands in distinction to clean futurism, the application of techniques of social science in predicting and shaping the future for the purposes of improving on the present. This type of futurism is widely practiced by designers, planners, policy makers, and other professions. The car is a link between the two futurisms. It is the focus of the Futurist leader Filippo Tommaso Marinetti's gleeful manifesto of 1909, in which he celebrates the car's dark side through his high-speed encounter with a ditch.[3] By now, we have learned that cars have other even darker sides including but not limited to fatalities, injuries, pollution, and depletion of natural resources.

As distant as the two are from each other, clean futurism has something to gain from the other Futurism. The dirty Futurists undeniably helped create the world in which we live. Their influence on our lives can still be directly felt in art and music, and especially in popular culture, including car culture. Many people, as we know, love cars and will continue to do so. They are physical objects, they move, they come in colors and shapes, they are your own space. They have a lot of compelling attributes that cannot be ignored. Our current clean futurists are right to anticipate and hasten the recuperation of other modes of mobility besides the car. But looking at the car through the lens of both futurism and Futurism creates a productive tension that brings new considerations to debates about mobility and our built environment.

[1] The Futurama exhibit at the 1939 New York World's Fair imagined the world twenty years in the future. It was designed by Norman Bel Geddes.

[2] The term "full-scale map of the world" comes from Jorge Luis Borges's short story "On Exactitude in Science" (1946).

[3] Filippo Tommaso Marinetti, "The Founding and Manifesto of Futurism," *Le Figaro*, 20 February 1909.

WHY 2035?

Marco Anderson

I ONCE SAW A PRESENTATION BY A FUTURIST NAMED GLEN HIEMSTRA.
Hiemstra proposed a mental exercise for putting oneself in the frame of mind to think about the short- and long-term future. He suggested that in order to really understand the possible futures we may encounter, we should think about a time fifty years in the past, and identify the differences between now and then. The extent of change over fifty years is a frame of reference that can be shifted from the past into the future. According to Hiemstra, fifty years in the past is just out of our immediate cultural memory, so we are able to think about fifty years ago as a static picture, separate from recent technological innovations and the distraction of ongoing change. The key to Hiemstra's exercise is that fifty years in the past is the best vantage point point from which to perceive twenty-five years in the past. By thinking about twenty-five years in the past, we can grasp subtle and surprising changes, and constants. If we project those forward twenty-five years, we open a view onto an illusive interim state that is crucial to planners and designers: the near future, halfway between now and the long-term future fifty years away.

The essays in this book examine changes that could occur to vehicles and their operating context over the next twenty-five years. The date we have chosen for our future time horizon—2035—corresponds to the target year for the vision for future transportation infrastructure that informs the Southern California Association of Governments (SCAG) 2012–2035 Regional Transportation Plan / Sustainable Communities Strategy. SCAG is one of hundreds of regional planning bodies, known as Metropolitan Planning Organizations (MPOs), across the United States that prepare transportation plans every four years in order to qualify for federal transportation funding.[1] The 2012 Regional Transportation Plan is an important source of information and research for the assumptions made in this book.

2035 is a halfway point between the current state of affairs and a significantly different future state in 2060. Therefore as, Hiemstra suggests, in order to put ourselves in the frame of mind to ponder 2060, and 2035, we should remember (or imagine, for those not old enough) the world, and specifically Southern California, in the years 1962 and 1987.

There was a time when personal vehicles were luxury items purchased with cash; by 1987, they were personal necessities often entirely financed.

THE ONCE AND FUTURE CAR

We can use Hiemstra's technique to think about features in personal vehicles. Most cars in 1962, 1987, and 2012 have four wheels that are connected via axles and a drive train to an internal combustion engine. The driver uses a steering wheel and pedals to control the direction and speed of the vehicle. Drivers and passengers maintain a forward-facing seated position while in the vehicle. Most vehicles have three discrete spaces: engine, passenger, and cargo. The latter two spaces, while distinct, have some-times merged in the case of vans, station wagons, and more recently, hatchbacks.

By looking to the past years of 1962 and 1987, it is easy to imagine both dramatic differences and incremental differences in all other aspects of vehicle design, manufacturing, usage, and pricing. While the characteristics noted above have held constant, vehicles in 1962 were largely mechanical devices (using such antiquated technology as brake cables, steering rods, and spring-loaded suspension) designed, engineered, and produced out of metal alloys. Mandatory installation of seatbelts was still three years away, intermittent windshield wipers had yet to be perfected, and few vehicles were equipped with head-rests to reduce whiplash neck injuries. Most vehicles ran on fuel with lead compounds to allow engine performance without pings and knocks.

The cars of 1987, on the other hand, represent an interim state between the "distant" past and the present. Electronic controls, including on-board computers, were becoming common. Emission controls had been present in vehicles for ten years, and the phase-out of leaded fuel, begun in 1973, was almost complete. Interior amenities and safety features had advanced significantly since 1962. These included air conditioning, sophisticated music systems, ergonomic seats, headrests, and seatbelts. Certain classes of vehicles that did not exist or existed in limited number in 1962 (such as SUVs and compact cars) were well-established product types by 1987. Significant progress was made in how cars are designed and built between 1962 and 1987. Computer-aided design and fabrication allowed designers to incorporate compound curves and significant aerodynamic features. Technological advances led to radically more involved computer monitoring and guidance of systems like suspension, brakes, and fuel systems.

Importantly, how we purchased and used our vehicles changed dramatically from 1962 to 1987. There was a time when personal vehicles were luxury items purchased with cash; by 1987, they were personal neces-sities often entirely financed. The goal of the financing used to be ownership, while the current trend favors use and access. In 1987, fewer than 7% of vehicles in the United States were leased. By 2012, the rate has increased to more than 20%.[2] In 1987, a family often shared one or two vehicles. Currently, in California, there are more cars than registered drivers, and it is not uncommon for teenagers in affluent or middle-class families to expect a car upon reaching driving age. (Interestingly, that trend has begun to reverse over the past few years because teenagers are apparently

Reality twenty-five years in the future will still be recognizable... The future of 50 years, however, will be radically different, and may be informed by dramatic changes that we can only imagine today.

less interested in driving than they used to be.) Commute time between 1962 and 1987 greatly increased, as did the designated speeds on highways and roadways.

Since 1962, and again since 1987, increases in average speeds due to increased lane widths and improved road engineering have negated improvements in passenger safety: While average crash fatalities per miles driven in the United States have decreased greatly, the absolute numbers have steadily risen. Between 1987 and the present, emissions due to increases in the number of miles behind the wheel, or vehicle miles traveled (VMT), have caught up with advances in emissions controls. Reductions in emissions since 1987 are also starting to tick back upward due to vehicle size, resulting in diminishing returns on emissions reductions through technological advances in gas engines. And improvements in average gasoline consumption will not counteract the negative impacts of CO_2 emissions.[3]

Based on this summary, the reader can anticipate that reality twenty-five years in the future will still be recognizable, and many of the innovations that will significantly change our lives in the future are already tangible and under development in a university laboratory or automobile design studio. The future of 50 years, however, will be radically different, and may be informed by dramatic changes that we can only imagine today.

[1] SCAG is the MPO for the six counties encompassing all of Southern California except for San Diego County, which has its own MPO. The six counties are Los Angeles, Ventura, Orange, Imperial, San Bernardino, and Riverside. The 2012–2035 Regional Transportation Plan / Sustainable Communities Strategy (2012 RTP/SCS) was adopted by the 89 locally elected officials in April of 2012.

[2] Percent of Lease Agreement for New Cars: Bureau of Transportation Statistics and Edmunds.com, courtesy of the Auto Club of Southern California.

[3] Reid Ewing et al., *Growing Cooler: The Evidence on Urban Development and Climate Change* (Washington, D.C.: Urban Land Institute, 2008).

POSSIBLE FUTURES: SOUTHERN CALIFORNIA IN 2035

The Car Future Group

The Car Future Group speculates about the interconnected forces that will affect the future of mobility in Southern California.[1]

THE REGION

Some urban areas will become more densely populated, with taller buildings and more people closer together than today, creating a greater range and variety between the most urban and suburban parts of the region. This will be partly due to a 2009 law to regulate greenhouse gas emissions through regional land use planning, and partly because of anticipated market pressures. However, the region will continue to be a polycentric one, supporting both dense and dispersed housing, office, and commercial centers spread throughout.

The health of the regional economy, cost of housing, average household income, time it takes to travel by different modes of transportation and cost of transportation will be the biggest factors in shaping the mobility and the built environment of the region. The increased variety in density and the connections between populations will influence all of the possible futures discussed below. Consequently, the answer to the question "What will be the environment for the car in 2035?" will depend on the level of population and employment density in particular parts of Southern California.

COUNTERPOINT: *This book does not deal directly with many radically alternative scenarios, including severe global depression, permanent drought in the Southwest, the Big One (massive earthquake), Peak Oil (global oil demand exceeding peak oil reserves), and rapidly rising sea levels due to climate change. However, these possibilities shouldn't be ignored.*

SOUTHERN CALIFORNIA IN 2012

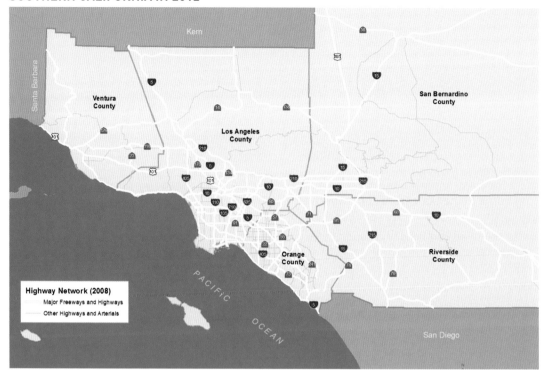

SOUTHERN CALIFORNIA IN 2035

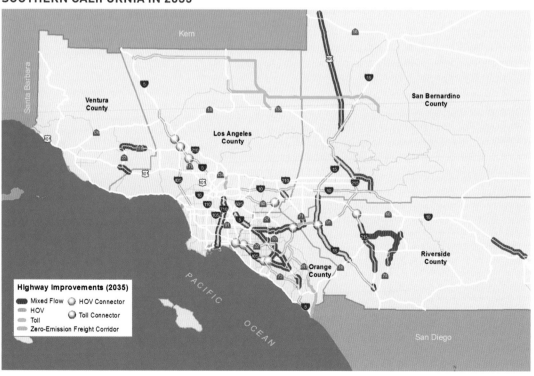

2012-2035 SCAG Regional Transportation Plan/Sustainable Communities Strategy.
© 2012, SCAG

PEOPLE

DEMOGRAPHICS: In 2010, one of every nine Californians was over the age of 65; in 2030, it will be one of every five.[2] Most of the retirement-age population of 2030 will have come to the state from somewhere else early in their lives. Of those younger than 65, however, the great majority will have been born and educated in California—in greater proportion than at any time since California became a state. By 2030, there will be two retirement-age Californians for every five persons of working age—nearly doubling the number of seniors compared to working-age people in 2010.

In 2030, the state's workforce will tend to be younger than the workforce of 2010, so a smaller percentage will have reached the age when they can expect their highest earnings and greatest choice of lifestyles. The majority of the workforce will be immigrants, primarily those who arrived before 1990, and their California-born children. The votes of baby boomer retirees will determine the transportation options that are available for the Californians in the workforce of 2030 who travel from home to work and back.

The Southern California population will spread itself widely across the region's landscape, as every previous generation has done. The mix of ages and incomes will be distributed in dense lumps of similarity, with workers traveling anonymously from place to place.

Today, many older retirees can recall riding around Southern California on brand-new freeways that had little congestion. The ease or the difficulty of getting around in 2030 will impact the decision to make a trip or not, and whether the pleasure of moving around Southern California will be more than just a memory.

The Southern California population will spread itself widely across the region's landscape, as every previous generation has done.

URBAN FORM

BUILDINGS AND HOUSING: Both demographic trends and rising transportation costs will impact how people live in a region currently oversupplied with large-lot suburban housing. While this type of housing may continue to be the most popular, demand for denser housing types throughout the region will increase. Large-lot single-family homes will continue to be developed in areas with cheap land; however, mixed-use single- and multi-family housing types will be developed in cities and town centers throughout the region.

PARKING: By 2035, we will have found a better way to designate parking spaces than by painted stripes, and different types of parking needs will be addressed more efficiently. Parking design and policy have received an enormous amount of attention in recent years. Smart technology, including sensors, computers, and electronic signage, will improve parking efficiency, and is already being deployed rapidly—though unevenly—throughout the region. Automated parking garages have already been approved for use in denser parts of the region.

Shared parking, public and private car share stations, and continued unbundling of parking from housing and employment centers will increase the options available for parking in a region where parking is already at a premium. This will also greatly increase the diversity of home and work parking solutions. For example, a small, 100% electric vehicle may be clean enough to store in the house in a dense urban neighborhood. Or driverless vehicles may be legally allowed to park themselves in a remote area detached from the suburban home.

URBAN FORM

In urban or urbanizing areas, regional parking policies based on requiring a developer to provide the current number of parking spots will be phased out by 2020. In addition, transit service and multi-mobility access will be robust enough to justify variable parking rates that change during the course of a day to meet demand and assure a constant 85% vacancy of parking in business districts.[3] Fully automated cars will park themselves in either automated or standard parking structures. In either type of structure, the cars will be more efficiently stored, allowing lower ceilings and more cars per level—which will be a boon to developers. The level of deployment of driverless cars will affect parking congestion.

By 2035, cars will be fully capable of staying in circulation after their owners or passengers have arrived at their destinations. One possibility is that autonomous, shared vehicles will only need to be stored while they are recharging. The rest of the time they could remain in almost constant circulation. This could have dramatic effects on parking requirements. For example, the car you use to get to work may be transporting other passengers while you are at work.

TRANSIT STOPS AND HUBS: Hubs will need to accommodate a greater variety of modes of transportation, and provide a more viable link between long and short journeys, and between transit and pedestrians. For example, bus rapid transit (BRT) stops currently pose a seemingly intractable challenge for integration into streets, due to overlapping transit services and the buses traveling in parking lanes during peak hours. These issues will be addressed in a more satisfactory way and the efficiency of transit will continue to improve with the availability of accurate real-time information for passengers. Within the urbanized areas, Metro Rail

URBAN FORM

Metrolink and urban streetcar hubs and their environs will continue to grow, attracting development and retail amenities. In more dispersed areas of the region, transit stops as we know them will be fewer, replaced by on-demand services.

JITNEYS: Jitneys, or small vans and buses, will provide first- and last-mile connectivity. They can offer a very agile and cost effective way to move around in residential neighborhoods and ferry individuals from home to a transit station/hub and then again from transit stop to workplace. As energy costs spiral, taxi operators might realize that running small electric or gasoline-powered vehicle, such as a neighborhood electric vehicle (NEV), for first- and last-mile operations makes sense. Optimally, enlightened cities will make it easier for individual entrepreneurs to operate jitney services. Currently, web-based services operating in San Francisco provide specialized insurance coverage that allows members to share their vehicles with other members. Using these services to crowd source billing, operation, and licensing functions for individual owner/operators is only a short step away.

How these services integrate with urban form will depend on how a specific jitney service is deployed. Smart shuttle services provided by employers may develop into a privatized network, or an entrepreneurially minded transit operator may develop a hybrid public/private model. On the other hand, jitney service may come from taxi and shuttle companies perfecting a ride-sharing pricing scheme that is easy to understand and acceptable to passengers. Along with these scenarios is one in which jitneys start as unlicensed operations in poorer areas of the region, and eventually establish themselves as legitimate operators. However

COUNTERPOINT: *In Southern California, the implementation of jitney service would require some significant issues to be solved by technology and policy. For one, by serving the most popular routes, jitney service further erodes per-passenger returns on public transit service. In addition, competition between jitney providers can lead to unlicensed drivers entering the business, and competition can create its own congestion. Varying levels of quality among providers can affect factors such as safety and cleanliness. Finally, the taxi industry and transit unions in Southern California may remain powerful enough to continue to derail any change in the status quo.*

URBAN FORM

this last scenario is unlikely, as taxi licenses are tightly regulated in North America. The establishment drivers would quickly "turn in" unlicensed operators. There are few examples of true jitney service in North America. Where flexible route transit services are deployed they are used in circumstances where fixed route service is lightly used and expensive to provide, such as in residential neighborhoods or rural areas. However if jitney service does become widely available, we will need fewer definitive bus stops and fewer bus shelters, since jitneys will pick people up on demand along their routes as they currently do in many other cities around the world.

SERVICE STATIONS AND REFUELING:
Gasoline-powered vehicles will remain in the majority in 2035, so service stations will remain functionally similar to today. However, they will offer a larger variety of fuel types. The spacing and availability of stations will greatly depend on the range of the vehicle fleet. The absolute number of refueling stations may go down slightly as electric vehicles become more common. These will be recharged at stations dispersed throughout the region in buildings of different uses such as homes and parking garages adjacent to places of work and shopping centers. In 2012, municipalities have expressed more reluctance to develop charging areas than they did in the 1990s, when they created facilities for electric vehicles before they were widely manufactured and accepted by the market. As a result, the electric cars of the future will have to rely more heavily on the private sector to develop recharging stations. Commercial vehicle refueling will become more differentiated from consumer refueling because commercial electric vehicles will have higher rated charging equipment, and will be available with hydrogen fuel cells before consumer vehicles.

VEHICLES

VARIETY OF CARS: A substantial number of older, *legacy* cars lacking the benefit of sensor-enabled safety features will share the road with *autonomous* vehicles that are self-driving. A much wider range of types of vehicles will share the roads, as will drivers with a greater variety of skill levels and attentiveness to the task of driving. Efforts are being made to design, produce, and promote smaller vehicles, but the trend in consumer choice has been in exactly the opposite direction, with market demand continuing to be strong for larger cars.

If current trends continue, new cars of the future will have significantly improved engine technology and safety. The efficiency of hybrid engine technology and lighter, more sophisticated construction techniques could continue to be applied to making larger and faster cars, as they have been over the past 20 years. However, other kinds of new technologies, such as automation, could either enable current trends or create new ones. It is also hard to predict the effect of demographic changes on the car market. One strong possibility is that we may concurrently see two opposing trends: one towards a proliferation of smaller and more urban friendly cars and another for the continued prevalence of large cars.

AUTONOMOUS VEHICLES: Over half of the fleet of new vehicles in 2035 will be fully autonomous, with regulations and market acceptance having supported the ubiquity of autonomous vehicles on highways, arterials, and residential streets.

COUNTERPOINT: *On-demand mobility means we will use different types of vehicles for different trips, and cars will not be privately owned, but rather shared and generic. Cars will have fewer empty passenger seats due to car sharing and alternative ownership. At the same time, suburban families will maintain multiple kinds of cars, such as larger cars for family outings and smaller cars for daily commutes.*

COUNTERPOINT: *No consensus has been reached as to when self-driving vehicles will be accepted by regulators and allowed to operate on local streets. In some ways the technology probably performs better at lower speeds, where the algorithm is relying more on sensors and slowing the vehicle, than on highways, where the algorithms are calculating complex variables of space, speed, and relation to other vehicles. However, high-speed travel presents less risk, because the mixed traffic is all moving in the same direction and because of the absence of pedestrians. Political regulation will depend on whether the public decides that self-driving vehicles remove human error or infringe on our driving liberties.*

VEHICLES

CAR DESIGN: As the overall vehicular system becomes more autonomous, the interior environment of the vehicle will become more like a small living room and allow for increased customization for closer integration with each individual user's lifestyle. Some predict a shift in car designers' focus away from the sculptural dynamics and styling that have traditionally been important to vehicle design. Apple's simple and understated product designs, such as for the iPhone, may hint at future vehicle exterior design: a simple exterior form with anonymous styling that users can customize.

Fleets of cars will travel together at a space of a few feet apart in autonomous formation, facilitating the user's ability to communicate, socialize, work, watch movies, and play games during their daily commute. Current research into improvements in the design of vehicle egress for handicapped people will result in cars with better-designed access in general. The way we enter and exit vehicles will be less standardized, in keeping with the increased variety of types of vehicles.

COUNTERPOINT: *The overall design of vehicles—the vehicle architecture—will remain similar. Vehicle exterior surfaces will be impregnated with phosphorus-like materials to store solar energy from daylight and would passively glow in the dark, contributing ambient illumination to the environment in high-density urban areas and therefore reducing the energy draw from the grid. To further facilitate the requirements for constant social networking, we will see the integration of molded organic LED materials into the exterior panel construction of vehicles. These would display real-time communications, dialog, and expression using changeable and animated color and graphic motifs, allowing individualization and personalization of the anonymous exterior design.*

Illustration by Jiha Hwang.

VEHICLES

AUTOMOTIVE INDUSTRY: Insurgent start-up vehicle companies will lead in innovative vehicle architectures. A minimum number of vehicles will still need to be sold in 2035 in order to see a vehicle "pencil out" for a manufacturer. So established car companies will continue to subsidize an array of experimental vehicles with their best-selling models. But because of efficiency gains in the manufacturing processes, materials, and engineering, manufacturers will be able to produce a larger variety of cars and be more responsive to changes in markets.

Car companies will become more like computer companies as distributed component designers and manufacturers responding to specifications and assembly processes will drive vehicle production. Marketing information will come from multiple sources, and costs will be more widely distributed. The major manufacturers will provide branding, distribution, major assembly, and some research and development funding.

Significant changes in the government's approach to the regulation of vehicles will allow for more dynamic architectures. A regulatory framework built around risk assessment and performance measures will regulate communication standards for on-board and off-board telemetry. By 2035, safety will be so improved that relaxed vehicle architectures will follow separate safety guidelines, based on systems redundancy instead of increasingly forceful collisions.

VEHICLES

BUSES AND TRUCKS: We will see a wider variety of sizes and types of buses and trucks, and they frequently will have assisted driving systems. Buses will range from long-distance rapid transit to local shuttles and a great number of small, less regulated private vans and jitneys. Like today, drivers of buses and trucks will have more rigorous training than drivers of cars. Buses will look more like streetcars, and streetcars will make a comeback in dense areas.

The bus and truck industry does not adapt quickly to change, including integrating new technology. In fact, the general form of the cargo truck has not changed in 50 years. Currently, smaller buses are designed to fit on large truck beds, leading to raised plat-forms and uncomfortable cabins. Moreover, existing cargo and emergency vehicle speci-fications dictate road standards. A major contributor to the current lack of evolution in truck and bus design has been the slow specifications-based purchasing processes required of public agencies. Changes to the purchasing processes would allow for more responsive design on the part of truck and bus manufacturers. An emerging market for privatized, shared public transportation could encourage variety and experimentation in the design and manufacturing of trucks and buses, which in turn would influence public sector purchasing decisions. Increased variety in density may also challenge current conventions and lead to a more diverse truck fleet in the region, as it has in Europe and Asia.

COUNTERPOINT: *Significant increases in the cost of energy will make long-distance transportation of finished goods economically unsustainable. This will induce a large-scale move to local manufacturing that will change the face of trucking. Long-distance trucking will reduce; short-haul, regional, and urban distribution will increase. We will see even more small delivery trucks and vans.*

VEHICLES

Chrysler GEM Peapod Neighborhood Electric Vehicle. Photo: AutoblogGreen.

SMALL CROSSOVER VEHICLES AND MOTORCYCLES: Crossover vehicles that are somewhere between a Segway and a golf cart, a Segway and a motorcycle, or a motorcycle and a car will proliferate. Some will have two or three wheels, some four. They will have a variety of ranges and speeds, and require different kinds of fuel; for example, electric motorcycles will be common.

Since 1998, Global Electric Motorcars (GEM) has been manufacturing one of the more common and better-looking neighborhood electric vehicles (NEV) to be seen on American streets. This small, battery-operated electric vehicle was designed by Dan Sturges. In 2011, the progressive company Polaris acquired GEM from DaimlerChrysler, who had made little effort to promote the vehicle. Polaris may see GEM as an opportunity to be innovative in this dormant but ready-to-be-exploited market for effective and economical means of local, personal mobility. Polaris is well positioned to create the next generation of NEVs with more sophisticated safety engineering.

VEHICLES

The future of a broad range of vehicles in between the standard four-passenger car and the bicycle, including NEVs, will depend on the actions of the regulatory agencies and the automotive industry. We will need to face the challenge of designing roadways to accommodate these vehicles. Similarly, we will need to craft licensing policies and traffic rules that allow them to travel safely alongside much larger and faster vehicles. A long-term negotiation to establish public and private cooperation will be the only way to optimize the use of these crossover vehicles and allow them to find a market.

FUEL TYPES AND ENGINES: The internal combustion engine will remain by far the most common for the next 20 years, but there will be more variety of fuel types than we have today, and more individual vehicles will have the capacity to use different types of fuels. Petroleum-based fuels will be further reformulated, perhaps with an increased Ethanol (cellulosic) content, and in 2035 these improved petroleum-based fuels will account for about 60% of the market. Most cars will be gasoline/electric or diesel/electric hybrids. Some will be capable of being plugged in, but non-plug-in hybrids, like the Toyota Prius, will still be very common. Zero emissions battery/electric vehicles will account for 5% to 10% of the fleet. Use of compressed natural gas will increase; it will be made more popular by the possibility for home-based refueling. Hydrogen vehicles will also be a factor, although in the minority.

COUNTERPOINT: *In 2035, nearly all road vehicles will have electric traction motors, which have the capacity to regenerate energy. The question is: What will be the energy storage mix of the fleet in 2035? A significant proportion of new vehicles will have some form of internal or external combustion engine requiring liquid energy storage. These hybrid engines will generate electricity to supply the electric traction motors. This allows a far more efficient use of the liquid fuel—whether it is gasoline, diesel, bio-mix, or something else— because of combustion engine optimization and elimination of the inefficient mechanical transmission used today. It also allows significant range of travel.*

Some vehicles designed for shorter journey usage will have battery storage of electricity or perhaps hydrogen fuel cells. Which of these two prevails will depend on which of the technologies wins the race for economic production, ecological cleanliness, and energy density. Battery storage will likely be predominant in most vehicles; and hydrogen fuel cells will be seen more in buses and trucks, where the high cost of the technology is a smaller percentage of the overall vehicle cost and having sufficient space to store the hydrogen tanks is less of an issue.

VEHICLES

TRAINS AND BUS RAPID TRANSIT VEHICLES: The proliferation of types of rail vehicles will continue, and there will more than likely be select deployments of streetcars in small areas such as Downtown Los Angeles and downtown Santa Ana. More Southern Californians will have passing acquaintance with modern rail vehicles, as Metrolink continues to update its rolling stock and offers workspace amenities such as wireless communication and charging stations for digital devices. As noted above, buses will be designed with more ease-of-use and look more like rail-based transit. Bus rapid transit systems will continue to be a feasible alternative to rail-based systems for relatively low-density areas of the region that cannot justify the investment in rail transit.

COUNTERPOINT: *High-speed rail is on the path of a 20-year plan for providing inter-city passenger rail service in California. However, fiscal and governance issues can still delay or stop the project.*

Regional rail service will improve; however, much of the current right-of-way for rail is still surrounded by long-term industrial uses, and will get in the way of regional rail stations becoming the nuclei of viable transit-oriented districts. This will vary greatly depending on the use and placement of freight rail. Corridors with freight rail operations will still have noise and pollution effects, higher risks, and wider unavailable rights-of-way.

ROADWAYS

HIGHWAYS: Within Southern California in 2035, the freeways and highways will have the same footprint or right-of-way (ROW). The quality of the surfaces of the highways will be extremely varied throughout the region. Many current high-occupancy vehicle (HOV) facilities and flyovers will be converted into high-occupancy toll (HOT) lanes. HOV and HOT lanes are now being built as continuous-access facilities and not as physically separated lanes. Self-driving vehicles will not be segregated from other vehicles on freeways. To segregate them is impractical and a waste of time and money. The technologies that will allow autonomous vehicles to work will allow them to mix invisibly with legacy vehicles.

ARTERIAL ROADWAYS: The most complex urban and transportation design challenge will play out on moderate- and high-density corridors in suburban communities.[4] These will need to accommodate the widest range of modes of transportation, and the widest range in the fleet: heavy/light, fast/slow, large/small, and autonomous/non-autonomous vehicles. They must serve regional and local needs in addition to accommodating pedestrians. Across the region, disparity in the quality of the road surface will be even greater, based on economic strength of local roadway jurisdiction.

In urbanized areas, the right-of-way (roadway footprint) will remain static, and in many cases we will see a critical mass of political will to reclaim street space for traffic calming, public space, and sidewalks. Wealthier communities in suburban areas will continue to see new arterial construction and better maintenance of existing roads. Deployment of signal prioritization and smart signals that communicate actively with cars will favor wealthier suburban areas.

COUNTERPOINT: *Significant investments have already been made in toll transponder infrastructure, so we may see a HOT lane easily converted into a lane for fully automated vehicles. Highway-running autonomous vehicles promise the greatest return on investment in congestion reduction and easy implementation. However, automation is more effective at lower speeds, therefore local driving in automated mode will make more sense.*

ROADWAY CONTROLS AND LANE MARKINGS: A great deal of research is being carried out these days on technologically enabled roadway controls such as cameras, sensors, and active controls that allow infrastructure to communicate with vehicles. Yet some planning and design case studies favor fewer controls, for example, streetscapes free of markings in high-density and low-speed environments. Again the ubiquity of self-driving vehicles and their operation in low- and medium-speed environments will be a major determining factor on what kinds of requirements will be placed on roadway controls and markings.

The implementation of the strategy for using roundabouts to achieve traffic calming will depend on the size of the intersections and the speed of traffic, with these treatments being more likely as neighborhood amenities. Traffic circles have fewer conflict points than conventional intersections and work without vehicles having to completely stop. Use of traffic circles in suburban and exurban arterial settings will again be encouraged by the presence of self-driving vehicles.

Segregation for bicycle facilities will increase, as will the sophistication of signals on bicycle infrastructure. Complete Streets approaches that integrate pedestrian, bicycle and vehicular travel will be implemented in varying degrees depending on density and local resources.

COUNTERPOINT: *The vehicle manufacturers will develop traffic controls, meaning that they will be deployed on the vehicles themselves rather than on the infrastructure. Using cloud computing, GPS-type systems, and car-to-car communications, the vehicles, rather than the infrastructure, will create systems redundancy that will result in public safety. Thus, self-contained virtual roadway controls are created that don't depend on expenditure by public agencies. This will allow much more rapid development and ensure that the technologies are continually updated and with no opportunity for certain cities or regions to be deprived of better traffic management because of political stasis. The technologies that allow autonomous vehicles to work will not demand many—if any—additions to the infrastructure such as roadway controls.*

ROADWAYS

FUNDING: The long-term funding mechanism of the American transportation infrastructure segment faces an uncertain future. This topic is probably the murkiest it has been in the last 50 years. In its 2012–35 Regional Transportation Plan, the regional council of the Southern California Association of Governments (SCAG) calls for allowing a local agency, county, or city to raise the gasoline tax with a simple 51% majority instead of the two-thirds majority required for all other taxes and fees. The agency will be required to meet the condition that the funds be spent only on projects that reduce congestion.

Transportation experts of all ideological and professional stripes agree unanimously that the current method of infrastructure funding is inadequate. The current model for gasoline tax collection and distribution was developed in the 1930s and is in need of updating. As gas mileage increases due to the new federal standards that require 54.5 mpg fleet-wide by 2025, Southern California will see a decrease of $12 billion in transportation infrastructure funding over the 20-year period because of a decrease in gasoline tax revenue. Moreover, electric vehicles currently pay no infrastructure maintenance tax. A future system will most likely supplement the gas tax with an indexed, inflation-adjusted user fee charged via on-board equipment or at the time of emissions testing and registration. In addition, several more transponder-based toll facilities will be used in Southern California, similar to the current Highway 91 express lanes.[5]

COUNTERPOINT: *Telecommunications and computing companies are the infrastructure providers of roadway pricing, and therefore strong proponents: They research, develop, and produce the technical expertise, hardware, and software needed to implement pay-as-you-go user fees. However, they have yet to significantly enter into the policy debate and do not actively participate in pursuing ways to fund the physical infrastructure. Fuel providers are currently so concerned with meeting demand for energy that they have not been actively involved in infrastructure funding development, so public agencies lack some important and much needed allies in the quest for funding for construction and maintenance of physical road infrastructure.*

A future system will most likely supplement the gas tax with an indexed, inflation-adjusted user fee charged via on-board equipment or at the time of emissions testing and registration.

MOBILITY HABITS

CULTURAL ATTITUDES: "THE RIGHT TO DRIVE": In Southern California, the notion that driving is a right will still be a factor in public policy for at least the next 15 years. However, the *right to drive* conveniently ignores the fact that the mobility challenged do not have the same right to mobility as others do. By 2035, the leading edge of the boomers will be entering their reduced mobility years, and may be reaping the planned transil investments they voted for through county-level half-cent sales tax measures in five of the six southern California counties.

More importantly, a wider spectrum of mobility options and vehicle ownership options will be available. This will remove the economic mandate of driving as the only credible method of access to economic activity. So by 2035, the *right to drive* will no longer be synonymous with *the need to drive my own car*. Autonomous vehicles will allow a more diverse range of people to get in a vehicle and safely get to wherever they want, so the *right to drive* could become the *right to mobility*. In fact, the market power of the baby boomers, and their now-caretaker children, will provide the market incentives to automo-bile manufacturers.

COMMUTING PATTERNS: Commuting habits will be less routine, resulting in traffic being spread out through the day instead of compressed during rush hour. Staggered work hours, dropping children off and picking them up from school, and "trip chaining" (where workers run errands as part of their trips to and from work) are examples that have already disrupted the traditional peak hour commute model. Some employers already have policies that expect workers to work at least eight hours, and be in the office from 10 a.m. to 2 p.m., without specifying

COUNTERPOINT: *Local trips will be made in small, electric vehicles. In the ideal urban community of 2035, no one should be farther than walking distance from any facility required on a daily basis—schools, shops, clinics, entertainment, and a local satellite business hub.*

MOBILITY HABITS

precise arrival times. The lack of routine will result in more difficulty in offering efficient transit services. On the other hand, the increased concentration of population density means people will travel shorter distances, so closer range mobility and public transit will be in greater demand.

In addition to commuting taking place throughout the day, instead of only during rush hours, telecommuting and remote working will be much more common. However, the implications on traffic are uncertain. Will more remote work result in more local trips, and in more overall travel during the working week, or reduced overall travel? A very large proportion of the population, especially the economically disadvantaged, will not have the option to telecommute because of the nature of their work.

LICENSING, DRIVING SKILLS, AND ENFORCEMENT: In 2012, driver licensing and vehicle miles traveled have been decreasing for the last five years. This decrease is observed even when the data is controlled for the effects of the post-2008 recession. There are numerous factors contributing to this decline, including high fuel costs and "graduated licensing," which limits drivers between 16 and 18 from driving with other minors in the vehicle without a driver over 18. However, this decline also reflects the increasing appeal of virtual connectivity and a greater interest in digital devices over automobiles for people in their late teens and early 20s.

The coexistence of autonomous vehicles and non-autonomous vehicles on the same roads, and drivers needing to be proficient in autonomous and non-autonomous modes, will require a greater variety of driving abilities. The diversity of types of driving modes means that drivers will, ironically, have to

COUNTERPOINT: *The allure of autonomous vehicles is that ultimately driving skills will no longer be important. Increasing automation will degrade, and eventually eliminate, manual driving skills.*

The diversity of types of driving modes means that drivers will, ironically, have to be more skilled in the short run.

MOBILITY HABITS

be more skilled in the short run—creating the need for new levels of drivers' licenses, stricter enforcement of traffic rules, and higher costs for licenses. Some on-board communication technology will be used to immediately assess fines and encourage surrendering driving control to the car.

ALTERNATIVES TO CAR OWNERSHIP:
Across the region, vehicle ownership patterns will grow increasingly varied. More on-demand mobility options and technology-enabled mobility will be available in denser areas. Smart phones will facilitate on-demand car sharing, electric charging rates will vary with current demand, and flexible insurance policies will cover co-ownership or renting out your own vehicle. On the other hand, a very large segment of lower income vehicle owners will still be buying cars with cash and engaging in informal car sharing.

Future vehicle ownership is extremely unpredictable. More efficient vehicle pricing, leasing arrangements, and usage could lead to fewer vehicles per capita, or it could lead to many families owning multiple different vehicles for unique purposes, such as short trips, commutes, and weekend errands. In either case, people will have better access to a variety of specialized vehicle types. Users may choose to own one or more cars, or they may choose to subscribe to a total mobility package that gives them access to what they want when they want it. They may own the vehicle that they use nearly all of the time for commuting and then lease other kinds of vehicles for occasions when the requirements are different, such as weekend trips.

COUNTERPOINT: *Car ownership has been a cultural touchstone for nearly a century, and globally it is still on the rise. A car remains the second largest purchase many people make in their lives. While the expense of cars provides a good reason to move away from car ownership, the fact that so many still buy cars also demonstrates a deep social attachment to them. However, analysts have conflicting opinions on the pace of this potential change away from ownership to other methods of access. It would take four semi-continuous years of sustained exorbitantly high gas prices to trigger a majority of Americans to a tipping point of more systematically "rational" and cost-effective options, such as moving away from car ownership.*

[1] The Car Future Group consists of Bill Trimble, Geoffrey Wardle, Steve Mazor, Kati Rubinyi, Christopher Gray, Marco Anderson, Terry A. Hayes, and Simon Pastucha, with input from others, including Stuart Reed, Ty Schuiling, Steve Finnegan, and John Thackara.

[2] The most informative projections available provide a profile for the year 2030. Comparable projections are not available for 2035, so the 2030 projections are used here. See John Pitkin and Dowell Myers, 2012, "Generational Projections of the California Population by Nativity and Year of Immigrant Arrival." Produced by the Population Dynamics Research Group, Sol Price School of Public Policy, University of Southern California. Text and supporting materials are published at: http://www.usc.edu/schools/price/research/popdynamics.

[3] In *The High Cost of Free Parking* (2011), UCLA professor Donald Shoup demonstrates 85% utilization as an optimal utilization of on-street parking. This number translates as one free parking space out of every seven spaces, or one to two free spaces per block. This assures visitors, and more specifically, customers an available space, and keeps them from circling the block to find a space, which creates congestion and pollution. That number has been confirmed through observation as an ideal utilization figure for parking lots as well.

[4] As defined in Caltrans' "Smart Mobility 2010," these arterials are generally wide, four to six lanes, and relatively high speed, 35–55 mph speed limits, often with 60 mph design speeds.

[5] The regional transportation plan includes a planned extension of the 91 express lanes: the I-10 and 110 high-occupancy toll lane demo projects will start operating in Los Angeles in 2012, and the Orange County Transportation Authority was considering high occupancy toll lanes on I-405.

CROSSING THE STREET IN 2025

The Car Future Group

Bill Trimble, a senior planner for the City of Pasadena, proposed the Crossing the Street in 2025 Project. Its purpose is to use fiction to explore many of the questions that planners, designers, and policy analysts ask when they consider the future of personal mobility, including the rate of change in vehicles, transportation infrastructure, and technology. The following two stories about commuting in Southern California in 2025 are based on a compilation of narratives developed by The Car Future Group.

In order to get in the right frame of mind to visualize the future, we thought about what specific intersections looked like 10, 20, and 30 years ago. We thought of the types of vehicles you would have seen on the road, and the pedestrians who would have been standing on the sidewalk. What infrastructure was present—crosswalks, pedestrian signs, curb cutouts? Then we thought about current trends in demographics, design, and technology, and imagined the same intersection 15 years in the future. The ten or so participants randomly chose the degree of density and economic context of the future intersection. What emerged were sharp distinctions between the anticipated futures of economically disadvantaged areas and wealthier communities. Generally speaking, infrastructural improvements were expected to follow the patterns of the last fifty years, in which areas of less density are favored, especially wealthier suburbs, while the infrastructure of denser, urban areas continued to deteriorate due to increased social inequity and the persistently uneven distribution of funding for roadway mainte-nance and improvements.

As a group of grade school students approaches the intersection, a young girl races ahead. The lights at the edge of the sidewalk blink, signifying traffic in the intersection. The crosswalks are clearly marked and the pavement is smooth and new. The slightly blue tint in the pavement reflects the non-petroleum-based low-emission asphalt. You can't see the pedestrian sensors under the pavement but they communicate with the newer automated vehicles to let the cars know that a pedestrian is crossing or that the light is red. The new synchronization systems sense the oncoming traffic, and resynchronize after it passes. Cars typically wait no more than 20 seconds at a light. The speed of the autonomous cars conforms to the electronically posted speed limit, which varies with time of day, traffic patterns, and weather conditions, and they can sometimes travel for miles without ever stopping at a light. This affluent, suburban area of Orange County is one of the few non-freeway locations where vehicles may be oper-ated autonomously because of the dense network

iReal by Toyota.

Uno III by BPG Motors.

of intersections with cameras, traffic signals, and detectors. Implementation of this system a couple of years ago was assisted through hard-won state and national grant funding.

The turn lane has a green thermoplastic coating to signify that it doubles as a bike lane. The right-most lane also has the coating and dedicated bicycle lights. A wide mix of cars, bicycles, and other vehicles flows out of the business district— a few fifteen-year-old hybrids driven by teenagers and young college kids and a number of brand-new, all-electric Mercedes and Audis are on their way to the freeway's autonomous toll lanes. Two- and three-seat neighborhood electric vehicles whiz by soundlessly. They share the road with hybrid trucks, which get a pitiful 30 mpg and cost $2000 a year to register but are still popular with those who have the room to park them.

Behind the kids is a gas station with eight to ten different types of pumps sorted by fuel type. On one side are the large gas, diesel, and natural gas pumps. On the other are the hydrogen and electric charging stations. The gasoline sold these days does not even seem like gasoline any more, since it contains 15% ethanol and many other additives to lower its carbon footprint. Some of the 240-volt medium-rate electric chargers can take several hours for a complete recharge, but more and more are converting to 480-volt fast chargers that can take an EV or PHEV battery from near dead to 80% charged in about 15 minutes. Since the rash of accidental electrocutions in the high humidity of the South a few years ago, the technical problems appear to have been worked out of these systems. This station, like most, also has E85 pumps and CNG and high-pressure (10,000 PSI) hydrogen.

The light for the cars turns red. The bicycle light stays green for another ten seconds to allow the bikes to clear the intersection, and one lone straggler crosses on an electric Uno, the music from his speakers accompanied by the whirr from the hub motor. As soon as the bicycle light for the other direction turns green, the automated BRT bus starts to cross. A few seconds later, the traffic signal for the cars finally turns green. LED strips embedded in the pavement of the pedestrian crosswalk start blinking, and the speakers overhead start their singsong beeping. Two senior citizens on personal mobility chairs whirr up behind the group at the crosswalk. The scooters sense that they are not in a dedicated mobility lane, so a low bell alerts the kids on the sidewalk that they are approaching.

The cars stopped at the intersection include both automated vehicles tied into the centralized traffic control system and several legacy vehicles driven the old-fashioned way. While the pedestrians are crossing, a driver approaches the intersection. This vehicle has no automated controls, and it isn't slowed down enough to stop. The driver, on a call with his automated stockbroker, runs the red light, nearly hitting the group crossing the roadway. The driver's phone buzzes with an automatic citation. While the driver looks at the citation, his phone buzzes again. He has been notified by his insurance company of an immediate rate increase. This is the third ticket he has gotten in the last two years for similar situations. It might be time, he thinks, to invest in a new 2026 Toyota with automatic control systems.

I am a 25-year-old clerical worker at Broadway and Vernon Avenue just south of downtown Los Angeles. I am trying to reach my ultimate destination in the huge job center in West Los Angeles that has far eclipsed all of the employment opportunities of the old and outmoded downtown area.

Every weekday, I catch a northbound bus along Broadway, and then catch the extended Metro Purple subway line to Beverly Hills, catch another Wilshire bus, and then a jitney that circulates southward. Most people in my area have abandoned active use of their cars, now that gasoline costs $10/gallon. Travel is by necessity; our discretionary trips are severely curtailed. Public funding has shifted from rail-based transit to super-articulated rubber-tired buses. On the major arterials serving job centers, region-wide parking taxes and tolls that are intended to deter passenger vehicle travel have had the greatest impact on the most economically disadvantaged areas. It hasn't helped that the secondary street network for legacy vehicles with limited intelligence is discontinuous and in poor repair. Available freeway onramps for car model years 2010 and earlier have been limited by Caltrans's aggressive "smart mobility" priority policies.

The ten-foot-wide sidewalk on Broadway is packed. Its level of service is F minus. Fuel costs have spawned a surge in walking, but I cannot move at a brisk and purposeful pace. People and other obstructions combine to make this morning's walking trip an adventure. A large number of elderly people on the sidewalk are on scooters and several people have Honda walk-assisters on their legs. Linked by tiny sensors hooked onto a person's earlobes, the walk-assisters, which have become almost as common as eyeglasses used to be, check balance and create responsive movements by mimicking leg muscle activity. The crowd shares the sidewalk with many wagons, most of them drones that follow behind their owners. The wagons are typically filled with produce or other items to swap. It once seemed inconceivable that we could adapt to fewer cars and less money this way, but life goes on. The new fad is to worry about every ounce of weight that might be pulled, pushed, or carried.

Because of the cost, people think twice about moving themselves and their goods from one place to another. In advertising, light is the new green.

I weave through the bags, wagons, and people to reach the corner, but I cannot cross because of the long line of articulated buses stacked up at the intersection. Only the old cameras and light detection systems are in place in this area, so unruly queues of super-articulated buses are the norm. Two extend almost the entire distance of a short city block. There is no way to cut in between these monster vehicles. Retreating from the crosswalk, I look for any sort of gap. Darting across Broadway is a risk. Since vehicle use is down, citations by the police for jaywalking have become a primary source of public revenue.

The curb and street are in sorry shape. Lots of potholes. In this part of the city, the little light cars that belong to those lucky enough to have them just cannot weather the pounding. I decide to make my move. I dart in and out from among the various shapes and sizes of buses, jitneys, and converted privateered minivans. The newer vehicles I pass are entirely covered by advertisements, which have become a standard part of any lease agreement. I am also facing platoons of refitted 2010-vintage SUVs with outboard suspension systems with huge springs. This primitive horde of vehicles shows little respect for pedestrians and any type of traffic control rules, perhaps a sign of a technological inferiority complex. Lots of cyclists navigate the roads here too, but the unmaintained pavement makes their passage precarious and unpredictable. You just never know what a cyclist is going to do, or be able to do.

Several of us see our bus. We make a break for it and I try not to fall prey to a pothole. I have lots of torn clothing as a memento of prior crossings. When I thrust my pass in front of the bus door sensor, a voice responds, "Admit one." I grab the overhead handrail and my day begins.

BENZ NEXT INTERIOR PICS YOU LIKE MY CHOICE READY TO HIT SWITCHES PUTTIN THE BAGS ON BLUEBER HILL REACHING THE PEAK TO SUCCESS SITTING LOW BOMB DIGGLE WIGGLE KIDO HAH SO FRESH AN SO CLEAN CLEAN BIANCA WARE CAR 13 BANK SCARFACE 100 GLODEN MI OTRA S10 MY BF RID3 DIS MY GIRLS 66 CHEVY N 04 TOYOTA TACOMA DIS R MY GIRLS LEGENDARY TIME TO GO CARS TRUCKS CAR HONDAS 2007 300 22 THE CUTLASS WELO SUCH A SHOW OFF CHEVY CAPRICE WAGON HYDRAULICS WHEEL PUMPS DAYTONS TV CHROME DV LOW SIEMPRE FIRME NISSAN 370Z TROY FACET PHOTOGRAP HIT ME BACK DIS IS MY GATOR CHEVY IMPALA HER NAME IS TJ N A GATOR CHEVY CAPRICE AIR RI SHAVED 1991 CAPRICE CLASSIC AFTER THE CAR WASH MOTO LOWRIDER BLUE MOTO BLUE CHOPPE THIS IS AN AWESOME CAR VTURBO BUICK REGAL HOMICIDE AND JAZMAINE CAMION SKITTLES SKITTL CAR MI DONK W 22 S 94 CHEVY JUICED ME AND MY 95 LOVEINIT LA MEXICAN MAFIA HATERS WHAT IMPALA LOWRIDER JOHANA HIS RANFLA 1963 IMPALA MY CAR MY ART WORK MY LIL LOW LOW THE BO 516 SUPERMARIO OLDS CUTLASS SUPREME 13X7 LOWRIDER OLDS CUTLASS SUPREME LOWRIDER 13 CHEVY CHEVROLET INTAKE INTERIOR 1963 IMPALA 4 DOOR HARDTOP BONESBLACKYUKON MY LOW LO 1963 LOW RIDER MY NISSAN SKYLINE ESPANOLA NM MY 94 CHEVY ON 22 WILL HONDA G35 SNOWED DREAMCARS XTERRA LOWRIDER MUSTANG ROLLIN ON TRUES VOGEES MY RIDE HJJ STEFAN LAMBE WORKING HARD LOWRIDER BIKE LOWRIDER BIKE PART LOWRIDER BIKE FROM WWW TOPLOWRIDER 20 MUSTANG WWW OGOGOG COM TRUCK XTREME IMAGE RIDE BIG MY 2ND BABY MY BABY MY 1ST BA HEAVY CHEVY MERCEDES BENZ NEXT INTERIOR PICS YOU LIKE MY CHOICE READY TO HIT SWITCH PUTTIN THE BAGS ON BLUEBERRY HILL REACHING THE PEAK TO SUCCESS SITTING LOW BOMB DIGG WIGGLE KIDO HAH SO FRESH AND SO CLEAN CLEAN BIANCA WARE CAR 13 BANK SCARFACE 100 GLODE MI OTRA S10 MY BF RID3 DIS R MY GIRLS 66 CHEVY N 04 TOYOTA TACOMA DIS R MY GIRLS LEGENDA TIME TO GO CARS TRUCKS CARS HONDAS 2007 300 22 THE CUTLASS WELO SUCH A SHOW OFF CHE CAPRICE WAGON HYDRAULICS 3 WHEEL PUMPS DAYTONS TV CHROME DV LOW SIEMPRE FIRME NISSA 370Z TROY FACET PHOTOGRAPHY HIT ME BACK DIS IS MY GATOR CHEVY IMPALA HER NAME IS TJ N GATOR CHEVY CAPRICE AIR RIDE SHAVED 1991 CAPRICE CLASSIC AFTER THE CAR WASH MOTO LOWRID BLUE MOTO BLUE CHOPPER THIS IS AN AWESOME CAR TURBO BUICK REGAL HOMICIDE AND JAZMAI CAMION SKITTLES SKITTLES CAR MI DONK W 22 S 94 CHEVY JUICED ME AND MY 95 LOVEINIT LA MEXICA MAFIA HATERS WHAT 63 IMPALA LOWRIDER JOHANA HIS RANFLA 1963 IMPALA MY CAR MY ART WO MY LIL LOW LOW THE BOSS 516 SUPERMARIO OLDS CUTLASS SUPREME 13X7 LOWRIDER OLDS CUTLA SUPREME LOWRIDER 13X7 CHEVY CHEVROLET INTAKE INTERIOR 1963 IMPALA 4 DOOR HARDTOP BONE BLACKYUKON MY LOW LOW 1963 LOW RIDER MY NISSAN SKYLINE ESPANOLA NM MY 94 CHEVY ON 22 W HONDA G35 SNOWED IN DREAMCARS XTERRA LOWRIDER MUSTANG ROLLIN ON TRUES VOGEES MY RI HJJ STEFAN LAMBERT WORKING HARD LOWRIDER BIKE LOWRIDER BIKE PART LOWRIDER BIKE FRO WWW TOPLOWRIDER 2007 MUSTANG WWW OGOGOG COM TRUCK XTREME IMAGE RIDE BIG MY 2ND BA MY BABY MY 1ST BABY HEAVY CHEVY MERCEDES BENZ NEXT INTERIOR PICS YOU LIKE MY CHOICE REA TO HIT SWITCHES PUTTIN THE BAGS ON BLUEBERRY HILL REACHING THE PEAK TO SUCCESS SITTI LOW BOMB DIGGLE WIGGLE KIDO HAH SO FRESH AND SO CLEAN CLEAN BIANCA WARE CAR 13 BAN SCARFACE 100 GLODEN MI OTRA S10 MY BF RID3 DIS R MY GIRLS 66 CHEVY N 04 TOYOTA TACOMA DIS MY GIRLS LEGENDARY TIME TO GO CARS TRUCKS CARS HONDAS 2007 300 22 THE CUTLASS WELO SUCH SHOW OFF CHEVY CAPRICE WAGON HYDRAULICS 3 WHEEL PUMPS DAYTONS TV CHROME DV LOW SIEMPR FIRME NISSAN 370Z TROY FACET PHOTOGRAPHY HIT ME BACK DIS IS MY GATOR CHEVY IMPALA HER NA IS TJ N A GATOR CHEVY CAPRICE AIR RIDE SHAVED 1991 CAPRICE CLASSIC AFTER THE CAR WASH MO LOWRIDER BLUE MOTO BLUE CHOPPER THIS IS AN AWESOME CAR TURBO BUICK REGAL HOMICIDE A JAZMAINE CAMION SKITTLES SKITTLES CAR MI DONK W 22 S 94 CHEVY JUICED ME AND MY 95 LOVEIN LA MEXICAN MAFIA HATERS WHAT 63 IMPALA LOWRIDER JOHANA HIS RANFLA 1963 IMPALA MY CAR ART WORK MY LIL LOW LOW THE BOSS 516 SUPERMARIO OLDS CUTLASS SUPREME 13X7 LOWRIDER OL CUTLASS SUPREME LOWRIDER 13X7 CHEVY CHEVROLET INTAKE INTERIOR 1963 IMPALA 4 DOOR HARDTO BONESBLACKYUKON MY LOW LOW 1963 LOW RIDER MY NISSAN SKYLINE ESPANOLA NM MY 94 CHEVY 22 WILL HONDA G35 SNOWED IN DREAMCARS XTERRA LOWRIDER MUSTANG ROLLIN ON TRUES VOGE MY RIDE HJJ STEFAN LAMBERT WORKING HARD LOWRIDER BIKE LOWRIDER BIKE PART LOWRIDER BI FROM WWW TOPLOWRIDER 2007 MUSTANG WWW OGOGOG COM TRUCK XTREME IMAGE RIDE BIG MY 2 BABY MY BABY MY 1ST BABY HEAVY CHEVY MERCEDES BENZ NEXT INTERIOR PICS YOU LIKE MY CHOI READY TO HIT SWITCHES PUTTIN THE BAGS ON BLUEBERRY HILL REACHING THE PEAK TO SUCCE SITTING LOW BOMB DIGGLE WIGGLE KIDO HAH SO FRESH AND SO CLEAN CLEAN BIANCA WARE CAR BANK SCARFACE 100 GLODEN MI OTRA S10 MY BF RID3 DIS R MY GIRLS 66 CHEVY N 04 TOYOTA TACOM DIS R MY GIRLS LEGENDARY TIME TO GO CARS TRUCKS CARS HONDAS 2007 300 22 THE CUTLASS SUCH A SHOW OFF CHEVY CAPRICE WAGON HYDRAULICS 3 WHEEL PUMPS DAYTONS TV CHROME LOW SIEMPRE FIRME NISSAN 370Z TROY FACET PHOTOGRAPHY HIT ME BACK DIS IS MY GATOR IMPALA HER NAME IS TJ N A GATOR CHEVY CAPRICE AIR RIDE SHAVED 1991 CAPRICE CLASSIC AFTER

THE CAR:

THE CAR:

AUTONOMOUS VEHICLES

Geoffrey Wardle

THIS BOOK IS ALL ABOUT THE FUTURE OF THE CAR. But if you live in a metropolis like Los Angeles or San Francisco, you might be wondering: How can there *be* a future for the car?

On the one hand, as noted elsewhere in this book, we believe that for the foreseeable future, California is one of the American states that will not see any huge investments in new transportation infrastructures—there isn't the political will to do so and even if there was, there is certainly not enough money to do so. (The one exception might be a limited high-speed rail network connecting San Francisco to Southern California, but this will perhaps compete more with regional air traffic than it does with road traffic.) This means that we are stuck with the infrastructure we already have. No more roads of significance will be built and anyway, experts in traffic management agree that building more roads does nothing to relieve congestion; it just moves the problem to another neighborhood.

On the other hand, apparently, most of us still prefer to get into our personal cocoon every day to drive to work than to use public transportation options. Despite significant improvements in bus, subway, and commuter rail services in our major Californian metropolises, the door-to-door convenience of using our cars outweighs the mind-numbing and blood-pressure-raising daily combat of competing against our peers as we inch forward on our urban highways and freeways.

However, a knight in shining armor on the horizon might ride to our rescue: the autonomous vehicle.

For many decades, visions of future transportation have depicted bubble-topped cars that waft along elevated highways while blasé looking families inside lounge around reading newspapers and playing games. For at least two or three decades, quite a few research groups around the world have experimented with various ways of allowing road vehicles to navigate themselves.

In the 1990s, a section of a dedicated, part-time high-occupancy vehicle (HOV) lane on a freeway near San Diego was upgraded to demonstrate prototype autonomous cars driving by themselves. These self-driving cars were limited in their abilities and relied greatly on expensive enhancements to the roadway. They relied on embedded technology in the infrastructure and utilized communication with the infrastructure and centralized command systems. In other words, these autonomous vehicles would require major investments to modify the existing infrastructure and to build a universal communication network. With no major investment on the radar and the specter of all of the various interested parties agreeing upon a universal operating platform for the communication network, autonomous vehicles looked like an implausible concept.

But wait! What if we did not need to modify the existing infrastructure and did not need a universal communications system? What if we just design the vehicles to figure everything out? Then there is no onus upon governments and taxpayers to invest in the infrastructural changes. It will be up to the vehicle manufacturers and their supply network to figure out the solutions. They could utilize open platform systems, and as a consequence, we wouldn't not get stuck with a platform that quickly becomes obsolete.

Between 1987 and 1995, the largest research and development project to date to advance autonomous cars was called the EUREKA Prometheus Project (Programme for a European Traffic of Highest Efficiency and Unprecedented Safety). This project involved universities and car manufacturers from across Europe. A famous participant in this project was Dr. Ernst Dickmanns, of Bundeswehr Universität München. In collaboration with Daimler Benz, he succeeded in developing twin robot cars that, in 1994, drove autonomously for 1,000 kilometers at up to 80 mph on normal Paris freeways. In 1995, Dickmanns created an S Class Mercedes-Benz that drove by itself at up to 110 mph on a 1,000-mile trip from Munich to Copenhagen and back.

In the United States, the Defense Advanced Research Projects Agency (DARPA) has challenged the research and academic communities to design vehicles that can find their own way from point A to point B. Google has also been very much in the news recently as it claims to have successfully driven a fleet of vehicles around on public highways without direct human control.

In 2009, the European Commission funded SARTRE, a three-year program to develop autonomous vehicles on unmodified freeways. In January 2011, successful trials of two vehicles running autonomously and in tandem were completed.

How can this possibly work? Well, the secret is in enabling the vehicles to recognize their geographic location, understand where their final destination is and how to get there, judge exactly where they are on the road at any point in time, recognize stationary and moving objects (trees, barriers, cyclists, parked vehicles, other moving vehicles, pedestrians, stray dogs, etc.), and compute how to navigate around and through this dynamic environment.

To do this, vehicles will need to be able to talk to each other to share real-time information about the changing environment. Effectively, all vehicles within a given proximity will describe to each other their immediate environment so that together a continually updated picture of the local environment is

In 1995, Dickmanns created an S Class Mercedes-Benz that drove by itself at up to 110 mph on a 1,000-mile trip from Munich to Copenhagen and back.

created. From this virtual, real-time environment map, complete with old mattresses, stray dogs, and road work gangs noted, they can then collectively compute the information to allow each individual vehicle to make decisions about its forward trajectory. As each vehicle proceeds, information about the environment it is entering will be shared by preceding and oncoming vehicles—just like columns of foraging ants relaying information about where the food lies ahead. With suitable levels of systems redundancy—as is familiar in the aerospace industry—autonomous road vehicles can be part of a robust system where erroneous contact with another vehicle or object is a thing of the past.

Any systems or subsystems failure in an airplane can be catastrophic. Therefore, multiple, parallel subsystems are engineered into an airplane to back up the principal subsystem. Similarly, in a car, a dual braking system is required. This means that if any part of the hydraulic braking system suddenly fails due to damage or corrosion, a full or partial secondary system will bring the vehicle safely to a halt. On an aircraft, every function will have at least two back-up systems, in the event that a secondary back-up fails. This approach to complementing controls systems with duplicates, triplicates, or even quadruplicates is referred to as systems redundancy. The number of normally redundant systems that are engineered into a vehicle or machine is dependent upon the calculated risk and consequences of failure. The systems that

PAY TOLL
0.5 MILES

INCOMING CALL

ANA

65

Illustration by Jiha Hwang.

will allow vehicles to be autonomous are already numerous, which helps reduce the likelihood of failure in the first place. Deliberately engineering in some extra redundant systems can lower the chance of failure to an acceptable level.

We already have many of the technologies well developed and many people are working furiously on the remaining pieces of the jigsaw puzzle. Indeed, some of the technologies are already features of vehicles in production and for sale now. For example, we have global positioning systems, which are accurate to within a few feet, for geographic location. Dynamic driving control systems can make decisions about braking or accelerating a car far faster than a driver can compute and command. We have proximity sensors that alert vehicles and drivers of other vehicles in blind spots or when we are backing up

We even have cars that can accomplish what many drivers can't: They can parallel park themselves!

too close to a car behind. These features are described as "accident avoidance systems." Many cars also have adaptive cruise control, which automatically applies the brakes when the vehicle on cruise mode gets too close to the car in front. We even have cars that can accomplish what many drivers can't: They can parallel park themselves!

What still needs development is the sensing and monitoring equipment that will allow a vehicle or group of vehicles to "read" their immediate environment. This will include algorithms to translate visual input to determine the difference between a streetlamp, a parked vehicle, a child running into the road, or a refrigerator bouncing off the back of a pick-up truck. Several large companies, including automotive companies, have been working furiously for some time to develop visual perception technologies.

Also needed are advances in cloud computing, which are on the way, and computing power, because those algorithms will be big ones. Recent breakthroughs in British and Japanese universities are set to boost the power of microprocessors quite radically over the next decade, maybe even beating Moore's Law.

But hold on, you say. What about taking my freedom away? I want to be in control of my car. Well, maybe we don't have as much control over our current cars as we think. For years, many cars, particularly very powerful ones, have had subsystems embedded in their central processing units that discretely override the driver's input commands if the car determines that it is approaching an unstable condition. Instant, rapid application of the brakes on individual wheels or a smooth reduction in throttle opening will occur without the errant driver even realizing. These electronic stability controls (ESC) are becoming ever more prevalent and the National Highway Traffic Safety Administration's rule #126 requires ESC to be installed in all passenger cars and light trucks, including vans and sport-utility vehicles, starting with the 2012 model year.

Gradual extensions of such subsystems can easily be extended to steering and throttle pedal inputs to avoid hitting another vehicle or exceeding a speed limit by a dangerous margin. The technologies to do this already exist. Several cars available in the United States today feature lane departure warnings or even lane departure interventions. These systems warn the driver if they drift out of the lane when the turn indicator is not engaged.

Some actually gently nudge the car back into the lane. If you meant to change lanes, but neglected to turn on the turn indicator (and none of us would ever do that, would we?), the driver can override the "gentle nudge" and complete the lane change. Other currently available cars have lane change warnings that use radar or cameras to warn if another vehicle is alongside when you turn on the turn indicator.

For years, cars have been programmable to set an alarm if a certain speed is exceeded. Currently, Ford offers a "My Key" program that allows parents to program a car to limit maximum speed and maximum sound system volume when their teen is driving. The car senses which key (the parent's or the teen's) is in the ignition and sets the preprogrammed limits.

In Europe, some city buses steer themselves along certain parts of the route, guided by a video camera and computer that tracks a white line painted along the road. This is a relatively simple version of what will be needed for the future. It works, and passengers apparently don't start screaming when the bus driver takes his or her hands off the steering wheel.

Okay, so I can imagine a future world when all cars drive themselves, but how do we get from today, where there are virtually no autonomous vehicles, to a future of only autonomous road vehicles? The intermediate technologies described above are the key to the changeover. As more and more of these discrete subsystems become embedded in our cars, in the name of safety or accident avoidance features—as anti-lock brakes were introduced 30 years ago—people will become more and more accustomed to the car correcting errors of driver judgment.

The AAA Foundation for Traffic Safety/ Automobile Club of Southern California recently surveyed owners of cars equipped with some of the previously mentioned and other systems (such as adaptive cruise control, backing aids, adaptive high-intensity discharge [HID] headlights, and voice activated navigation). They found that the majority became accustomed to the system quickly, found themselves relying on the technology, and would want the system on their next car. In fact, several subjects responded that they had had collisions when backing up a car that was not equipped with a backing aid because they were used to the system providing warnings in their car. Most respondents felt that the new technologies made their cars safer.

Once these systems become robust and trusted by drivers, one can imagine that driving without much attention at all would no longer be a disaster. Gradually, we would reach a tipping point where we would just let the car make all the major decisions. At that point, it is probable that most drivers would be quite happy to relinquish total control of the car as they began to appreciate the reduction in stress it yielded. The other realization would be that commuting time could be used for something far more productive like sleeping, reading, or communicating. Having crossed this "tipping point," things would

It is probable that most drivers would be quite happy to relinquish total control of the car as they began to appreciate the reduction in stress it yielded. Commuting time could be used for something far more productive like sleeping, reading, or communicating.

really start to happen quickly and the truly significant advantages of totally autonomous road vehicles would manifest themselves.

And what are these? We are likely to be stuck with the infrastructure that we already have. Therefore, we need to use that infrastructure much, much more efficiently than we have done thus far. Caltrans, the Californian State agency responsible for transportation infra-structure, believes that we have more than enough roads, highways, and freeways for now and the future, if only we could stream all the vehicles much more efficiently along the thoroughfares. This means smoothing the traffic flows and moving the vehicles much closer to each other. Take away the erratic human driver, prone to inattention and error of judgment and, worse still, slow reaction times, and suddenly the dream of more efficient traffic flow seems realiz-able. Vehicles that are guided by electrons rather than neurons can travel together in very close proximity because reaction times become effectively instantaneous.

By 2035, new cars that are equipped to be totally autonomous, with a suitable level of systems redundancy, can be assumed to be so unlikely to crash into another autonomous vehicle that they can be built significantly lighter. This is because they can be devoid of the massive over-engineering that is required today to protect inattentive drivers from the consequences of their and other drivers' lapses. No heavy safety structures, no air bags, no side curtains, no massive bumpers, no side intrusion structures, no telescoping steering columns—indeed no steering columns at all!

A significant question is, how many legacy cars will be mixing with the autonomous vehicles in 2035? It can be argued that no amount of electronic wizardry can completely protect one from the drunken fool in the legacy non-autonomous Cadillac Escalade. So in 2035, will autonomous cars still have to be built for collisions with the cars of today? This will depend upon when the "tipping point" occurs. This will be less of a technical issue and much more of a political, economic, and social issue. How aggressively will government fiscal policy encourage drivers to switch to autonomous vehicles and what incentives will the vehicle providers offer to make people make the switch? Will any legacy vehicles be left by 2035? It can also be argued that an autonomous vehicle, able to keep out of the way of other autonomous vehicles moving in a dynamic and unpredictable environment, will be capable of avoiding the errant, human-controlled Escalade, by being able to calculate instantly the optimal escape route.

Ultimately, cloud computing amongst scores of vehicles will create cooperative flows of traffic through the infrastructure rather than competitive surges and resultant shock-waves. Indeed, on surface streets, one can anticipate that traffic signals and pedestrian crossings will become redundant. Vehicles will never have to stop until they have to pick up or drop off their occupants. They will perfectly choreograph their way around other vehicles or pedestrians, regardless of the direction of travel.

If you want to see a wonderful model of this constant, choreographed traffic flow around randomly moving interruptions—albeit in slow motion—please visit Bangalore or any other major Indian city. Because of decades of skills honed on motorcycles in crowded, narrow streets, the modern Indian car, bus, and truck drivers have already developed these choreographed traffic skills. Nobody ever stops—for anything; no anger, no rudeness, no problem if someone drives the wrong way down a street or an errant marketer pushes his barrow of vegetables across the street without looking. The traffic just moves around the perturbation.

So the software algorithms that need to be developed (probably in Bangalore) will emulate the Indian driver; the resulting electron networks will just be significantly faster than even the finely honed Indian software developer's neural networks.

Finally, with cars being able to drive themselves, ride on demand and car-sharing schemes can take on whole new dimensions,

offering the possibility of greatly reducing the number of vehicles that need to exist. Once a journey has been completed, a car can go back into immediate circulation to transport someone else.

Suddenly, the future of the car looks much rosier. Indeed, the prospect of smooth, high-density streams of renewably energy-efficient vehicles that precisely match the requirements of each individual journey suggests a personal mobility solution that is safer, more energy efficient, more ecologically responsible, and certainly more convenient than any transit system. Come on, Detroit!

"Today, the only use for a horse is for sports."
Jim Hall, 2953 Analytics, a Birmingham,
Michigan automotive market analysis firm.

THE 2035 LOOK

Geoffrey Wardle

Car of the future, by Carl Vetillard.

AS A CAR DESIGNER, I OFTEN GET ASKED WHAT CARS WILL LOOK LIKE IN THE FUTURE; will they be soft and streamlined or will they look sharp and industrial? Will they be minimalist in their sculpturing and detailing or will they be exaggerated and ornate?

Like predicting any other aspect of the future, the further ahead we look, the more difficult it is to say with any certainty how things will be. So it is with cars. There are many influences on the way cars look, some related to market forces, some by the herding instincts of the relatively small car design community, and some dictated by the underlying technical and manufacturing capabilities of the time. Then there is the generally evolutionary nature of the automobile industry.

So, in order to write intelligently about how cars will look in 2035, we can learn some things by drawing inferences from past experiences and others by considering what the likely trends will be for the different influences and driving forces in the future.

EXTRAPOLATING FROM THE PAST

If we look through the history of automobile design, we can recognize distinct periods when cars seemed to look a particular way. For the first couple of decades of the automobile industry, cars took on a wide variety of appearances because no perceived

wisdom yet dictated the way cars should be. Cars were still essentially an industrial experiment, with widely different approaches to propulsion, layout, steering systems, and the number and placement of wheels. In these early days, if there was a particular look, it borrowed much from the various types of horse-drawn wagons and carriages.

In 1910, the gasoline engine was by no means the certain propulsion system of choice. Steam and particularly battery-electric cars were more popular. Battery-electric cars were clean, quiet and extremely easy to use and particularly favored by women for urban driving. It was, ironically, the invention of the electric starter motor in 1912 that quickly swung public favor toward the internal combustion engine. Now the major inconvenience of the technology—thumb-breaking starting procedures with a hand crank—had been thwarted and the major advantages of range and instant operation won out. Already, here is an instance of a minor technological advance having a major influence on how cars evolved and looked. Electric cars of the time had a very different and arguably more advanced look than their gasoline powered rivals. Had Delco not invented the electric starter motor until, say 1918, electric cars could have reached a tipping point and automotive history and the cars it spawned would look radically different today!

By the second decade of the twentieth century, a general format for the layout

A car manufacturer
often only supplied
the running chassis.
The body was built by
another enterprise,
chosen by the
customer. The radiator
was therefore a way
for Ford, Chevrolet,
and Mercedes-Benz to
make sure their brand
was always displayed
prominently.

of automobiles with internal combustion engines had started to emerge, influenced by such notable cars as the 1891 Panhard-Levassor (1) of France and epitomized by the 1908 Model T Ford (2).

This format generally placed the passengers facing forwards, two-by-two between the front and rear axles with the motor, typically, ahead of the passengers under some kind of hood. The motor was connected to the rear driving wheels via a gearbox and drive shafts passing underneath the passenger floor. There were still plenty of exceptions to this format, particularly for the quite numerous battery-electric cars then in existence.

Typical for the breed, the first Model T Fords were open cars, with weather protection provided by folding canvas roofs on steel or timber frames—much like the horse-drawn buggies of the time. As the front-mounted internal combustion engine became the norm, ornate cooling radiators became an early design feature. While body shapes were still quite rudimentary, the different manufacturers created their own distinct outlines and details to the radiators of their cars. As a result, both "brand identity" and the concept of the "face" of the car became defining features. Incidentally, in those days a car manufacturer often only supplied the running chassis. The body was built by another enterprise, chosen by the customer. The radiator was therefore a way for Ford, Chevrolet, and Mercedes-Benz to make sure their brand was always displayed prominently.

These early cars generally ran on narrow, large diameter wheels and tires with high ground clearance because early roads were still unmade. The passenger-carrying bodies were mounted on top of a ladder-frame chassis, to which all the mechanical parts were attached and which also took care of all the suspension forces. This meant that the overall height was quite tall compared to modern cars, and the passenger had to climb up to get in.

Wealthier car buyers expected more weather protection than cars like the Model T provided, so closed bodies became more common for expensive cars. These tended to be quite upright and boxy affairs, with vertical side windows and windscreens. If a bespoke body-builder or coachworks built the body, some subtle forms were introduced to the panels and mudguards that were redolent of the traditions of horse-drawn carriage building from which these coachbuilders had evolved.

The 1922 Lancia Lambda [3] was the first significant car to jettison the separate chassis by designing the body to become a load-bearing structure. This allowed the car to be much lower to the ground to make it easier for passengers to get in and out and to vastly improve the dynamics of the vehicle in tune with the greatly improved road surfaces. The wonderful 1934 Citroën Traction Avant [4] (Légière 15) epitomized the Lancia's influence toward the low-slung look and was greatly enabled by its advanced, pontoon monocoque body in combination with front-wheel drive.

Greatly encouraged by European coachbuilders and the great Harley Earl, founder of General Motors' Art and Color studios, from this point on the exterior appearance of cars morphed from practical to more contrived.

All the hitherto separate elements of the car exterior started to become more considered in their shape. Figoni & Falaschi Talbot [5], the exotic French coachbuilders of the 1930s [6], and the parallel fascination in the United States with Art Deco and streamlining pushed this integration of forms to more extreme shapes, although the wheel fenders, hoods, trunks, and radiator openings were still identifiable elements.

The onset of World War II froze car design trends for some years, but as soon as the war finished, there was an eagerness to bring modernity to the automobile. Car designers of the day had become very aware of the aerospace industry's progress through the hostilities, and it was not long before forms and details associated with aircraft were to be seen on cars. Perhaps the single most important trend that this encouraged was the complete integration of the wheel

fenders into the main body form and the disappearance of the vertical opening to the radiators at the front of the car. The 1948 Cisitalia [7], designed by the great Italian coachbuilder Pininfarina, was perhaps a pivotal car in this trend. An example can be seen in the Museum of Modern Art in New York.

In Europe through the 1950s, car design trends were no doubt influenced by economic austerity. They tended to carry on from the Cisitalia, looking to create harmony of forms, simplicity and economy of details, and an efficiency of architecture. External dimensions were kept as compact as possible to reduce material costs and fuel consumption while maximizing the accommodation inside for passengers and baggage. Design through necessity.

Meanwhile, in the United States, a very different mood of optimism and economic growth prevailed. The resulting designs were much more flamboyant, heavily inspired by science fiction, space travel, and an industrial

5

6

7

cultural inclination toward built-in obsolescence. American car design was driven to excessive ornamentation in the form of fins, chrome, dual-tone paint schemes, phallic details, and elaborate glass shapes. Design through fashion. (1959 Chevy Impala Coupe (8) and a suitably finned and protuberanced Chrysler (9).)

Although they shared some influences, by and large, two different kinds of auto industries emerged on either side of the Atlantic Ocean in the fifties, sixties, and seventies.

In Europe, the fifties and sixties produced cars that were generally soft in exterior form, extremely so in the case of the Renault Dauphine (10) and the Jaguar D-Type (11) or moderately so, for instance the Citroën GS (12) and the Volvo Amazon (13).

Although they shared some influences, by and large, two different kinds of auto industries emerged on either side of the Atlantic Ocean in the fifties, sixties, and seventies.

8

9

10

11

12

13

14

15

Any American influence was seen in very moderate fins at the rear and more ornate front grille decorations.

Arguably one of the greatest car design geniuses of all time, the Italian Giorgetto Giugiaro dropped a huge rock in the pool in the late sixties. Having designed some of the most sensual soft-formed cars in the early part of his career (the Alfa Romeo Canguro (14) show car of 1965 springs to mind) he started to experiment with quite dramatically sharp-edged and shallow-formed cars, first as concept vehicles for car shows and then in cars that he was contracted to design for production, such as the Original Volkswagen Golf/Rabbit (15).

Because he had such an exquisite Italian sensibility to proportion, form, and detail, these remarkably stark designs had their own beauty. Quite quickly, Giugiaro's work inspired a trend toward sharper edged and flatter paneled cars. Through the latter half of the seventies and the early eighties, most cars coming out of European manufacturers were quite architectural in their appearance.

By the late seventies, though, car designers were beginning to tire of the Giugiaro school of design and became fascinated again by softer forms, which they applied to the more disciplined architecture that Giugiaro had perfected. In parallel, the energy crises of the

seventies had turned the attention of auto companies on both continents back to energy efficiency and aerodynamics. By the late eighties and early nineties, soft form cars were predominant (16a, 16b). However, as it turns out, cars do not have to have very soft outer forms to be highly aerodynamic. The art and science of automobile aerodynamics is much more subtle than that. In fact, some of the most notable low-drag cars to be introduced at the turn of the eighties were quite formal in their exterior design, for example the Audi 100 (16c) and Audi 5000, which had soft forms where they were needed but were quite severe in other aspects.

Over the last 20 years, the greatest progress in automobile manufacturing has been the development of highly reliable vehicles and remarkable improvements in performance, handling, and standard features, all across the spectrum. Now, it is quite unusual for a "bad" car to enter the market. A $14,000 Toyota is really not much less competent than a $50,000 Audi. Speed, grip, refinement, perceived quality of materials, details, and electronic features separate the two, but they share fundamental competence. This means that more than ever competing companies have to differentiate their brand identities through the appearance of their vehicles—inside and out.

16a 1991 Toyota Celica.

16b Ford Taurus.

16c Audi 100.

As emerging generations lose interest in cars, maybe the car designer, in the traditional sense of one who wrestles with all the established conventions of automotive taste, will be a thing of the past.

As the global market becomes increasingly and brutally competitive, it is more difficult for a company to make its cars stand out from the competition without resorting to visual gimmicks. The appearance of many cars seems to be excessively reliant on gratuitous visual flourishes. This breaks with the past focus of designers on judicious development of satisfying proportions, carefully controlled forms, graphic harmony of different elements, and an intuitive appreciation of negative spaces. Audi, Volkswagen, and one or two others still seem to adhere to these high design principles. But most other brands now seem to have abandoned high automotive design principles in favor of visual noise.

That trend pendulum might swing the opposite way. Or, as emerging generations lose interest in cars, maybe the car designer, in the traditional sense of one who wrestles with all the established conventions of automotive taste, will be a thing of the past. Perhaps the appearance of cars will increasingly become commoditized or even wild as technology allows customers more and more opportunities to "design" their cars online.

WHERE DO WE GO NEXT?

Let us consider the future leading to 2035 in chunks. For each chunk of time, overarching driving forces that are not related to vehicle design per se will be nevertheless influential—economics, politics, and societal issues. Other changing influences will be more specific to the auto industry's evolution, such as technological developments and market forces. Together, these will contribute to how vehicles will look.

Writing this chapter in 2012, one thing is quite clear: the rate of change of the automobile industry is going to be faster and more significant between now and 2035 than perhaps the entire history of the car. Of course, quite major, even catastrophic events, which are hard to predict, could completely change the direction of development. For instance, a major conflict in the Middle East that upends the global oil industry is possible, with predictable outcomes. A massive series of solar flares that knocks out two-thirds of the world's communication satellites would have a less predictable influence on our global progress. Similarly, a huge nuclear accident in Europe or Michigan would have a massive impact on the fortunes of auto companies.

2012–2015

In this period of time in the near future, influential forces external to the industry are fairly easy to summarize: continuing, global, economic sluggishness; known, looming fuel efficiency legislation; continued emphasis on pedestrian safety in Europe; the continuing growth of the Chinese auto industry's capabilities; and the strength of the South East Asian car markets generally.

Technological factors that will impact cars over the next three years will include the mainstream introduction of plug-in, *parallel* hybrid vehicles, such as the Toyota Prius. In addition, there will be more plug-in *series* hybrids similar in concept to the Chevy Volt.

New, all electric (battery-electric) cars will trickle onto the market. (We are still some years away from the economics of battery production making sense for consumers and manufacturers alike without subsidies being part of the equation.) Diesel hybrids are starting to be introduced into the European market, producing vehicles with quite remarkably low fuel consumption. These might spread to North America.

Connectivity between vehicles, their external environment, and the Internet will continue to be developed. More advanced accident avoidance technology—sub-systems that will assist drivers in keeping out of accident situations or even wrest control from the driver when the car's sensors determine that a collision is imminent—will be introduced.

These external and technological factors are going to have only modest, incremental influences on the architecture of cars— the underlying passenger and mechanical layout of the vehicle that determines proportions, dimensions, profiles, window, and door positions.

A trend toward slightly smaller frontal cross-sections will continue in order to help fuel efficiency through lowering aerodynamic drag, which explains the recent industry trend to introduce more small, car-based SUVs (crossovers) (17).

On the other hand, in the Chinese market, size matters and so does bling. While Europeans and Americans will continue looking for modesty in size, we can expect more cars, SUVs, and trucks to be lengthened and more boldly decorated for the Chinese market.

Over the next three years, no significant new vehicle segments will be created—i.e. new categories of vehicles in the market such as the Smart Car (18), which was introduced a few years ago, the crossover, and the hybrid.

The exterior styling of cars in the next three years will probably be a continuation of gratuitously noisy forms and excessive and out-of-place graphic arrangements. The shape of the headlamps, for instance,

17 Range Rover Evoque.

18 Smart Car.

19 Lexus.

will have no relationship to adjacent details, and forms will be forced around all this incongruence (19).

An anime-influenced penchant for cartoony-looking vehicles, personified by the Nissan Juke (20), will remain for a while.

Large diameter wheels (21) will probably reach their peak by 2015 as the disadvantages of their considerable weight and inertia outweigh any real customer benefits. This is a visual pendulum that needs to start swinging the other way.

20 *Nissan Juke.*

21 *Fisker Karma.*

22 *Chinese car 2015.*

While Europeans and Americans will continue looking for modesty in size, we can expect more cars, SUVs, and trucks to be lengthened and more boldly decorated for the Chinese market.

2015–2025

As we move beyond 2015 toward 2025, however, events will be changing. Fuel-efficiency legislation that was merely on the horizon will be baring teeth. Public and political frustration at increasing levels of traffic congestion around the world will have caused various forms of road pricing to be introduced. This will start to change some people's attitudes about how they use their cars. Continuing climate changes that raise sea levels and create increasingly extreme weather events will begin to take the general, global population toward a tipping point. Regular folks will realize that each of us has to create a much smaller carbon footprint.

While it took the Japanese car industry two decades to be regarded as serious rivals by American and European manufacturers, and maybe 15 years for Korean auto brands, everyone expects that the Chinese auto industry will penetrate world markets faster and, quite possibly, more comprehensively. This will certainly affect the bottom end of American, European, and Australasian markets, where a plethora of unfamiliar Chinese brand names will offer vehicles at low prices to increasingly large numbers of disinterested car users (22). While Chinese car companies are quite capable of designing good-looking cars, intense competition between Chinese exporters will likely produce some strange looking vehicles in an attempt to compensate for their nonexistent technical and functional differences. However, we should not assume that Chinese car manufacturers would limit their ambitions to the low end of the market. Chinese consumers themselves are already major consumers of existing premium brands and the Chinese industry is very keen to supply up-market brands too. Chinese companies competing with Lexus, Audi, BMW, and Jaguar Land Rover will force these companies to really hone their brand identities in order to survive. As a result, existing premium brand companies may start to consider distinctly American, German, British, or Swedish looks, according to their country of origin.

A plethora of unfamiliar Chinese brand names will offer vehicles at low prices to increasingly large numbers of disinterested car users.

The rapid rise and success of the Chinese auto industry will undoubtedly be the death-knell of existing European, American, and Japanese car companies that are not super-fit. They will either disappear or be acquired by Chinese companies, as Volvo and MG/Rover already have.

In the developed Western economies, little in the way of new transportation infrastructure will have been built in comparison to what we have today. As a result, most of the progress in the transportation field will have been in utilizing existing infrastructure more efficiently, hence the interest in road-pricing and car share systems. Many of the car companies will be realizing their existing business model is not sustainable. They should be asking themselves how they could make a good return on their investments when the total appetite for buying cars is falling, even though the demand for personal mobility is rising. They might be starting to consider new ways of relating to their customers. Perhaps they will be focusing more on selling us passenger miles delivered, rather than just the hardware.

For the next two or three decades, whatever propulsion system we choose for our vehicles, the cost of energy for moving those vehicles is going to be a very significant part of our weekly expenditure. There will likely be times when the availability of gasoline and diesel becomes unreliable, because perturbations in the marketplace will no longer be buffered by plentiful reserves.

The answer? We will become very, very strategic about when we use vehicles for transport and what sort of vehicle we use for a specific journey.

A mild preview of the future can be seen in Europe and the mature Asian economies where deliberately high taxes on gasoline and diesel fuels have popularized smaller, more energy efficient cars. Europeans like the convenience of cars like anyone else. They like fast cars too. However, they forfeit size, weight, and inefficiency to maintain their addiction.

At the time of writing this, gasoline prices in the United States are climbing again toward the $4–5 per gallon levels that started to see people adjust their automotive buying habits a few years ago. As prices start to break new records—$8 per gallon, $10 per gallon (typical current European cost today), $12 per gallon and even higher—adjustment will no longer suffice. We will start to look differently at the whole notion of owning and using cars or multiples of cars.

THE RIGHT TOOL FOR THE JOB

Today, when we purchase a vehicle we tend to assess all the uses we might possibly want the vehicle to perform, even the uses we might never actually put the vehicle to. For instance we might, for our annual vacation, go camping in the Sierra Mountains. So we decide to buy a four-wheel-drive, semi-off-road-capable, five-seat SUV with a powerful, five-liter multi-cylinder engine to make sure we have enough power to scale the mountain tracks. We also feel comfortable that we could, if needed, tow a U-Haul trailer or make a trip to IKEA to pick up those kitchen cabinets we might buy. Oh, and if The Big One happens, we can be the first to get out of town!

Of course, what the vehicle will primarily be used for is to drop the kids off at school and then to take us those 30 miles across town to work and back again—alone.

So let's look at another option. If gasoline is $8 per gallon, why don't we buy a small, four-seat car with a 1.8-liter engine that will carry the kids to school and perhaps return 35 mpg on the commute to and from work instead of the 15 mpg that the SUV would achieve? When we go to IKEA for those kitchen cabinets, we can get the store to deliver them, or we could buy them online. If we do go camping for the summer, we'll look into renting an SUV or figure out a way of hitching a small camping trailer to the car. It will probably manage to negotiate the mountain roads; it just won't be as much fun. Europeans seem to enjoy camping in the Alps just the same, even if they drive a small Fiat with a huge roof rack!

At $12 per gallon of gas, 35 mpg sounds pretty poor. Maybe, we should be thinking 70 or 80 mpg? What sort of vehicle would achieve that? Well, how about a quite small vehicle with one main driving seat and a seat behind that two children could squeeze into or some groceries. The vehicle would be rather lightweight and streamlined for aero-dynamic efficiency, no wider than needed to give its occupants some side-intrusion protection. Propelled by a small gasoline or diesel engine, it would still be able to keep up with freeway traffic and would actually be quite fun to drive as well. With increasing numbers of vehicles being fitted with col-lision avoidance technologies, mixing with other, larger vehicles would seem less risky.

Beyond $12 per gallon, we will be looking at even more radical solutions to small vehicles and be quite choosy about when we decide to use a vehicle for personal transporta-tion. Perhaps we could own more than one vehicle to provide optimal transportation solutions for different travel occasions. But many economic pundits predict that more of us are going to be less affluent than before, so for most of us, owning multiple vehicles is not going to be a reality. As you may read elsewhere in this book, many experts

If gasoline is $8 per gallon, why don't we buy a small, four-seat car with a 1.8-liter engine that will carry the kids to school and perhaps return 35 mpg on the commute to and from work instead of the 15 mpg that the SUV would achieve?

are predicting that the trend in Southern California will be for denser urban living conditions. So, not only will we not be able to afford to own several vehicles, we will have no space to store them when we are not using them.

Put all these factors together and we can start to see that for the majority of us in Southern California, we are going to be more discerning about when we decide to drive and what we drive. Our criteria for choosing our personal vehicle will be very different from today and for many, parking vehicles will be far more restricted by available space, which in turn will mean rising parking costs.

As a result of these powerful external forces, the kinds of vehicles seen on the roads will change significantly. Car manufacturers will be strongly incentivized to supply the kinds of vehicles that consumers realize that they really need—and want.

The largest, most obvious unmet opportunity in the marketplace until now has been for the 85% of car journeys with only the driver—the urban and ex-urban commuter and the long-distance business traveler. Toward 2020, stiff new fuel-efficiency legislation, urban parking shortages, and the growing public concern about our environment will finally open up this market segment and we will see growing numbers of one-seat, one-plus-one-seat, and one-plus-two-seat cars that will be freeway capable, rewarding to drive, comfortable, and highly fuel efficient. Twizy type (for metropolis errands and commutes) should look like a one-plus-one—more upright, agile, and fun (23); XL1 type (for long-distance commutes or business journeys) should look low, narrow, sleek, beautiful, fast (24).

Many other categories of cars will be getting more compact to make them lighter and sleeker to significantly reduce energy consumption. For instance, we will see new expressions of America's favorite: the go-anywhere, all-terrain SUV-type vehicle (25). The current Mini Cooper Countryman is the precursor to many other compact, lightweight but highly capable-looking micro-SUVs.

If current social trends continue, today's emerging young generations will have much less interest in cars as a principal expression of themselves. They will see cars mostly as utility devices. Their significant interest in leisure activities derived from social networking will likely spawn a new generation of vehicles like today's Scion XB. The emphasis will be on a comfortable, flexible interior volume in which several friends can journey around town together. However, these vehicles will still be packaged and engineered to be highly fuel efficient, no bigger or heavier than necessary to do the job (26).

The largest unmet opportunity in the marketplace until now has been for the 85% of car journeys with only the driver.

23 By Jun Imai—2022
Twizy and VW XL1 type vehicle.

24 By Nick Gronenthal—2022
XL1 type. For long-distance commutes or business journeys.

25 By James Yamazaki—2025
Small, highly capable vehicle.

26 By Geoffrey Wardle—2022
Scion XB type vehicle emphasizes efficient packaging, easy ingress/egress, and is friendly, inviting, and charismatic.

ALTERNATIVES TO OWNERSHIP

A much higher number of people will be comfortable with ride sharing as computer apps seamlessly and reliably allow even strangers to instantly find someone else planning a nearly identical journey. This will lead many more people to start considering why they need to own a car at all. Enterprises like today's Zipcar car-sharing clubs could become much larger and more ubiquitous. This in turn will create a demand for vehicles designed for continual use by different drivers who lease rather than own them outright. These vehicles will need to be tough and durable but still very attractive. Perhaps their appearance will reflect the car-sharing club's brand identity instead of the manufacturer's brand. Also, the cars will be designed to recognize the driver and instantly adapt to that driver's preferred seat and mirror positions, interior ambience, entertainment options, and even interior trim colors and exterior colors. These car-share enterprises will provide a mixed fleet of vehicles, so their members can access the precise kind of vehicle that they need—a one-seat commuter, a five-seater for family or social journeys, a van for trips to IKEA, etc.

This growing business for leasing vehicles to members on an as-needed basis could be the model that changes the way the whole automobile industry and its customers do business. In effect, passenger miles delivered—rather than specific vehicles—in "Total Mobility Packages," where they have access to various vehicle categories as and when needed. These new vehicle categories and usages will be designed around significant technological developments, many of which will enable serious reductions in weight, greater energy efficiency, increased connectivity to the external environment, and major contributions to reducing accidents.

A much higher number of people will be comfortable with ride sharing as computer apps seamlessly and reliably allow even strangers to instantly find someone else planning a nearly identical journey.

ENGINEERING AND DESIGN IN THE MID-FUTURE

To this end, far more cars will have electric motors to propel them, with internal or external combustion engines (turbines) on board to generate electricity. Range extension through series hybrids promises an optimal balance between simplicity and energy efficiency until battery development delivers cheap, energy-dense, environmentally clean batteries. Such a power-train system also allows the car designer more flexibility in how they distribute the various components around the vehicle for the benefit of passenger convenience. Mostly, however, the optimal tuning of modestly sized gasoline or diesel engines to run at a single speed to generate a constant amount of energy yields ultra fuel efficiency and clean emissions.

A variety of liquid or liquid gas fuels will be offered, depending on geography, to power these ultra-efficient power trains, in the form of different blends of responsible bio-fuels, natural gas and oil-based products. During

27 By Geoffrey Wardle —2025
SAAB Concept Sketch.

28 By Young Jin Hough —2015
Korean brand with a German premium look.

this time period, hydrogen will sputter into mainstream to either become established in the mainstream or to be used solely for highly specialized applications.

Discrete accident avoidance systems, vehicle-to-vehicle communications, and cloud computing algorithms will facilitate the emergence of semi-automated vehicles. Such vehicles will be capable of sensing and avoiding other vehicles and obstacles without driver input and, in appropriate situations, will be able to find their way toward final destinations. These vehicles will have all the primary and secondary driving controls familiar to us today and more. They will represent a significant step toward completely automated vehicles, and allow the public to contemplate how their cars could differ if they did not have any physical controls at all. Drive-by-wire control systems will routinely include steering and braking systems—a precursor to complete automation—allowing safety advances (for instance, no awkward steering columns to manage in a frontal impact collision).

During most of this time period, from 2015 to 2025, cars for production will still be designed around the assumptions of a

seated driver using controls that look similar to the ones we have today, even if they are connected to the vehicle in a different way. Nearer 2025, cars will be introduced that are capable of driving completely robotically. By this time, completely automated vehicles will have been demonstrated in concept form for some time.

In an effort to save significant weight, new forms of glazing to replace heavy glass will be developed from plastics and polycarbonates that have glass-hard, scratch-resistant surfaces. As a secondary benefit, such glazing materials could offer designers greater freedoms to generate more elaborate and sculptural window surfaces.

This major effort to reduce energy-sapping weight will also apply to aerodynamics. While there is little more to learn about the basic forms of vehicles, gains can still be made from airflow management around and through front faces, rear ends, undersides, and the relationship between overall vehicle shapes and the ground. For example, one easy way to reduce overall aerodynamic drag is to make sure that the frontal area is kept as low as possible, i.e. the vehicle should be no wider and taller than needed to accommodate its occupants comfortably.

The overall quest in this era to reduce weight and rolling resistance will force designers to reduce wheel-sizes. Between large diameters reducing frictional losses at the bearings and smaller diameters reducing un-sprung weight and inertia is a sweet spot. Even in 2012, we have broken through that sweet spot. A narrower tire reduces rolling resistance at any diameter. Therefore, many designers will make every effort to emphasize perceived stability with tires and rims pushed toward the outer corners of their vehicle designs but with narrower treads.

Tire technology and better wheel dynamics through lower inertia and gyroscopic forces will ensure no loss in grip. More avant-garde designers might decide that it is time to move on and de-emphasize wheels (wheels are a nineteenth-century anachronism), or even hide them altogether (27).

In terms of the visual language of cars in this time frame, quite a diversity of shapes, proportions, and surface treatments will be available. Between entry-level commodity cars and premium brands that emphasize cultural attributes, a noisy sea of designs will be in the middle. Competing companies will be fighting to get noticed by the middle-class market that is still relatively interested in cars beyond just transportation. In their up-market push, Chinese automakers will have premium brands that emulate premium European and American brands, just as the Korean companies are successfully doing now (28). In a great variety of vehicle types, auto companies will seek to create recognizably different brand identities with styling that utilizes a range of form languages, including soft, sharp, architectural, organic, restrained, charismatic, conservative, and funky. We see the beginnings of this today with vehicles like the range of Minis, the Range Rover Evoque, and Volvo C30, which are charismatic and strongly identified with their brands yet not gratuitously gauche.

2025–2035

The major change by 2025 is likely to be the robust arrival of fully automated road vehicles—cars, trucks, big-rigs, and buses that do not need a human driver, ever. During the ensuing years, automated vehicles will become nearly ubiquitous, and this will completely change the way we think about cars. It will usher in a completely new era in personal mobility and a potentially glorious rebirth for car companies in business at that time.

With the arrival of fully automated vehicles, insurance companies' interpretation of risk management, along with data showing a significant reduction of inter-vehicle impacts, will support legislating far less stringent passenger safety requirements. In turn, greatly reduced passenger safety legislation in fully automated road vehicles will make them significantly lighter—for instance, with no air-bags, no side intrusion barriers, no crumple zones, and no collapsible steering columns. This will make vehicles much cheaper to

The major change by 2025 is likely to be the robust arrival of fully automated road vehicles—cars, trucks, big-rigs, and buses that do not need a human driver, ever.

design, develop, and build, incentivizing the car industry to delete manual vehicles from their product range.

The Total Mobility Package business model can really take off now. From a customer perspective, on-demand access to any kind of vehicle needed for a specific journey can work seamlessly with precise delivery and exchange of vehicles when and where needed.

The rapid spread of Total Mobility Package industry/customer relationships, lessons learned from light-weighting vehicles with energy efficient powertrains, and the rapidly increasing use of automated vehicles will greatly reduce the total energy consumption of the global road fleet.

In terms of propulsion systems, electric motors will be ubiquitous, driving wheels through simple mechanical transmissions or directly mounted in the wheels (hub motors). Propulsion energy sources will still vary according to geography and politics. Onboard energy storage will tend to be batteries for small-to-medium-sized urban cars and range extension devices for larger cars and those intended for longer-distance inter-city travel (such as cars, trucks, and long-distance buses).

29a By Alan Chao—2027
Interior of 4 seater, where front and rear passengers are facing each other.

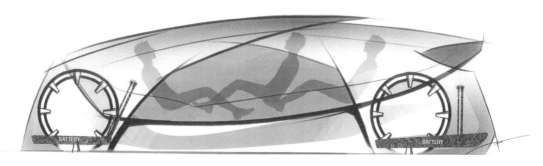

The vehicle-manufacturing segment of the industry will also fragment due to incentives to modularize vehicle component sets and the removal of ultra-expensive crash safety development, which will remove barriers to entry for smaller or start-up enterprises to join the industry. Advanced manufacturing technologies (local manufacturing, new materials, new forming, and 3-D printing processes) will completely decentralize vehicle production (even if products and brands remain global entities).

Vehicles will no longer be designed around a driver. The relative lack of passenger safety requirements will allow occupants to be positioned in completely new configurations. For instance, brand new vehicle segments will have passenger and cargo arrangements optimized for sightseeing, business meetings (29), meditative journeys, rest, efficient work (30), limousine work (31), and leisure (32).

The demonstrable energy savings of the new road vehicle fleet will allow some relaxation of aero-efficiency, giving greater freedom to design vehicles around more generous occupant spaces, where appropriate. The higher aerodynamic rolling resistance and weight of the more voluminous multi-occupant vehicles will be offset by a large number of single or dual occupancy hyper-efficient urban commuter vehicles.

Significant new opportunities to change the appearance of cars will also come from completely new manufacturing paradigms. Components, structures, and panels will be manufactured from 100% recyclable or new

29b By Alan Chao—2027
Exterior of a vehicle with relaxed seating positions and glazing optimized for viewing surrounding landscapes, cityscapes.

30 By Whoon Min—2030
Vehicle interior set up for one or two people to use their commute time for work.

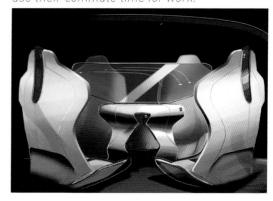

31a By Fero Tobak—2027
A driverless, luxury Rolls-Royce
"Town Car" conveyance.

31b By Fero Tobak—2027

32a By Gabriel Wartofsky—2027
A vehicle highly adaptable for outdoor
leisure activities.

As new manufacturing materials are developed, designers have an opportunity to wean customers away from shiny to other attractive finishes.

materials derived from organic, renewable sources that allow industrial-grade performance and accuracy of components. These, along with additive manufacturing processes (3-D printing) and other new forming processes will allow local manufacture of vehicles.

Human beings are naturally attracted to shiny things. But that attraction in things automotive comes at a huge cost. Creating a deep, long-lasting luster requires staggeringly high industry investment in paint shops; massive time, cost, and energy in making high fidelity press tools to stamp flawlessly smooth steel panels; and some really expensive chemicals to coat the steel to protect it from corrosion and help the paint stick. Containing the environmental fall-out from all these chemical and paint processes is a part of the high costs.

As new manufacturing materials are developed, designers have an opportunity to wean customers away from shiny to other attractive finishes. We can look to all of the inspiring buildings that take our breath away without shiny paint. Natural material finishes, such as aluminum, wood, concrete, and fabric, captivate us in the works of Renzo Piano, Richard Rogers, and Toyo Ito. The glass is the only glossy element.

Perhaps the most striking change in 2035, though, will be a very different idea about the place of the car in our everyday lives.

In 2012, even though its image is getting a little tarnished in Europe and North America, the car is seen on a pedestal—an imaginary extension of our egos, penises, breasts, power, wealth, status, masculinity, aggression, taste, the list goes on. One could also say the same thing about grand architecture and massive homes.

By 2035, it is quite possible that the car will be regarded more as a practical tool for getting around—more like mobile architecture. At the same time, perhaps buildings will be seen more as a practical tool for living in. Perhaps the two will collide and the boundaries between buildings and cars in our day-to-day lives will blur. As my good friend the genius Dan Sturges would say, enter the era of *mobiliture*.

> *The boundaries between buildings and cars in our day-to-day lives will blur.*

HYBRID: THE NEW NORMAL

Tom Smiley

LONG BEFORE 2035, hybrid cars won't be referred to as "hybrid" but will simply be cars. This process has already begun and will continue through the next few decades. The first hybrid car, the Honda Insight, hit the road thirteen years ago. It looked like a blob and only had only two seats. The car was designed for an urban, no-kids demographic, one the automaker imagined to be much larger than the .025% it really is. For the hybrid to succeed, the car had to change. The first hybrids to be taken seriously by Americans were the Toyota Prius and the Honda Civic Hybrid. The cars were still too small for most Americans, but they fit the needs of 0.1% of the market. In 2003, hybrids finally grew to a size heavily demanded by Americans, and so the launch of the Toyota Camry Hybrid, Ford Escape Hybrid, and the second generation Prius earned more widespread market acceptance. The single attribute shared by all three of these vehicles is a "midsize" interior volume. For Americans, midsize is "just right": it matters less if they're sedans, SUVs, or pickup trucks—a four-door midsize vehicle gives them a Big Gulp interior with a maneuverable exterior. With the launch of the Camry, Escape, and second generation Prius, hybrids became vehicles that most Americans could buy without sacrificing usability. As gas prices increased, hybrids went from being exotic to being mainstream.

Unlike what many marketers would like you to think, a hybrid engine won't make birds sing as it drives down leafy roadways. A hybrid fuel system doesn't make a car faster, and certainly all that weight doesn't make it more agile. In fact, beyond increased gas mileage, the only thing a hybrid really does is add cost and reduce usability by stuffing half of the trunk with batteries. But for the middle class, the savings in gas outweigh

With the launch of the Camry, Escape, and second generation Prius, hybrids became vehicles that most Americans could buy without sacrificing usability.

the drawbacks in cargo space and agility. So hybrids are finding increasing success in the middle class, as they keep the gas bill down while accommodating 1.5 kids and the dog. With gas prices currently hovering around $4 a gallon, hybrid models are now 3% of the U.S. market.

Hybrid powertrains are expensive, adding thousands of dollars to the price of a vehicle with little benefit other than mpg. So even with ten-year development times, hybrid vehicle manufactures will strive to time the availability of these vehicles perfectly with an immediate rise of gas prices. They are aware high gas prices are by far the most significant driver for sales. Four-dollar-a-gallon gas is still not expensive enough to justify widespread adoption of hybrid technology because turbocharging an engine can more efficiently keep the monthly gas bill under the magical $200 level.[1] For now most families can keep their monthly gas bill manageable with these simple technologies and avoid the cost of a hybrid, but the hybrid is poised for a boost. Demand for fuel from India, China,

The hybrid is poised for a boost. Demand for fuel from India, China, and developing countries will cause the price of gasoline to increase dramatically.

and developing countries will cause the price of gasoline to increase dramatically. Notwithstanding arguments about exactly how fast this will happen, it's safe to say that it's inevitable, and will occur before 2035, at which time hybrid engines will be dominant in all types of vehicles popular with the middle class.

No vehicle represents the "self-reliant" middle class lifestyle better than the pickup truck. The general shape and layout of the pickup truck hasn't changed in a hundred years and probably won't change much in the next twenty-three, so it's safe to say they will largely look the same in 2035. Today's pickup trucks still have powerful V-8 engines, in the great American tradition, but there is already a shift in the pattern. With gas at $4 a gallon, Ford's EcoBoost V-6 has proven itself on the market to be a viable compromise between power and fuel economy. But this won't last. With whatever the price of gas will be in 2035, the solution to the same problem will be a full hybrid. Existing hybrid pickup trucks are only partial hybrid "assists." In the future, a full Prius-like hybrid pickup truck will not only be available, but will be the default pickup truck. The fuel mileage benefit will be dramatic, and even in fleet models, the increased cost will make sense to consumers due to the dramatic reduction in fuel costs. Premium trucks will not be distinguished by larger engines but rather by larger batteries capable of charging through regular power outlets. Traditional diesel and gasoline-only trucks will be unheard of in 2035.

For those lucky enough to work behind a desk, the midsize sedan has always been a facilitator of a lifestyle. For the daily commute to weekends driving the family around, the interior room of a mid-size sedan has always fit the demands of the middle class, and this will not change in 2035. The hybrid powertrain is already a staple of the mid-size sedan market, and as the price of gasoline rises, we will see this powertrain become dominant, as a straight gasoline engine will no longer make fiscal sense. The fuel costs for a prestige car with a straight gasoline V-6 engine are already becoming an unsustainable burden for the middle class. With gas prices of a completely different order in 2035, the everyday mid-size hybrid sedan will gain plug-in functionality and be so economical and practical as to eradicate the V-6. By then, manufacturers will design hybrid cars with added performance, while 100 mpg (if plugged in each night) will help keep gasoline bills manageable even if gas hits twenty or thirty dollars per gallon.

Beginning in the late 1990s, sport utility vehicles (SUVs) overtook station wagons as the family vehicle of choice. With the rise in fuel prices, lighter and more fuel-efficient car-based SUVs, known as crossovers, replaced traditional truck-based SUVs. Today, every elementary school is overrun with these vehicles twice a day, because the height, size, and interior space comfort parents who see these cars as complete safety. At the moment, turbo charging is helping these notoriously fuel-thirsty vehicles keep the expenses "reasonable." By 2035, virtually all SUVs will have a hybrid-type powertrain with the added benefit of a plug-in system. This will be required because

A full Prius-like hybrid pickup truck will not only be available, but will be the default pickup truck.

even the hybrid powertrain is not enough to offset the rise in fuel prices. With a plug-in type system, SUVs will continue their reign as the suburban neighborhood transport of choice. Minivans are an entirely other matter. Strangely, minivan sales are typically not affected by fuel prices. Four-cylinder and fuel-efficient models tend to sell poorly even with gas prices at $4 a gallon because minivans are primarily used for local trips to the grocery store, school, and the proverbial big box retailer. They do not accrue miles in the same way a commuter car does. This low usage, combined with fewer units sold than sedans, trucks, or SUVs, will make minivans one of the last vehicles to be available as a hybrid. Minivans may never benefit from the more advanced plug-in technology, but by 2035, most vehicles, including minivans, will be hybrids.

[1] Driving behavior changes beyond a $200 per-month-expenditure. This rule of thumb comes from data from the U.S. Energy Information Administration, and the U.S. Department of Transportation. It is a rough estimate and tracked over time with CPI adjustments. The figure is derived from gallons of gasoline sold, miles driven, and number of licensed drivers.

This low usage, combined with fewer units sold than sedans, trucks, or SUVs, will make minivans one of the last vehicles to be available as a hybrid.

THE CONNECTED VEHICLE

Mohammad Poorsartep

DECEMBER 9, 2035, WAS A CRAZY DAY.
I dressed in five minutes, late for an important meeting. I got into my car and it was so pleasant and soothing to hear the song "You're Never Late" streaming out of the stereo as I opened the door. I love my new car...it's so thoughtful.

I was driving down the I-5 freeway when my car suggested a detour because, just a few seconds ago, two trucks had gotten into an accident and the system predicted traffic delays. Now I was going to be even later for my meeting! While navigating the detour, I activated my voice command to buy concert tickets to celebrate my anniversary that evening. Bad luck again: the tickets were sold out. My heart began pounding and my blood pressure rose. The car's health sensors noticed that I did not like what I was reading, and the system started looking for alternatives. The computer in the car offered me another event, which was a fine suggestion.

As I approached my destination, I received notification on the screen that the parking lot at my destination was full. I reserved a spot in the nearest lot with available spaces and, from my car, booked a two-way ticket for the jitney that would take me to the building where my meeting was. The system told me I would only have to wait a couple of minutes for the van to arrive. I was going to be late for the meeting but, luckily, my car had already sent an e-mail to all meeting attendees, letting them know I would be there within minutes, despite the traffic and parking problem. As my car parked, I joined the meeting by videoconference, uploaded my presentation, and then switched over to my handheld device as I stepped out of my car.

This scenario may well seem like a passage from a science fiction novel, but technology development is well underway to make all the above capabilities available for the future car. For the automobile industry, cars enabled by the technological innovations described here fit under the broad umbrella of "connected vehicles."

In the early 1990s, the United States Department of Transportation (USDOT) initiated a program first called "IntelliDrive" and later rebranded as "Connected Vehicle" to look at vehicle-to-vehicle (V2V) communication and vehicle-to-infrastructure (V2I) communication. In 1995, Ford and GM started a coalition called the Crash Avoidance Metrics Partnership that now includes Mercedes-Benz, Nissan, Toyota, Hyundai/Kia, Honda, and Volkswagen. The coalition, in collaboration

The Connected Vehicle program spearheaded by USDOT—with safety as its primary objective—has developed wireless communication technology by involving partners from the academic, private, and public sectors.

with USDOT, investigates and accelerates the implementation of new technology on vehicles to avoid automobile accidents.

The Connected Vehicle program spearheaded by USDOT—with safety as its primary objective—has developed wireless communication technology by involving partners from the academic, private, and public sectors. The program focuses on dedicated short-range communication in 5.9 GHz band that will support three types of application:

SAFETY APPLICATIONS are designed to increase situational awareness of the driver that will lead to reduction or elimination of crashes through V2V and V2I data transmission of driver advisories, driver warnings, and vehicle and/or infrastructure controls. These technologies may potentially address up to 82% of crash scenarios with unimpaired drivers, preventing tens of thousands of automobile crashes every year. However, the safety applications are not limited to passenger vehicles and further research will incorporate heavy vehicle crashes, including buses, trucks, and rail.

MOBILITY APPLICATIONS provide a connected, data-rich travel environment. The network captures real-time data from equipment located onboard vehicles and within the infrastructure (e.g., traffic signals). The data is transmitted wirelessly and used by transportation managers in a wide range of dynamic, multi-modal applications to manage the transportation system for optimum performance. This will lead to congestion reduction and other similar benefits.

ENVIRONMENTAL APPLICATIONS generate and capture environmentally relevant real-time transportation data and use this data to create actionable information to support and facilitate "green" transportation choices. Travelers may decide to avoid congested routes, take alternate routes, use public transit, or reschedule a trip—all of which can make their travel more fuel-efficient and eco-friendly. Onboard equipment can advise drivers on how to optimize the vehicle's operation and maintenance for maximum fuel efficiency.

We will be one step closer to a future with fewer traffic accidents and reduced traffic congestion.

In August 2011, the Connected Vehicle program's Safety Pilot Driver Clinics began to test the new V2V safety applications with ordinary drivers in controlled roadway situations. The evaluations explored drivers' reactions to safety applications using a variety of cars under a range of test conditions. The results achieved from this study revealed that more than 90% of drivers were in support of having the technology in their cars.

The Safety Pilot Model Deployment in Ann Arbor, Michigan, used nearly 3,000 vehicles equipped for wireless communication between vehicles and roadside equipment. Passenger cars, commercial trucks, and transit buses used a mix of integrated, retrofitted, and aftermarket V2V- and V2I-based safety systems. The data from the project will be analyzed for safety benefits. USDOT, and the broader transportation industry, will use the results in their efforts to develop additional safety, mobility, and environmental applications utilizing wireless technologies.

In late 2013, after development, testing, and deployment in pilot projects, the National Highway Traffic Safety Administration will begin a rule-making process for connected vehicle technology on passenger vehicles. If mandated, car manufacturers in the United States will be required to install the technology on all new vehicles (there will be retrofit solutions for older vehicles), and we will be one step closer to a future with fewer traffic accidents and reduced traffic congestion.

If you're a driver in the United States, it's likely that you have heard of, or experienced, OnStar, Synch, or other similar services in your vehicle. This is another form of a connected vehicle, for which the narrower term is "telematics." With telematics, you are not necessarily connected to other vehicles. You are connected, through a cellular network (e.g., CDMA, GSM, LTE, etc.), to data "clouds" that transmit information such as vehicle diagnostics and location, or receive information such as traffic conditions, weather, or even your friends' Facebook statuses.

This technology has become an increasingly important topic within the automotive industry since the cohort of Millennials—a new generation of drivers obsessed with instant information access—has entered the market.

Though it may seem that vehicle connectivity is driven by a paradigm shift in society, bringing the Internet to the car will be a first step in a longer journey. For consumers, having the ability and freedom to drive and safely access information is appealing. This will allow car manufacturers to leverage such demand and offer a long list of new applications and services. New technology will enable the following uses for vehicle connectivity:

+ Diagnostic applications, via a remote link to the vehicle, will offer monitoring of vehicle health, maintenance, and customer service to the owner.

+ Infotainment services, provided by a third party, will result in more customized music, news, weather conditions, and social networks. Integration of such services into the vehicle ecosystem will offer a personalized experience for each individual driver based on his or her preferences.

+ Navigation and location-based services (LBS) will enable the vehicle to intelligently select routes, or make informed suggestions of nearby businesses of interest to the driver.

+ Annual rates for insurance will become a thing of the past as drivers are charged based on their actual, and not estimated or perceived, usage. Plans will be tailored for each individual customer based on their driving behavior, miles driven, location, or other factors.

+ Payment services will streamline payments for tolls, parking, and other services during daily commutes.

+ Safety and security applications, such as automatic crash response, will transmit accurate life-saving information pertinent to an accident to emergency first responders. Such information can also reduce fraudulent insurance claims and their associated cost.

These examples only scratch the surface of what will be possible through vehicle connectivity. As car-sharing schemes and electric or even autonomous vehicles become prevalent and preferred, connectivity will become a crucial enabling platform for other vehicle technologies. Imagine using a shared vehicle that can adjust the driver's seat to your pre-set preference as you enter the vehicle, an electric vehicle that can sell its stored energy during peak time when you are not using it and automatically charge during off-peak times to save you money, or a self-driving car that you can summon with your smartphone.

Connectivity will help all modes of transportation provide an integrated and information-rich travel experience, whether you are using buses, trains, taxis, or your car. Travelers or commuters will be empowered to choose between different modes of transportation by comparing, in real time, factors such as cost, time, energy use, convenience, and pollution, among others.

Bringing the Internet to the car will be a first step in a longer journey.

Today's personal transportation system is expensive and inefficient. We are isolated and stuck in traffic jams in costly, over-engineered, and underutilized cars that spend a lot of time sitting parked. On a worldwide scale, nearly eight million traffic accidents claim more than one million lives and injure roughly twenty five million[1] people annually. Congestion fritters away 80 million hours of productive time[2] and causes the emission of 220 million metric tons of carbon a year.[3]

Advances in communication technology, coupled with other vehicular technologies, are poised to reduce or even eliminate these negative consequences of mobility, and additionally, offer a better user experience while acting as a springboard for other emerging technologies.

We are isolated and stuck in traffic jams in costly, over-engineered, and underutilized cars that spend a lot of time sitting parked.

[1] "Global Status Report On Road Safety," World Health Organization, 2009.

[2] "Gridlock Driving Up Wasted Time," CBS News/AP, 2009.

[3] Todd Davis and Monica Hale, "Public Transportation's Contribution to U.S. Greenhouse Gas Reduction," Science Applications International Corporation, 2007.

FUELS AND REFUELING

Steve Mazor

CALIFORNIA MOTORISTS, like those in the rest of the United States, are spoiled. We can go to almost any intersection and buy fuel. Even at $4 per gallon, this fuel is inexpensive, has a high energy density, and is easy and convenient to dispense. Of course, I am talking about gasoline and, for a few motorists, diesel; both are produced from petroleum.

We are constantly told that we need to stop using petroleum-based fuels and switch to alternatives, but why? Multiple good reasons include air quality, global climate change, energy security, and the economy. The air is much cleaner today than it was 30 to 40 years ago, mostly due to improvements in passenger vehicle technologies, including fuels. However, achieving true clean air and especially maintaining it despite growth in population, and growth in miles of travel, requires further emission reductions from all sources, including passenger vehicles. Transportation is the largest single manmade source of greenhouse gasses (CO_2), and passenger vehicles accounted for 26% of it in 2006. When carbon-based fuels such as gasoline, diesel, natural gas, propane, and ethanol are burned, the exhaust is essentially H_2O and CO_2. To reduce CO_2, you need to

In 2035, petroleum-based fuels, such as gasoline and diesel, will likely still be the major players, accounting for about 60% of the market for passenger vehicles.

As fuel prices go up, people will adapt, often in surprising ways, but independent mobility must be maintained.

burn less of these fuels, either by using low- or non-carbon alternatives or by increasing the efficiency of the vehicle. We also need to develop a reliable supply of affordable energy, such as compressed natural gas (CNG), ethanol (cellulosic), bio-diesel, electricity, and hydrogen, that is produced locally and is not subject to the events that occur outside our own sphere of influence. Using a diverse set of fuels lessens our sensitivity to upheavals such as unrest in the Middle East, refinery problems in the Midwestern United States, and storms in the Gulf of Mexico. And finally, from the consumer's point of view, the main driver for alternative fuels is the economy. People need to be able to afford to go when and where they need and want to go. As fuel prices go up, people will adapt, often in surprising ways, but independent mobility must be maintained.

Taking into account these factors, what will the future hold for us in 2035? What fuels will we be using in our cars and how will we get them?

In 2035, petroleum-based fuels, such as gasoline and diesel, will likely still be the major players, accounting for about 60% of the market for passenger vehicles. However, we may not recognize these fuels. California gasoline has been reformulated at least six times since the 1970s, and we can expect further refinements, perhaps including an increase in ethanol content from 10% to 15% or more. We would expect diesel to change too, including further reductions in sulfur and increased blending with bio-diesel. It is possible (but doubtful) that petroleum-based diesel fuel could be banned outright, because diesel exhaust has been determined to be a carcinogen.

There will be significant growth in the use of electricity to power passenger vehicles. Plug-in hybrids (PHEVs) will be common since the California Air Resources Board is introducing a new category for their zero emission vehicle program called Transitional Zero Emission Vehicle (TZEV) that will require significant numbers to be sold. It is likely that some PHEVs will not use gasoline or diesel at all. There have been several demonstrations of vehicles using CNG-powered gas turbines as generators to maintain the charge in a battery pack, similar to the Chevrolet Volt. Zero-emission battery-electric vehicles will make up 5% to 10% of the fleet, and the current non-plug-in hybrids, like the Toyota Prius, will be extremely common.

Charging for electric vehicles (EVs) and PHEVs will be accomplished in a variety of ways. The most common will be home recharging with rates discounted for charging at night. This may even be automatic. Park your EV/PHEV and at the time the utility company deems "off-peak," your charger will connect itself, mechanically or inductively, and recharge the car. Apartment dwellers will have the ability to home-charge with credit-card-activated pole-mounted chargers located in the parking lot. Public charging stations offering 240-volt charging will be common, and 480-volt fast-charge stations that can recharge from 20% to 80% in a few minutes will be placed at strategic locations. AAA will have trucks with fast chargers on

Emergency refueling with high speed EV charging, gasoline, diesel, and CNG. Photo courtesy of AAA.

board to rescue motorists with dead batteries and reduce "range anxiety."

Since the United States and Canada have abundant reserves of natural gas and it burns cleaner than petroleum-based fuels, expect growth in natural-gas-fueled passenger vehicles. Today, the Honda Civic GX is the only OEM natural-gas-fueled car available, but this is will change.

The current network of Compressed Natural Gas (CNG) refueling stations will grow, and the public can anticipate CNG dispensers will appear at traditional fueling stations. However, home-based refueling is possible and likely in homes pre-plumbed with natural gas. Systems like Honda's current "PHIL," which slowly compress the low-pressure natural gas feeding your home to provide

Since the range of CNG vehicles is greater than electric vehicles, it is possible that CNG vehicles will almost never need to be fueled anywhere but at home.

A prototype facility located on the campus of California State University Los Angeles would use a combination of solar- and wind-generated electricity to produce hydrogen from water, and then compress it to 10,000 PSI and dispense it into vehicles. This facility would also have two EV charging stations. Image courtesy of Steve Mazor.

an overnight refill, will be more broadly available. Since the range of CNG vehicles is greater than electric vehicles, it is possible that CNG vehicles will almost never need to be fueled anywhere but at home.

The use of ethanol has the potential to grow from 10% to 15% through an increase in the amount blended into gasoline, and in the growth of the use of E85, which is 85% ethanol blended with gasoline. However, the headwinds against ethanol grow daily, as it almost certainly raises grain and food prices and therefore increases hunger in the food-importing world. The difficulty of E85 is that it cannot really use pipelines, as ethanol is hydroscopic (attracted to water, including groundwater), and so is highly unlikely to be implemented in any volume as it must be trucked everywhere and has a terrible carbon footprint as a result. For performance and safety reasons, ethanol cannot be used at 100%. Starting a car fueled with 100% ethanol on a cold morning is problematic, but more importantly it burns with an invisible flame, which can be hazardous for emergency responders in the event of a fire. Adding 15% gasoline provides that dramatic orange flame and billowing black smoke familiar to any of us who have watched an action movie. A major advantage of ethanol versus other alternatives is that it can be dispensed as a liquid with similar equipment to that used for gasoline.

Many see hydrogen as a panacea, and they may be partly correct, but many difficulties remain. The appeal of hydrogen is that when used to power a fuel cell, the only exhaust is pure water and thus hydrogen-fuel-cell-powered cars are the only other currently known zero-emission-vehicles besides electric vehicles. Hydrogen used in an internal combustion engine can qualify a vehicle as being Transitional Zero Emission, similar to many plug-in hybrids.

Hydrogen is the most abundant element in the universe (as far as we know so far), but at least here on Earth, it does not exist in pure form in any usable quantity. Instead, it is chemically bound with other compounds, most notable as the "H" in H_2O (water). It takes energy to separate hydrogen from whatever it is bound with. Today, splitting natural gas produces most hydrogen, but this leaves a residual of CO_2 (carbon dioxide), the most common greenhouse gas. But somewhere down the road, hydrogen could be an energy carrier in a 100%-renewable energy system. How could this work? Electricity from solar, wind, or other renewable sources could be used to electrolyze hydrogen from water, instead of natural gas, leaving only pure oxygen as a residual. The oxygen can be released into the atmosphere, since when the hydrogen is burned, as in a combustion engine or used to power a fuel cell, it is combined with exactly the same amount of oxygen producing the same amount of water as you started with. The water goes back into the environment and you restart the cycle.

Many other methods, some more promising than others, are under development to produce hydrogen from water. These include the use of high temperatures, enzymes, and catalysts.

WHAT WILL THE REFUELING NETWORK BE LIKE?

In 2035, we will have a much wider variety of refueling scenarios than are common today. Home refueling will be routinely available for electric vehicles and compressed natural gas vehicles. Urban areas will have mega-stations with the complete gamut of refueling capabilities including gasoline, diesel, CNG, E85, hydrogen, and 480-volt EV fast charging. Other areas will have stand-alone fuel-specific facilities. Automated systems on vehicles will locate the closest facility with the correct fuel and will be able to calculate the wait time for access to a charger or fuel dispenser. AAA will provide emergency refueling service similar to their current practice of providing one or two gallons of gasoline to stranded motorists, except all fuel types will be included. Fleets of vehicles, including government, private, and public car-sharing fleets, could have centralized automatic refueling systems specific to the vehicles and technology in their fleet.

The bottom line is that a wider variety of fuel types and many more ways of refueling our vehicles will be available. Between now and 2035 (and beyond), the marketplace, heavily influenced by regulators, will determine which fuels will grow and which will fade away. My long-term bet is on 100%-renewable hydrogen, but only time will tell for sure.

Automated systems on vehicles will locate the closest facility with the correct fuel and will be able to calculate the wait time for access to a charger or fuel dispenser.

FEWER, CHEAPER, LIGHTER: THE EVOLUTION OF VEHICLE MANUFACTURING

Eric Noble and Bill Surber

CONTEMPORARY CAR MANUFACTURE IS MOSTLY A MONEY-LOSING OPERATION. This fact alone could ultimately suffice as motivation for the adoption of new vehicle construction techniques. However, tightening safety standards, dramatically increasing fuel efficiency mandates, and consumers' undying desire for ever better products are all leading to improved methods of engineering and building cars. These forces will inevitably have distinctly positive effects on the design and sustainability of future automobiles.

While our primary focus here is the forward evolution of vehicle construction options, it is instructive to frame the current manufacturing business model before moving on to how it can be improved.

Since the 1932 Ford, most cars and light trucks have been made by bending sheet metal into particular shapes (stampings), and then combining (welding) those stampings like puzzle pieces into a whole, encompassing floor, apertures, and the paintable exterior surface we see. In the beginning, such body shells sat atop separate frames, but for the last 50 years, most passenger cars have had the frame integrated into the sheet metal body. This form of construction is known variously as body-frame-integral (BFI), monocoque, or unibody and is the dominant car manufacturing process used today worldwide.

Unibody construction requires astounding levels of capital and tooling investments. A typical unibody consists of 300 stamped sheet metal parts, each requiring three to five two-piece die sets. Even with a carryover floor and some parts sharing, a typical car's new sheet metal requires 400 new dies, not including doors, hood, and trunk lid. Die costs often exceed $150M per program. The

The problem today lies in allocating the monumental cost of using these old unibody construction methods. In the past, carmakers counted on such costs being amortized across tremendously high sales volumes per model.

stamped components from those dies must then be fixtured (held) and welded together, requiring another $80–85M in body fabrication tooling. Contemporary stamping presses (which push the dies together to shape the sheet metal parts) cost around $65M each, and the remaining plant equipment to assemble the stamped parts into bodies is another $600M. This brings the typical unibody construction investment, including tooling and equipment, to over $800M, and the resultant output is still just bare steel.

The next step in traditional car-body-building is liquid paint (something nearly all other major industries have discarded in favor of powder), which is sprayed onto the sheet metal structure. Car factory paint shops are therefore still complex, highly sensitive operations requiring an investment of more than $250M additional to the cost of the plant.

Together, automobile unibody stamping, assembly, and painting operation expenditures often exceed $1B, a staggering sunk cost for carmakers and their investors. The magnitude and, indeed, servicing of this investment effectively constrains automotive initiatives to existing factories and construction techniques. As a result, carmakers' new models, however innovative in concept or even powertrain, are condemned from the outset to a flawed business model, essentially unchanged from that of their predecessors. To the extent startup carmakers (and governments underwriting them) also assume conventional vehicle construction, this methodology serves as a barrier to entry in the industry.

The problem today lies in allocating the monumental cost of using these old unibody construction methods. In the past, carmakers counted on such costs being amortized across tremendously high sales volumes per model; investment, as a percentage of total revenue, was miniscule. The industry's postwar heyday saw single models of Chevy, Ford, and Plymouth selling a million units per year, their makers able to amortize very large fixed investments in very short periods, even a matter of months. As a result, designs and body styles could be updated annually, the tooling cost already recuperated. Today's diverse, competitive marketplace has resulted in an explosion of the number of vehicle models. As a result, high per-vehicle annual volumes are gone, though the production building blocks and methodologies built around them linger on.

The average sales per model in most vehicle markets in the developed world have fallen consistently for decades, and with them the profitability of carmakers. In the United States, average sales per model fell below $60K per year around the recent turn of the century, and are still dropping, far below the threshold of profitability for unibody construction. The reasons for this decline in annual model volumes can be summarized

The average sales per model in most vehicle markets in the developed world have fallen consistently for decades, and with them the profitability of carmakers.

as more carmakers, making more models, chasing the same number of buyers. Thinning margins from diminishing model volumes have led auto companies, on the expense side, to a nearly manic focus on cost cutting and, on the revenue side, to a messianic hope of the next "big hit" that will save the day by rapidly paying off its own tooling and then subsidizing the rest of the unprofitable model lineup. When that happens too seldom, they go bankrupt or get subsidized, or both.

While the sort of economic natural selection taught in business schools could rationally be expected to cull the car company herd, nations view automakers as key employers and rarely allow them to fail. America, Japan, Korea, Europe, Brazil, Russia, and China have all rushed to the aid of captive (and prospective) carmakers on a regular basis and in a myriad of creative ways. Whether such subsidization can—or should—continue in the face of broader economic issues is increasingly uncertain.

Meanwhile, automakers desperately seek lower costs, consumers fresher designs, and regulators greater efficiency and safety than unibody construction can reliably offer. This leaves all parties potential beneficiaries of moving beyond stamped steel construction. At some point, the confluence of these pressures will force this change to occur.

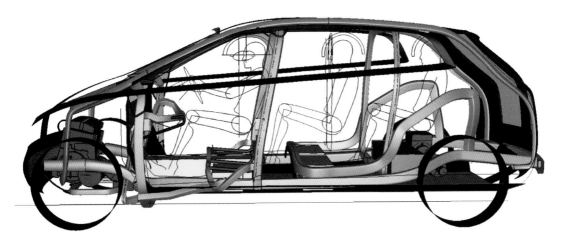

7-seat, hybrid, family vehicle with hydroformed steel space frame. Note very low parts count, excellent load paths, full safety protection, and use of inexpensive, overlapping joints for steel tubes. Composite outer— and inner—body panels would be attached. Illustration by Brian Booth.

What, then, will future vehicles be made of? The obvious answer is that material choice will be based upon particular requirements in the vehicle, instead of on servicing the sunk costs of old equipment and methodologies. As the value of capital (and mass) reduction rises, lower density materials will selectively replace steel for the body system, facilitated by advancing methods of producing and forming these materials. How then, will future cars "hold up the paint"?

First, lower density, low cost composite materials (think "fiberglass" not carbon fiber) will replace steel in the car body's "secondary" areas, such as floor, dash panel, and rear package shelf. These "unseen" areas of the vehicle are obvious, initial candidates for composites precisely because such parts are not appearance-critical, and want to be as large as possible—something composites do well.

Next in line for conversion to composites is the vehicle's exterior body. It is hard to overstate the historical difficulty in molding "appearance" panels using composites. Cars' visible surfaces must be very smooth (Class A) and defect-free. Traditional composite molding processes, such as hand lay-up (think ski boats), resin transfer molding (RTM), and structural reaction injection molding (SRIM), have yielded inconsistent surface results and low production throughput, and will, therefore, not be part of the new regime for vehicle construction. Conventional sheet molding compound (SMC), as used on Chevrolet's Corvette, is certainly more rapid, but has historically demonstrated surface degradation in paint ovens, necessitating repeated re-work, and also requires rather high forming pressures. Better methods for replacing stamped steel with composites are required.

A uniquely promising process for creating composite panels fit for automotive exterior use appears as an enhancement of an industrial molding process for fiberglass. In this process, a thickening system enables the compound to mold at very low pressures, allowing forming tools to be cheaply fabricated rather than machined from expensive billet (as sheet-steel stamping dies are), which very substantially reduces tool and equipment cost. This process is capable today of producing large, secondary vehicle structure panels to replace sheet metal, and is under development for automotive Class A exterior surface requirements. A U.S. company, National Composites, did ground-breaking commercialization work in this material and process, and progress today continues globally.

CHART 1: AVERAGE MODEL YEAR PERCENTAGE OF TOTAL LIFE CYCLE SALES

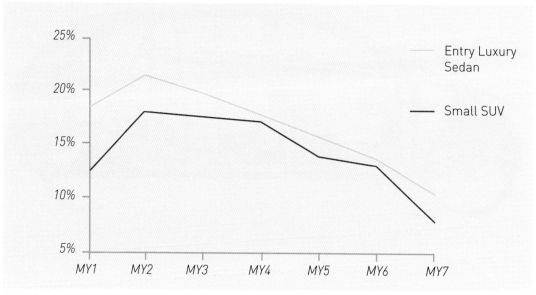

Rapidly changing consumer tastes and external environments give models in most vehicle segments a peak-and-die life cycle. Source: 2010 UHAS Study and Carlab.

As composites march toward their takeover of the vehicle body system, great progress in replacing wet paint is also being made. Specific to composites, in-mold paint is being explored, and post-mold powder painting techniques are being rapidly developed. It is likely that the paint booth will be obsolesced at some point not long after the stamping presses are.

If the car body will move to composites, what will the underlying structure be? Here, some observers wrongly assume the answer is also non-metallic. Most vehicle skeletons (the inner frame), however, will remain metal for the foreseeable future, because only metals have the unique combination of stiffness, ductility (crash energy absorp-tion), and relatively low cost required. This metallic, primary structure (rocker/sill, rails, pillars, etc.) must be composed of hollow members to achieve weight efficiency. As crash performance standards increase (which they will until the dominance of autonomous vehicles begins to eliminate crashes altogether), these frame members will transition to higher strength, tubular (not stamped unibody) steels, with some judicious application of aluminum. Essentially, these are tubular metal space frames akin to those

often seen as "roll cages" in race cars, but in volume production using fewer, larger tubes and modern forming processes more easily adapted to increasing safety and crash standards. Such hydroformed (exactly shaped from inside with pressurized fluid) tubular steel frames are already replacing inner sheet metal stampings in portions of current production vehicles. Total skeletons will come next, and be cloaked in composite skin.

Studies of vehicle-acquirer behavior consistently show styling and content tastes change much more frequently than carmakers debut new models.

Just how much could so-called "loose panel" composite construction, draped over a steel skeleton, alter the business case for making cars? Preliminary cost studies indicate savings of 25–35% piece cost and 70–80% investment reduction for a composite/steel skeleton assembly, compared with conventional stamped steel unibody. Further, these studies assume a perfectly realistic volume of only $60K per year for composite/steel while allowing $250K/year for steel unibody (a best-case scenario for traditional car factories). Once implemented, the new method will clearly outstrip the old one economically.

Beyond the obvious benefit of potentially lower prices, the consumer benefit of dramatically lower vehicle production costs is simple: more changes more often. Studies of vehicle-acquirer behavior consistently show styling and content tastes change much more frequently than carmakers debut new models. Proof here lies in the simple fact that fresh new models sell much better than aging ones (chart 1).

Automakers are today severely handicapped in meeting evolving market demands because they're stuck slogging through what is typically half a decade of production in an effort to pay off each model's hundreds of millions of dollars in unibody investment. Space frame/composite body cars promise to cut that required life cycle by more than half.

If consumers of unibody vehicles too seldom enjoy new generations of vehicles, so too do engineers and designers. The new fuel systems, better safety, improved efficiency, and fresh aesthetics that car companies painfully need all must wait for the cadence of a full model change. If such model changes can happen at twice the rate, so too can progress in these important areas.

The benefits of moving away from stamped steel construction, however, go far beyond shorter vehicle life cycles. Weight, the enemy of both performance and fuel efficiency, is dramatically lowered by moving to composite panels and steel space frame assembly. Calculations have shown that a typical, seven-seat family vehicle can, conservatively,

Calculations have shown that a typical, seven-seat family vehicle can, conservatively, shed more than 10% of its mass by moving to such construction. In the face of what has been, and will likely remain, the creeping obesity of cars (chart 2), this is a serious weight reduction, and one with very positive implications on sustainability.

shed more than 10% of its mass by moving to such construction. In the face of what has been, and will likely remain, the creeping obesity of cars (chart 2), this is a serious weight reduction, and one with very positive implications on sustainability. Counting on consumers to wake up and realize the cars they demand are far larger than they need is fantasy; meeting people where they are, with big, affordable vehicles that are simply lighter, is pragmatic. And possible.

In all facets of society, technology has enabled "better, faster, cheaper" products across a wide range of uses. Meanwhile, the car industry has been consumed with trying to force fit the ancient, stamped steel,

CHART 2: AVERAGE CURB WEIGHT

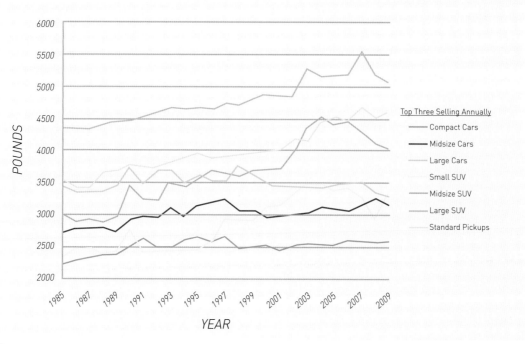

Despite materials advances, increased safety and feature content consistently add mass to even the top sellers in every segment. Without a move away from stamped steel construction, affordable vehicles will mostly continue this trend. Source: Carlab.

"$1M/year Impala" operating model to the new reality of $50K/year per model, a 95% reduction. The business and operating models do not scale to that degree, meaning $10K/year Nissan Leafs, Chevrolet Volts, and other potentially revolutionary vehicles will continue to be financially hamstrung (or moribund) by unibody construction.

Newer, reduced scale processes, utilizing contemporary composite molding technology, and the recognized advantages of metal space frames are capable of transforming the auto industry. Ironically, the speed of this transformation will be tempered by carmakers' (and governments') ongoing obligation to serve capital investments in the old machinery and equipment.

IS AN ENVIRONMENTALLY NEUTRAL CAR POSSIBLE?

John Thackara
Originally posted 11.15.10
on Design Observer (designobserver.com)

THE FUTURE OF THE CAR HAS BEEN ELECTRIC FOR—WHAT—FIVE YEARS NOW? Ten? The answer is for over 110 years, for it was back in 1899 that La Jamais Contente (The Never Satisfied) became the first vehicle to go over 100 km/h (62 mph) at Achères, near Paris.

Since then, as we have produced hundreds of millions of non-electric cars—and despoiled the biosphere in the process—all manner of non-petrol cars, including electric ones, have come and gone. Tesla in the United States and Norway's Think are just the latest in a long line of newcomers.

They, too, will fail to break the grip of the gas guzzler for one reason: they do not challenge the production system and business model of an incumbent global industry that is so mature that it can only make incremental changes as new pressures arise. Electric cars such as Tesla fall into this category: they are an incremental improvement, not a replacement for an *ecocidal* global industry.

This writer has long been skeptical that small private vehicles would have an important role to pay in a sustainable mobility mix.

But Riversimple has made me pause for thought.

At a presentation in Leicester, United Kingdom, where a deal has been struck with the city council for 30 vehicles to be piloted there in 2014, we were told that the formal purpose of this new start-up is "to build and operate cars for independent use whilst systematically pursuing elimination of the environmental damage caused by personal transport."

Not reduce but *eliminate* environmental damage? How could that be possible?

The company's founder, Hugo Spowers, explained that every aspect of the company's operation—not just its vehicle technology—is based on whole-system design. It has evolved from a linear resource-consuming model, in which natural capital resources are not replenished, to a cyclical system, in which waste streams provide all material inputs, and all loops are closed.

The car itself has five novel features: a composite body, four electric motors, no gearbox or transmission, regenerative

The way the system has been designed, it will be in everyone's interest to keep cars on the road as long as possible. Riversimple will be the first car manufacturer for whom success will not mean persuading you to buy a new car every three years.

braking, and power provided by hydrogen fuel cells. The vehicle is decoupled from a single power platform or refueling infrastructure. Its network electric platform has been so designed that future breakthroughs in other power sources can easily be incorporated later.

But Riversimple's technology is just the start. Its cars will not be sold outright. Customers will buy mobility as a service rather than a car as a product. There will be no maximum or minimum mileage allowance and, critically, a bundled service covers a number of costs such as road tax, vehicle maintenance, and fuel.

The way the system has been designed, it will be in everyone's interest to keep cars on the road as long as possible. Riversimple will be the first car manufacturer for whom success will not mean persuading you to buy a new car every three years.

Customers will interact with Riversimple and its user community through a personalized digital interface accessed from the car, on their computer or via their mobile phone. They will be able to manage their account, request maintenance, ask questions, locate the nearest refueling station, and so on.

To ensure that energy and resource efficiency remain at the heart of everything the company does, lower environmental impact is financially rewarded.

A sale of a service model is therefore pushed upstream into the supply chain. The supplier of the hydrogen fuel cell, for example, is likely to remain its owner. Manufacturer and supplier thereby have a shared interest in the longevity and reliability of the vehicle, and of the system as a whole.

Riversimple's production model, too, is distributed. Its carbon composite bodies allow profitable manufacturing with plants producing 3,000 to 5,000 units each year. This regional distribution of production will enable the delivery of improved service for regional markets at reduced cost. (The company is in early stage discussions with other regions across the world to roll out this strategy through joint venture partnerships for local manufacturing facilities).

The next consideration is service. A local car is effectively tethered to its locale, so the critical scale for establishing a commercial market is one service station serving that locale, rather than the whole nation. Riversimple's service infrastructure, too, is cellular—city by city.

The surprises continue. Everything in Riversimple is open source. The company is adopting an open intellectual property model, based on that used in open-source software. The design of this and future vehicles will be shared, thereby allowing anyone to collaborate in the design and build of the cars under an open-source license.

No matter how much better Riversimple's standards are, it won't be enough to win a standards war. If ubiquity is of greater benefit to Riversimple than competition is a threat, the need is to lower the entry barriers for making money from making cars. Riversimple is therefore licensing its technology for free to the open-source foundation 40 Fires. As a bonus, it will maximize design input from passionate experts and be the fastest route to replacing the internal combustion engine.

Riversimple is owned by six Custodians. Instead of the typical fiduciary responsibility of a board maximizing shareholder value, the role of the Custodians is to balance and protect benefits to stakeholders. Among these is the environment, which is kept on an equal footing with investors and commercial partners. Checks and balances are built into the system through the appointment of a Stewards body, which is responsible for auditing and monitoring the governance.

The structure and responsibilities of conventional corporations create a confrontational dynamic with most stakeholders. Therefore shared ownership is another key feature of the Riversimple system. Its ownership model is inspired by long-standing and successful businesses such as VISA International, John Lewis Partnership, and Mondragon. All stakeholders have a formal role in the organization, to all parties' benefit.

Is Riversimple another design-studio fantasy? Hardly. It is significantly backed by the family of Ernst Piëch, part of the dynasty that founded Porsche.

Oh, you wanted to see the car? Here it is:

ORIGAMI MODEL T

Sang-eun Lee

INDUSTRIAL ORIGAMI MANUFACTURING PROCESS

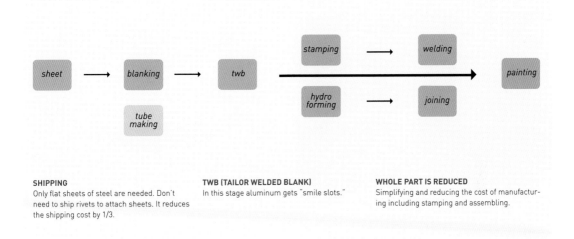

SHIPPING
Only flat sheets of steel are needed. Don't need to ship rivets to attach sheets. It reduces the shipping cost by 1/3.

TWB (TAILOR WELDED BLANK)
In this stage aluminum gets "smile slots."

WHOLE PART IS REDUCED
Simplifying and reducing the cost of manufacturing including stamping and assembling.

IN 2008, FORD CELEBRATED THE 100TH ANNIVERSARY OF THE MODEL T, which was first built in 1908. Students at Art Center College of Design participated in a project sponsored by Ford to design a car to be sold for under $7000 by utilizing an innovative manufacturing process. The car was intended to garner mass popular appeal like the Model T did 100 years ago.

I came up with Origami Theory, the idea that you can create volume by folding a flat sheet. The process is cost-efficient and environmentally friendly. I started researching origami-inspired products and I found the Industrial Origami company, which builds products by folding metal sheets. I contacted them and we started working together to make an Origami Model T. We collaborated very successfully throughout the course at Art Center, and the final model was selected as one of six finalists for the Ford-sponsored project.

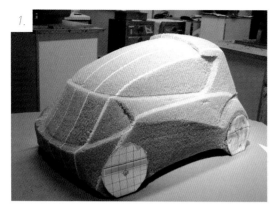

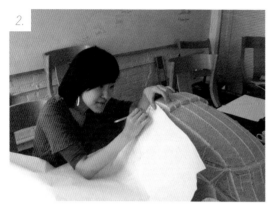

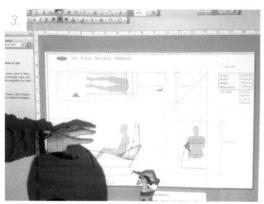

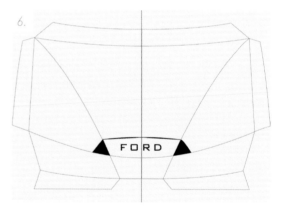

1. Patch papers on the mock-up to see how the surface would fold.

2. Tailor paper to the foam mock-up.

3. Design a chassis that suits the origami car body.

4. Study paper folding on the front-face design.

5. Keep refining front-face and side folding to match the corner lines.

6. Front-face and rear-end illustrator templates. These templates make the origami steel car possible.

7.

10.

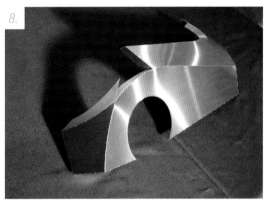

8.

11.

9.

12.

7. Completed paper mock-up.

8. Very first stainless steel side panel.

9. Origami folded wheel.

10. Attach the completed five panels to each side.

11. Attach each panel to the foam mock-up with glue.

12. Make two small holes on the corner of each piece and stitch the pieces with wires to complete stainless steel origami car body.

EYE SHADOW AT 80 MPH

Jeremy Gilbert-Rolfe

"CAR" IS SHORT FOR "CARRIAGE," one of those things (as with so much that is obvious) that I realized belatedly when reading a nineteenth-century novel, but it is surely the case that people think of cars now as much as things they wear or occupy as vehicles that carry them around. Certainly grandees used to have coaches with their coats of arms on them, but one does not get the sense that people in general identified with carriages in the way we take it for granted that they do with cars. Moreover, one also has the impression that this identification has become ever more complicated over the years, as car design has had to become more responsive to the logic of its fundamental purpose and the materials out of which cars are made. I'll suggest here that much that is important about cars and our relationship with them comes down to questions about speed and plastic. Counter-intuitively, perhaps, or so it seems to me, as cars' bodies have become more functional from an engineer's perspective, their decorative function for the bodies they transport has also increased beyond any conceivable precedent, rather than declined or returned to the relative anonymity of the original black box on wheels but without the horse with which it all began. The larger the roles played by speed and plastic, the more elaborately and closely we relate to what we drive. High speed as a norm brings the body into a relationship with what's going on which is much closer to the speed of thinking than of walking, and plastic is like skin, making possible a direct connection and association between the aerodynamics of the lived and the manufactured.

In an essay on Los Angeles written about twenty years ago I described it as the capital city of suburbs and characterized by its freeways, a system made of curves which carries people around at speed and on which streams of traffic converge without stopping, in contrast to the lowly "surface streets" which follow the city's grid, a system of right-angles which requires that one set of cars stops while others go.[1] The freeway is made of speeding up and slowing down, a system of intensities, while driving on the surface streets is, in contrast, a matter of starting and stopping, a system of on and off. The only thing that brings things to a stop on the freeway is an accident, whereas if you get all the way to your destination on surface streets without stopping that means you got lucky, you missed all the stop signs and people dithering while parking; stopping is part of going where surface streets are concerned. The freeway, elevated above the surface street grid, is touched by human feet only as the result of an accident or during its own maintenance and repair, otherwise it's a street for wheels and smooth movement. The surface street reflects its origins as a pedestrian way, on which corners can be turned with ease by feet moving without effort at right angles to where they were just a split second ago.

The contemporary car is made for the freeway. It is first of all an image that radiates the promise of moving smoothly through space, offering minimum resistance to the wind. When cars were invented the wind was not an issue, and when it was that had to do with whether it could be tipped over when the wind was strong, not with how it would propel itself through space. Now wind resistance is part of the sales pitch. In between, it was for several decades a decorative feature that represented something more like an aspiration than a reality. "Streamlining" added the look of speed to cars that were for the most part not helped to conserve fuel or go faster all that much by being made

to remind us of early jet aircraft, but they symbolically embodied a desire for speed. Now their design does help them to save fuel and go faster, and they're not so obviously streamlined as cars of the fifties. At the turn of the twentieth century the car was a horseless carriage with an internal combustion engine instead of a horse. By the middle of the century it had turned into a symbolic reference to air travel, the jet engine having completed the streamlining of airplanes begun in the late thirties as propeller driven aircraft reached towards speeds that caused them to fall apart if they weren't aerodynamically adequate. My Prius looks like a car, because that is what a car looks like nowadays (a paraphrase of the remark Gloria Steinem made to a journalist who said, at her fortieth birthday party, that she didn't look like she was forty: "This is what forty looks like these days"). It has a good relationship with the wind, it does not look like an airplane, although it does perhaps look halfway between the ancient black boxes of the car's early history and the limited aerodynamics of a helicopter. The point here though is that the passage from the non-aerodynamic to the actually aerodynamic involves an interim phase of the symbolically dynamic. Once established as an idea, it will

eventually become a reality. This is the way in which ideas normally enter reality. The contemporary car is a consequence more of the visual decoration of the fifties than of anything having to do with engineering. The fifties showed designers what they'd have to work within if they were to make a car that sold. They had to work within the constraints provided by a demand for speed, which found its shape long before it got its engineering up to a speed commensurate with the speed desired.

It may not be there yet, but one loses so much peripheral vision above eighty miles an hour that one supposes that as cars get even faster their drivers will have to leave more and more driving to robots. When that time comes everyone will be able to do safely what drivers on the freeway do anyway. As I also said in the earlier essay to which I referred above, drivers on the Los Angeles freeways treat the interiors of the cars they drive as private spaces and ignore the fact that they're actually surrounded by windows, and do all sorts of things in them even though they're going fast. This includes shaving faces and legs, but my favorite is applying make-up. When applying make-up the person involved is looking at something close up (a vanity mirror or, better, the rear-view mirror) while negotiating a deep space into which he or more usually she is plummeting while negotiating the similar passage of lots of other cars. The very phrase "eye shadow at eighty miles an hour" says all there is to say about the relationship between speed as an image and fact, now conjoined, in the car as a vehicle for much more than the transportation of bodies. As noted, at speeds that high one has hardly any peripheral vision, one can only see straight ahead...

The car which she is driving offers a stable space in which she can make up her eyes even as it propels her at a speed so high as to require thinking that is instantaneous, actions that are simultaneous with the thought that propels them, and is largely made of plastic. A no doubt now obscure work, which I happen to have read because it was written in part by my dad and in the year I was born no less, confirms that by that date (1945) "a considerable amount of plastic mouldings [were to be] found in the construction of the everyday automobile" and that "with the increasing demand for materials the cost should fall to such a level as to make the adoption of plastics an economical proposition."[2] Plastic can be cast, extruded and molded and is the closest thing to skin we've managed to invent so far, being at once smooth and flexible and, on demand, seamless. In *Beauty and the Contemporary Sublime*, a book concerned to update the differential through which aesthetic judgments are articulated and argued, I suggested that molded (or cast) plastic forms have more in common with the bodies of living things than forms that are constructed, because like ourselves they have, or seem to have, a continuous skin rather than to be made of separate surfaces brought together at their edges.[3] I compare a contemporary television cabinet with earlier ones to make that point, but I could of course have compared cars made since sometime in the forties at the latest with the earlier ones which resembled the sort of cars we had when we still called them carriages most of the time. The reader will note that this too is an example of the idea preceding the actualized aspiration, as it is only very recently that the car's smooth

curved surfaces themselves came to contain a fairly high proportion of plastic—the proportion of a car's content that's made out of plastic now being much more than twenty percent. The difference between the car's skin and its driver's, when it comes to flexibility, is one of degree—and here we may note, in passing, how smoothness has stood for speed since before the car and the jet aircraft: carriages called on the image of speed which preceded the automobile, that of the horse, whose surface is also smooth and shiny.[4]

Inside the car ergonomics join the driver to the controls and sit her comfortably in a semi-reclining position found most suitable for rocketing through space. The hansom cab driver sat upright; the car driver leans back, as if watching a movie. The car is the convergence of more than one kind of embodiment, one enfolding the other, at its center a subjectivity that is in no small part conditioned by the industrially produced body which its biological and living body occupies and it controls. Putting make-up on at speed is as natural a thing to do as applying it before a mirror in one's bed- or bath-room, which means that we have no difficulty relating to a near that remains constant while the far is a zone of extreme instability. Similar in that respect, perhaps, to the relationship between one's experience of what's immediately in front of one's eyes and the ungraspable zone of shifting and unstable turmoil that lies immediately behind them and inside one's head.

Trains cut the travel time by one third compared to roads.[5] Suddenly, for the first time, it became possible to measure distance reliably in terms of time, and speed began to define the space humans inhabit. I don't know what the ratio between freeways and surface streets is, but expect it's about the same or a bit wider—twenty miles per hour on surface streets and sixty-five on freeways, for example. We are, however, well past the point where we fear that acceleration might have a deleterious effect on the body. When decent roads were first laid in the eighteenth century (turnpikes) it became customary to break the journey between London and

Edinburgh and stay overnight at Leeds, half way, because it was generally thought that no one should subject the body to a constant speed of ten to fifteen miles an hour for that many hours at a time. By the time the railway replaced the turnpike (eighty years later or so) taking a break was no longer thought necessary. The body that rode the train was up for a twelve hour more or less straight shot at an average speed of about thirty. By the time the first world war broke out trains were in sight of going 100 mph, but the aircraft that flew over the trenches were flying at about thirty miles an hour and the by then nearly forty year old horseless carriage was achieving maximum speeds of about the same. The driver who puts on her make-up at speed is the beneficiary of a nearly two hundred year old process in which the body has become habituated to speed at every level. When she flies to New York or London the plane she's in flies at an average speed of five hundred plus miles an hour. Her body's used to it. And almost every piece of information she receives about anything comes to her electronically, which is to say, instantly. She is used to an information flow that puts things together as quickly as her involuntary responses inside her head do, and speeds which leave the walking body out of any calculation or experience of their velocity. Armies march at four miles an hour, and they only started going that fast in the nineteenth century (120 steps a minute for fifty minutes, which allows for a ten minute break every hour). Measuring by human steps has gone. It is not automatically to what one compares movement up and down in music, as one did not so long ago, or distances. It has been replaced by electronic instantaneity and the knowledge that we can effortlessly travel faster than the speed of sound (1100 mph) if we want to. The distance between four and eleven hundred is too great, our bodies have become accustomed to another world, in which they occupy and move through space using their hands as much as their feet, where walking is a condition in which one is either on display or in one place or doing it for fun. The driver putting on her make-up is multitasking but actually all the tasks except for the application of the make-up are the same, they all involve occupying the world

through a technological mediation which constitutes almost the entirety of the physical context: the car places her in a relation to the world which starts when her feet and hands become continuous with the car's controls, she speaks and receives messages on a hands-free phone, listening to the radio or music when not talking, the outside is reduced to what needs to be attended to, the interior of the car is a zone in which the body and the car become continuous. Soon we'll have total robot cars. She'll be able to get in, give it its orders, and concentrate on the make-up and talking to the office. For now, we are more and more obliged to blend into a relationship of inseparability with what we drive, from which we get our sense of time and space. We no longer think like pedestrians, the inside of our heads a whir of activity but the landscape still—likewise text on a screen is not grounded in the page as a thing. At the same time the car, which acknowledgment of the realities of global warming has caused to be really aerodynamic instead of just looking like it—accompanied, inevitably, by that simul-taneously developed lumbering insistence on denial, the SUV—is no longer a symbol of the entirely decorative but instead folds all that it once celebrated into a kind of passive-aggression that suits a capitalism that is at once out of control and clearly subject to enormous contradiction (global recession, massive concentrations of wealth, irrevers-ible poverty, etc.). Softer on the outside than earlier cars, it unites its driver with itself far more intimately and thoroughly than in the past, strapped in, multitasking thanks to a phone and radio and the car's ability to respond immediately to the slightest change of inflection on the part of the driver's hands or feet. It is the embodiment of the body's inseparable relationship with technology rather than the earth in our epoch. Her body is made out of that relationship. When putting on her eye make-up, she doesn't give a thought for how fast she is moving relative to the speed at which she'd be travelling if walking. Being in a medium expensive car, she experiences the interior as entirely stable—relatively speaking, static—allowing her to get the mascara on without being rocked about, an absolute convergence

Lamborghini interior by Versace. Photo credit: supercars.net.

of stillness and speed where the one has nothing to do with the other. No previous generation could embody such a contradiction, because it didn't live it, and could not therefore be made of, and experience itself as, it.

In *Beauty and the Contemporary Sublime* I make the point that people nowadays want to live as and within video images. Go to a shopping mall and what you'll see is people in a video-colored environment wearing video-colored clothes and eating video-colored food. Nowadays especially, we start with technology when imagining ourselves, and in this respect it seems germane to note that when thinking how we look and what we are we imagine ourselves in pretty much the same way as we think about our cars, from within and from a distance and in both cases as photographic, or more precisely video, images. Years ago, when they first put the Acura on the market, they tried out an ad campaign that didn't have the usual pictures of the car going down a country road and then pulling up at a fancy hotel, etc. Instead it had a pool with rocks in it and music and a voice-over. I was watching TV one morning

and was delighted to hear a grumpy ad man slag off the ad. "If I saw that ad," he said, "I'd think great, someone made a car that looks like rocks in a pool," and went on to explain that people didn't want crap like that they wanted a picture of the car driving along so they could imagine themselves in it, and he was obviously right for the same reason that no one would advertise a dress using something that wasn't a picture of the dress either. As I said at the beginning, people wear their cars. And as I also say in *Beauty*, the difference between the fashion model and the rest of us is that we have models model clothes to make the clothes look better, we buy the clothes to make us look better. The first task of the car ad is to make us think that the car will make us look better from a distance, it will be sexier than us while embodying our incorporation of the technological into our body's ability to live comfortably through and at the speed of the contemporary world.

The car's interior is where we become inseparable from that world and its speed in exactly the same way that, for the rest of the day, many of us remain inseparable from its instantaneity as we labor at keyboards from nine to five. Inside the car we are immediately present to a space defined by high speed and individual maneuvering. Inside the office we are in a similar relationship to the world to which we are connected by a screen as opposed to a windshield. I have been accused, correctly, of using the terms "instantaneity" and "immediacy" interchangeably in my critical writing in general.[6] I think they are interchangeable as far as the contemporary body is concerned, and that it's that quality or condition, potentially one of being so open to the world as to be continuous with it rather than outside it, that the contemporary human body and the contemporary car body both embody. I have said elsewhere that Martin Heidegger's analysis of the contemporary world is exact, but that we like much about it that he hates and that it actually is a technologically conditioned version of what he said we should have.[7]

Two things seem worth mentioning in conclusion to this brief note on the exchange between a machine with a partly plasticized metal exterior and a human subject who almost certainly imagines her mind to be somehow like a computer while also living through computers more or less all the time—not, as the eye make-up confirms, when in direct contact with another living body, as an image to be sure, but at almost all other times.[8]

The first point has to do with an anecdote about being astonished by how designers work. I asked a couple of my colleagues who teach car and transportation design whether there was a famous study having to do with the variance within the speed at which a person might walk for say a mile on a flat surface and that of a car driving along the same surface. When driving on the flat at a steady speed one notices the speedometer hover around a number rather than sitting solidly on it and I assume the same thing's true of a person walking. Neither of them had ever encountered such a study nor, I gathered, saw any need for one.

This is an astonishing thought for someone coming from the humanities (where, in the last two decades of the last century, we developed the concept and theory of the post-human). I'd never think, nor would or could any artist, of any vibration or speed without comparing it to the speeds of the body. There is a whole question here of where the sense of speed that informs and precedes whatever automobile engineers or body designers do with it. Inside the car breathing meets the speed of the electronic, perfect instantaneous reflexes are required in order that one may negotiate what's on the other side of the windscreen while attending to one's appearance, so nerves and lungs are totally at one with the car, but only tiny physical movements connect the motions of the body's surface to the speed of the car itself. This confirms that the relationship between inside and outside is absolute, and perhaps why it is symbolically important—the ergonomic and medical explanation being a rationalization of symbolic necessity—that the driver be semi-reclining. It also suggests that the car can't be thought of as something that the driver uses. The relationship is too intimate, primary function automatically rendered secondary. No one "uses" a blouse, no one "uses" a car. This is because the verb "to use" is both a given and insufficiently precise. "Use" implies too much distance and freedom of choice. Ultimately it is, I think, a question which takes us far from the present topic, or right underneath it, and has to do with whether music (aesthesis in its most fundamental form) derives from language and natural selection, as Herbert Spencer thought, or from a pre-linguistic phase and sexual difference rather than natural selection, which was Charles Darwin's opinion.[9] From the archaic and not necessarily computerized (in principle and practice, not of course in fundamental fact) world of the humanities I'd suggest there is a parallel here between the world of the designer and that of the painter. Piet Mondrian is famous for saying that the painting doesn't happen on the painting's surface but between that and its viewer. To describe a painting is to describe an event made of interactions between a recipient who projects and a complicated sign that initiates and sustains its own reception. From that perspective I am inclined to suggest that, as with any painting, it is not as easy as it may seem to say where the car starts and its use value begins, as opposed to what it actually is and what it makes the person who uses it be, at which point reciprocity complicates the idea of a user and used almost out of all recognition.

The second point I'd like to make follows from the driver's posture too. The car places the driver in a posture that has more to do with watching television while writing than with doing anything while walking. The car's speed is only one of the things with which its driver's concerned. With this in mind I'd like to suggest an analogy between the dashboard and the keyboard. What does the keyboard deny? The pleasures that come from writing by hand. Writing on a keyboard starts with language detached from the movements of the arm just as driving a car starts with the transfer of the body from walking or standing to movements of the hands and feet that have no direct physical reference to the actions they initiate, almost all of which pass through the electrical in order to become, as were those of the body that caused them to occur, mechanical. The future of the car is to become a complete robot. The driver will get into it and tell it where to go and get on with her make-up and messages without having to look out of the window if she doesn't feel like it. At the same time computers are getting good enough at voice recognition so that, punctuation aside, we may soon be able to write without touching the keyboard let alone using a pen. While both driving and writing we'll be almost entirely physically separate from the vehicle we're using. At the same time our mutual continuity with what we drive or through which we produce text will be greater—more immediate and instanta-neous—than ever. This is a reminder that we never design things. We want the blouse to make us attractive, we were attracted to it for that reason or with that in mind, it is an idea about attractiveness, not a piece of cloth but an image which followed from a fabric which was turned into a sign that surrounds a body and presents it. To talk of that as a kind of "use" is to leave out all that attracted us to it, which would mean that it might lead to a situation we could anticipate but not quite

It makes perfect sense that the ultimate destiny of the car should be that it evolves to a state where its function as a mode of transportation is of no more concern to its driver than whether the blouse she's wearing keeps out the rain. In other words that its ultimate destiny should be to realize at the level of engineering what it has always actually been with regard to the things that people find important, namely, whether it works as a symbol.

imagine in detail. Its designer set up the conditions for an event, symbolically implicit but by no means anything that a description of how it was cut and sewn could elaborate or make explicit. It makes perfect sense that the ultimate destiny of the car should be that it evolves to a state where its function as a mode of transportation is of no more concern to its driver than whether the blouse she's wearing keeps out the rain. In other words that its ultimate destiny should be to realize at the level of engineering what it has always actually been with regard to the things that people find important, namely, whether it works as a symbol.

POSTSCRIPT: THE DRIVER AND THE RIDER, THE SCOPOPHILIAC CONSEQUENCES OF HORSES AND CARRIAGES

Carriages insulated the driver from direct experience of the road to some extent while riding a horse intensified it. This difference, taken to an extreme, is maintained in the relationship between cars and motorcycles. Car suspension has gotten better and better, but just as one could always feel first of all the horse so too the bike rider feels the bike, more and more the faster she goes. Intensification and the immediacy of the physical experience is a primary feature of riding a bike, dispersing and displacing both (into a variety of tasks and distractions) the characteristics of driving a car. The aspect of the comparison on which I'd like to concentrate here has to do with the bike rider and the bike as an image, as opposed to the driver sitting behind the windshield of her car.

What I have to say here is indebted to my colleague and collaborator Rebecca Norton, and we'll probably return to the comparison elsewhere. Here, I note that it goes straight to the question of how the image is present to its viewer. Norton has observed that the bike rider cannot wear the bike like a blouse. Where the driver of the car is seen only as a head and shoulders, in the bike rider's case it is precisely the head and shoulders that are covered up, by a helmet and a thick leather jacket. Norton has suggested that the sexy equivalent of the girl in the cute car exposing her shoulders behind glass, inviting scrutiny as part of an aesthetic of inaccessibility, is the girl on the bike invisible from head to waist but wearing a short skirt. Anonymity where in the driver's case we can see her face, and an aesthetic of elusiveness rather than inaccessibility, we see the woman in the car when she's across from us at a stoplight. On the freeway we don't see her at all. What passes us is a car, maybe a glimpse of a profile as she goes past, maybe in our rear-view mirror. On the freeway we only see the bike rider in the rear-view mirror, as she draws alongside, and then as a behind receding into the distance. I quote directly from something I wrote about the short skirt in 1988: "The short skirt is the item of clothing that threatens to disappear."[10] The rider appears as Darth Vader in the rear-view mirror and then swoops past, momentarily a profile but quickly an image of a behind mounted on a wheel receding in front of one towards the vanishing point which she implies and also displaces, towards disappearing... As I also say in the essay from which I just quoted, "the short skirt announces an era of disclosure as opposed to an epoch governed by the principle of implication and promise."[11] With any image of sexual attractiveness, it would have to be the case that elusiveness and distance were a feature of the promise of flirtation offered in the first place. The woman in the car belongs to the tradition of attraction as a matter of implication and promise, the object of attrac-tion present to her viewer as an image of the at once distant and immediately present. She is really best seen when her car is standing still. Her car's design implies speed and her face and shoulders and bust imply the rest of her. When she's putting on her make-up she's quite sure almost no one is looking at her, and if so only in passing and indirectly, her car is a private space. The woman on the bike is an image of attractiveness that reminds us—playfully, because reminders about the erotic are only convincing when playful—that with disclosure comes, as one would logically expect, a proportionally intensified possibility of and capacity for elusiveness. Nothing private about the space of the bike, no chance of staring at her for long on the other hand either. Motorcycles are far more nimble on the freeway than cars. Quite unlike a short skirt, the car remains a space to be occupied, complementing its driver the way a Victorian dress full of boning complemented and formed its wearer without actually revealing very much of her. The eye shadow will take effect as an affect when she gets out and walks up to someone.

[1] Jeremy Gilbert-Rolfe, "Born to Be Mild," *Beyond Piety: Critical Essays on the Visual Arts 1986–1993* (Cambridge and New York: Cambridge University Press, 1995).

[2] F.J. Camm, H.W. Gilbert-Rolfe, and D.C. Nicholas, *Newnes Plastic Manual* (London: George Newnes Ltd, 1945), 204.

[3] Jeremy Gilbert-Rolfe, *Beauty and the Contemporary Sublime* (New York: Allworth Press, 1999), 121–22.

[4] As this goes to press an intellectual property case between the computer firms Apple and Samsung has just been resolved in the former's favor, and I note that the chief item at issue was the rounded edges of the Apple product, which they claimed Samsung had stolen. This is to give Apple a copyright on what is inherent to plastic, as if the Pope had declared that only his favorite artist could use the grid.

[5] Wolfgang Schivelbush, *The Railway Journey: The Industrialization of Time and Space in the 19th Century* (Berkeley: University of California Press, 1987), 33–34.

[6] Rex Butler, "Beauty, The Sublime, and Time," in *Art After Deconstruction: Jeremy Gilbert-Rolfe*, Rex Butler, ed. (Brisbane: Editions 3, 2012).

[7] Jeremy Gilbert-Rolfe with *Frank Gehry, Frank Gehry: The City and Music* (London: Routledge, 2000).

[8] I develop this point a little in *Beauty*, with reference to how people always imagine the mind and the psyche in terms of the dominant technology of the era (a telescope for early Humanism, the steam engine for Freud, for example) and also to writing, which is a technology which has both ordered and expanded spoken language, inventing the perfect and pluperfect tenses and much else on the same order. Our subjectivity is not only conditioned and a product of language, it is more exactly a product of writing. See Gilbert-Rolfe, *Beauty and the Contemporary Sublime*, 126–28.

[9] Elizabeth Grosz, *Chaos, Territory, Art: Deleuze and the Framing of the Earth* (New York: Columbia University Press, 2008), 32–33.

[10] Jeremy Gilbert-Rolfe, with Stephanie Hermsdorf, "A Thigh-Length History of the Fashion Photograph—An Abbreviated Theory of the Body," *Bomb* (fall 1988), reprinted in Jeremy Gilbert-Rolfe, *Beyond Piety*, 263.

[11] Ibid.

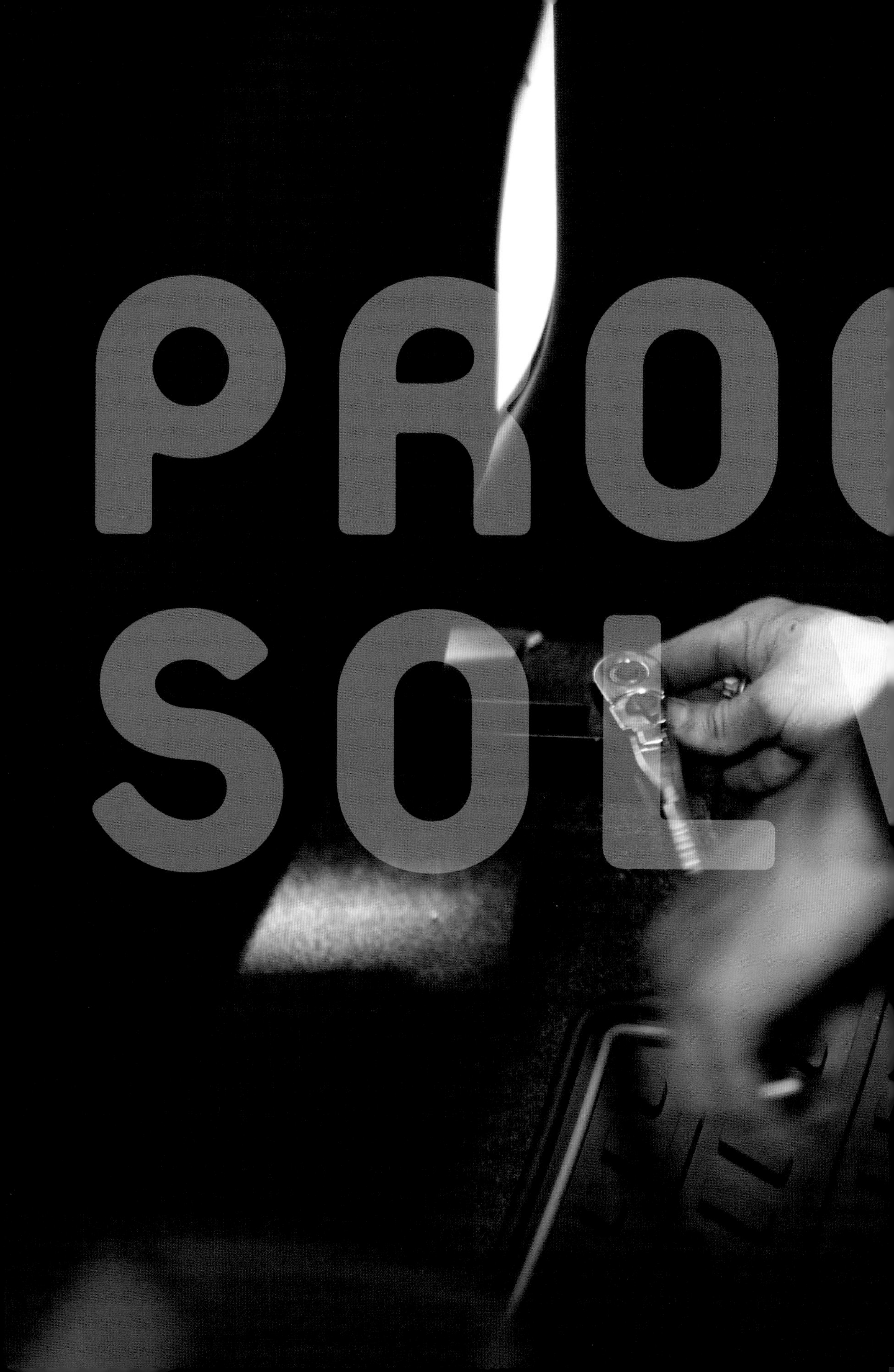
PRO
SOL

BLEM
VING

TUNERS: INTERVIEW WITH ROBERT TALLINI, ROAD RACE MOTORSPORTS

Kati Rubinyi

ROBERT TALLINI *was recommended to me when I was looking for an expert to discuss tuning—the craft of customizing cars to achieve high performance. He has been racing cars for over 20 years, and his business, Road Race Motorsports, is located in Santa Fe Springs, California. They design and fabricate products that optimize the performance of customers' cars for use on streets. They also have a fleet of their own cars that compete on racetracks. I asked him what Road Race does and why, and what the future holds in store for tuning.*

PROBLEM SOLVING

We modify Mitsubishis for a type of race called Time Attack. It started in Japan and is one of the most popular forms of motorsport in the world. It's not a wheel-to-wheel race; it's who can drive the fastest lap while maintaining traction. We are trying to balance a number of things, and it's really about experimenting, seeing what works and going back and adjusting in order to maximize horsepower, minimize weight, and maintain safety. We work on shaving weight: we want to make the car as light as possible, and we're also balancing the weight corner to

corner, so we move around the shocks and we weigh each corner. The most important thing is getting the weight even from front to back, and second most important, from side to side. The bigger the tires the better, but they have to be appropriate for the car. The width of the car also has to stay within a certain dimension.

We also move the ECU—the electronic engine control unit—because it has to stay cool and high enough in the car that it is never submerged in water. The electronic control unit is the key to giving you more horsepower, so we add piggybacks to the ECU in order to override the manufacturer's parameters. If you can re-flash the existing ECU, you can have everything you desire, and there are a couple of ways to do this. One is to remove the ECU completely and replace it will another engine management system. In a racecar, that lets you do more, but it's more complicated to do and not as bulletproof as the other option, which is to add onto a commercially made control unit. Two of our cars have a new, custom-made engine management system, and the other one has a piggybacked system. We also add a computerized accelerator—a launch control.

TUNING

We also modify a lot of different cars that are not necessarily for racing, but just because people want more horsepower from their cars and improved performance. As for the future, performance will always be a big deal. We talk to a lot of young people in their 20s and 30s, and there are always those guys who want to drive fast cars. It's an expression of manhood and machismo, and you can look back to the hotrod craze of the 1950s up to the street racers. You can see from the past that there's an age group that is always going to be compelled to buy the cheapest cars available and somehow transform them into something well beyond where they started. Some of the cars we have out here are 150 horsepower, and most of these guys are not satisfied until they've doubled that horse-power; and that would have been true in the 1960s, 1970s, 1980s, and so on.

Everybody's expectation is to take a $13,000 car—kind of bottom of the rung, from any manufacturer—and make that into a giant-killer. But we also have guys that are 40 or 50 who'll buy a car for practical reasons, but are not pleased with the pep and the pickup. They ask what we can do to improve the performance of the car. They're not interested in the looks of the car as much as getting more from the engine, and they are willing to spend money on it.

Some manufacturers design and build their cars to be tuned more than others. Mitsubishi, for example, has a racing heritage. They

have a halo product that they rest all of their laurels on: an Evo. Then they build a whole line of cars underneath at varying price levels. Below the Evo, you have a Rally Art, which is still turbo-charged but with less performance. Then they have their 2.4-liter Lancer GTS, which is five or six rungs down the ladder. But they're all the same body. That's great for us because guys who can only afford the bottom tier are still aspiring to have better perfor-mance. It's not the same with, say, Nissan. They have a lot of great cars, but they're all kind of random. For example, they have a 370Z. It has it's own body, it's own everything. Then they have an Altima, which is over here; the GT-R, which is an incredible supercar, is way over there. They have SUVs; they have a Cube. Talk about randomly filling niches. It's worked for Nissan, but you can't make a Cube into a 370Z.

Everybody's expec-tation is to take a $13,000 car—kind of bottom of the rung, from any manufacturer—and make that into a giant-killer.

LEFT: Starting work on a Suzuki SX-4 that was shipped from New Jersey to Road Race Motorsports in California. The owner is paying $20,000 for having his winter car tuned to become the fastest and most efficient it can be while staying street legal and in compliance with New Jersey's inspections. Road Race will strip down the inside completely so it just has racecar seats in the front. They will turbocharge the engine and double its horsepower with an engine modification kit they designed specifically for this type of car. The car will be ready to be shipped back to the owner in eight weeks.

ECUs

The biggest trend I've seen is that ECUs and computers are more and more difficult to change. Manufacturers are limiting what you can get away with. Even over the last four or five years, there have been some significant changes in the operating language: the OBD1, OBD2, and CanBus. The industry has some kind of an agreement where, within a year or two, they'll elect to change to a new operating language. The State of California forces a standards committee, the Society for Automobile Engineers, to do it. The standards make it more and more difficult for us to extract the most power.

But there's always a computer geek lurking in the wings. They don't even have to be in the industry. It's just a little bit of time before that system's hacked into. First it's hacked into enough to be able to read it and see all of the parameters, and shortly thereafter somebody's able to write it. There is a lot of brilliant people around—they could be working for Boeing, but they're intent on helping their little community of, say, Subaru guys who want to manipulate things. Every iteration that comes out, someone manages to overcome it. We find them on forums. They raise their hands; they want to become a folk hero in that community.

TRANSMISSIONS

Another thing that's been problematic is the transmission changes of the last few years, going to CVTs (continuously variable transmission) and things like that. Transmission has become a limiting factor because they are designed to take just enough of the power that the manufacturer has assigned to the engine. We can make the car twice as powerful in a manual version of the car, but if it has a CVT, it does not allow for that extra torque to be utilized. It'll start by throwing warnings at you, and if you choose to ignore those warnings or bypass them with electronic gadgets, they will eat up the chain or the belt and the transmission is done. Most car enthusiasts wonder why they came out with these transmissions. In Mitsubishis, eight out of ten have a CVT, while only 20% are manual. They always offer a manual version because they know the pure enthusiasts will gravitate toward that. Their way of looking at it is the CVT will sell to the masses and the enthusiasts will get the few manuals. With the newer manual models, there is an added plus for us tuners because the manufacturers don't offer enough in the right packages, so people come to us for modifications. That is another big trend.

We know the advantages of the CVT: the mileage and the smoothness when it shifts. It appeals to a broad audience. But all the operating environments are going to some variation of automatic transmission. Even a Ferrari, for God's sake, doesn't have a clutch pedal anymore. You go from that to a Ford

Fiesta, which they call a six-speed automatic, but it's just basically supposed to shift itself. Ten years ago the manual was cheaper. They're still pretending you should pay a premium for an automatic, but in reality, a manual is rarer and is the higher performance version. On the other hand, the new transmissions are allowing for big improvements in gas mileage. There are mandates now for an average of 35.5 miles per gallon in a fleet by 2016, and 35.5 is a lot.

AUTOMATED DRIVING

Cars mean a lot more to enthusiasts than people think, and when you say technology is helping you control it, that's fine. You can assist me with braking and steering, and I will accept it. But if you're taking my free choice away, I don't want it. Say, for example, a racecar comes with an antilock braking system (ABS) that doesn't respond in the most efficient way possible. We pull the fuse out. But we keep the fuse with us because if we have a race and it's raining, and we think the ABS will help us go faster, we put the fuse back in. Same thing with traction control or anything else. First thing we do is turn off traction control because with these kinds of cars, traction control will cut in such a way that way too much time lapses in between. But if I were in a rain race, I would put up with that because the speed would actually be enhanced.

Take away free choice and the enthusiasts are done. They're going to be driving old cars

You can assist me with braking and steering, and I will accept it. But if you're taking my free choice away, I don't want it.

if they can, or they're going to find ways to turn off all that stuff on new cars. I would assume that as automation technology emerges, there's going to be a premium charge for it, as in "The Mercedes knew the truck stopped." Good for them. But for the enthusiast, we'll take advantage of any chance to undo or remove it. There's a lot of satisfaction in driving a vehicle that has some performance to it. Just the exhaust note alone is something that motivates people. We spend time on that stuff. We even listen to the exhaust notes on this road out here that's wide open. It does have an impact. There's still a horsepower war. If you're going to take away my ability to drive, why entice me with 500 horsepower?

Automated controls sound good when I don't want to pay attention to driving. But not all drivers are good drivers, and not everyone knows where they're going. It's going to be very hard to account for all those factors.

LEFT: This phase of the work is about addressing all the car's systems for safety and performance. Road Race is installing larger brakes, a roll-bar, and increasing chassis rigidity. The car was originally produced with barely 100 horsepower at the wheels, but the horsepower of the two-liter engine is doubled by customizing their base turbocharger kit further for this project. Steel floor plates create a smooth surface at the bottom of the car so the driver can position his feet. The last step is using aircraft fastener clips to attach new custom fiberglass body panels, bumpers, side-skirts, and a rear diffuser.

One of the most technologically advanced cars in the area of ECUs is the Nissan GT-R. Nissan had originally put something in there where you could not get all the performance out of the car until the GPS told them you were at the track. Customer complaints made Nissan repeal that. People were saying, "I bought a $100,000 high performance car and you guys have Big Brothered me into using it in a sanctioned place via GPS."

People still see cars as a source of freedom. Even when you start taking that away and putting my money in public transportation, I will continue to tinker on my own car. With the manufacturers, there's the warranty side, but the public relations and marketing side of the companies know that people want the ability to personalize their cars. A lot of the time I get cars for free. I get an e-mail saying, "Hey, if you can build a turbo kit for this car, I'll buy it, but otherwise I won't." When I answer, I don't blind-copy the car company, I copy them! They use the e-mail with their upper managers to demonstrate what's going on. And we're doing research for them, informally.

500-horsepower car, I can't utilize it during my drive to work. But with a set of tires for the track, that car can go out once a week or once a month. More and more of these organizations are popping up. A while back there was one called Speed Trail USA, and you could go 150 miles per hour safely. That might work for someone with a 500-horse-power car. Then there's the Big Brother factor, where they can track you wherever you are. With OnStar, it calls a satellite every five minutes.

Road Race Motorsports.

TRACK EVENTS

Track events are another growing phenomenon. Even the young guys are starting to accept that racing around on public roads is not a good idea, so on any given day a lot of track events are held at local venues, where you can go out and run your car in a controlled environment. If I have a

TO GO CARS TRUCKS CARS HONDAS 2007 300 22 THE CUTLASS WELO SUCH A SHOW OFF CHEVY CAPRI WAGON HYDRAULICS 3 WHEEL PUMPS DAYTONS TV CHROME DV LOW SIEMPRE FIRME NISSAN 370Z TR FACET PHOTOGRAPHY HIT ME BACK DIS IS MY GATOR CHEVY IMPALA HER NAME IS TJ N A GATOR CHE CAPRICE AIR RIDE SHAVED 1991 CAPRICE CLASSIC AFTER THE CAR WASH MOTO LOWRIDER BLUE MO BLUE CHOPPER THIS IS AN AWESOME CAR TURBO BUICK REGAL HOMICIDE AND JAZMAINE CAMI SKITTLES SKITTLES CAR MI DONK W 22 S 94 CHEVY JUICED ME AND MY 95 LOVEINIT LA MEXICAN MA HATERS WHAT 63 IMPALA LOWRIDER JOHANA HIS RANFLA 1963 IMPALA MY CAR MY ART WORK MY LIL LO LOW THE BOSS 516 SUPERMARIO OLDS CUTLASS SUPREME 13X7 LOWRIDER OLDS CUTLASS SUPRE LOWRIDER 13X7 CHEVY CHEVROLET INTAKE INTERIOR 1963 IMPALA 4 DOOR HARDTOP BONESBLACK YUKON MY LOW LOW 1963 LOW RIDER MY NISSAN SKYLINE ESPANOLA NM MY 94 CHEVY ON 22 W HONDA G35 SNOWED IN DREAMCARS XTERRA LOWRIDER MUSTANG ROLLIN ON TRUES VOGEES MY RI HJJ STEFAN LAMBERT WORKING HARD LOWRIDER BIKE LOWRIDER BIKE PART LOWRIDER BIKE FRO WWW TOPLOWRIDER 2007 MUSTANG WWW OGOGOG COM TRUCK XTREME IMAGE RIDE BIG MY 2ND BA MY BABY MY 1ST BABY HEAVY CHEVY MERCEDES BENZ NEXT INTERIOR PICS YOU LIKE MY CHOICE REA TO HIT SWITCHES PUTTIN THE BAGS ON BLUEBERRY HILL REACHING THE PEAK TO SUCCESS SITTI LOW BOMB DIGGLE WIGGLE KIDO HAH SO FRESH AND SO CLEAN CLEAN BIANCA WARE CAR 13 BA SCARFACE 100 GLODEN MI OTRA S10 MY BF RID3 DIS R MY GIRLS 66 CHEVY N 04 TOYOTA TACOMA DIS MY GIRLS LEGENDARY TIME TO GO CARS TRUCKS CARS HONDAS 2007 300 22 THE CUTLASS WELO SUCH SHOW OFF CHEVY CAPRICE WAGON HYDRAULICS 3 WHEEL PUMPS DAYTONS TV CHROME DV LOW SIEMP FIRME NISSAN 370Z TROY FACET PHOTOGRAPHY HIT ME BACK DIS IS MY GATOR CHEVY IMPALA HER NA IS TJ N A GATOR CHEVY CAPRICE AIR RIDE SHAVED 1991 CAPRICE CLASSIC AFTER THE CAR WASH MO LOWRIDER BLUE MOTO BLUE CHOPPER THIS IS AN AWESOME CAR TURBO BUICK REGAL HOMICIDE A JAZMAINE CAMION SKITTLES SKITTLES CAR MI DONK W 22 S 94 CHEVY JUICED ME AND MY 95 LOVEIN LA MEXICAN MAFIA HATERS WHAT 63 IMPALA LOWRIDER JOHANA HIS RANFLA 1963 IMPALA MY CAR ART WORK MY LIL LOW LOW THE BOSS 516 SUPERMARIO OLDS CUTLASS SUPREME 13X7 LOWRIDER OL CUTLASS SUPREME LOWRIDER 13X7 CHEVY CHEVROLET INTAKE INTERIOR 1963 IMPALA 4 DOOR HARDT BONESBLACKYUKON MY LOW LOW 1963 LOW RIDER MY NISSAN SKYLINE ESPANOLA NM MY 94 CHEVY 22 WILL HONDA G35 SNOWED IN DREAMCARS XTERRA LOWRIDER MUSTANG ROLLIN ON TRUES VOGE MY RIDE HJJ STEFAN LAMBERT WORKING HARD LOWRIDER BIKE LOWRIDER BIKE PART LOWRIDER BI FROM WWW TOPLOWRIDER 2007 MUSTANG WWW OGOGOG COM TRUCK XTREME IMAGE RIDE BIG MY 2 BABY MY BABY MY 1ST BABY HEAVY CHEVY MERCEDES BENZ NEXT INTERIOR PICS YOU LIKE MY CHOI READY TO HIT SWITCHES PUTTIN THE BAGS ON BLUEBERRY HILL REACHING THE PEAK TO SUCCE SITTING LOW BOMB DIGGLE WIGGLE KIDO HAH SO FRESH AND SO CLEAN CLEAN BIANCA WARE CAR BANK SCARFACE 100 GLODEN MI OTRA S10 MY BF RID3 DIS R MY GIRLS 66 CHEVY N 04 TOYOTA TACO DIS R MY GIRLS LEGENDARY TIME TO GO CARS TRUCKS CARS HONDAS 2007 300 22 THE CUTLASS WE SUCH A SHOW OFF CHEVY CAPRICE WAGON HYDRAULICS 3 WHEEL PUMPS DAYTONS TV CHROME DV L SIEMPRE FIRME NISSAN 370Z TROY FACET PHOTOGRAPHY HIT ME BACK DIS IS MY GATOR CHEVY IMPA HER NAME IS TJ N A GATOR CHEVY CAPRICE AIR RIDE SHAVED 1991 CAPRICE CLASSIC AFTER THE C WASH MOTO LOWRIDER BLUE MOTO BLUE CHOPPER THIS IS AN AWESOME CAR TURBO BUICK REG HOMICIDE AND JAZMAINE CAMION SKITTLES SKITTLES CAR MI DONK W 22 S 94 CHEVY JUICED ME AND 95 LOVEINIT LA MEXICAN MAFIA HATERS WHAT 63 IMPALA LOWRIDER JOHANA HIS RANFLA 1963 IMPA MY CAR MY ART WORK MY LIL LOW LOW THE BOSS 516 SUPERMARIO OLDS CUTLASS SUPREME 1 LOWRIDER OLDS CUTLASS SUPREME LOWRIDER 13X7 CHEVY CHEVROLET INTAKE INTERIOR 1963 IMPA 4 DOOR HARDTOP BONESBLACKYUKON MY LOW LOW 1963 LOW RIDER MY NISSAN SKYLINE ESPANOLA N MY 94 CHEVY ON 22 WILL HONDA G35 SNOWED IN DREAMCARS XTERRA LOWRIDER MUSTANG ROLLIN TRUES VOGEES MY RIDE HJJ STEFAN LAMBERT WORKING HARD LOWRIDER BIKE LOWRIDER BIKE PA LOWRIDER BIKE FROM WWW TOPLOWRIDER 2007 MUSTANG WWW OGOGOG COM TRUCK XTREME IMA RIDE BIG MY 2ND BABY MY BABY MY 1ST BABY HEAVY CHEVY MERCEDES BENZ NEXT INTERIOR PICS Y LIKE MY CHOICE READY TO HIT SWITCHES PUTTIN THE BAGS ON BLUEBERRY HILL REACHING THE PE TO SUCCESS SITTING LOW BOMB DIGGLE WIGGLE KIDO HAH SO FRESH AND SO CLEAN CLEAN BIAN WARE CAR 13 BANK SCARFACE 100 GLODEN MI OTRA S10 MY BF RID3 DIS R MY GIRLS 66 CHEVY N TOYOTA TACOMA DIS R MY GIRLS LEGENDARY TIME TO GO CARS TRUCKS CARS HONDAS 2007 300 22 T CUTLASS WELO SUCH A SHOW OFF CHEVY CAPRICE WAGON HYDRAULICS 3 WHEEL PUMPS DAYTONS CHROME DV LOW SIEMPRE FIRME NISSAN 370Z TROY FACET PHOTOGRAPHY HIT ME BACK DIS IS MY GA CHEVY IMPALA HER NAME IS TJ N A GATOR CHEVY CAPRICE AIR RIDE SHAVED 1991 CAPRICE CLASS AFTER THE CAR WASH MOTO LOWRIDER BLUE MOTO BLUE CHOPPER THIS IS AN AWESOME CAR TUR BUICK REGAL HOMICIDE AND JAZMAINE CAMION SKITTLES SKITTLES CAR MI DONK W 22 S 94 CH JUICED ME AND MY 95 LOVEINIT LA MEXICAN MAFIA HATERS WHAT 63 IMPALA LOWRIDER JOHANA RANFLA 1963 IMPALA MY CAR MY ART WORK MY LIL LOW LOW THE BOSS 516 SUPERMARIO OLDS CUTL

THE
STREET:

THE STREET:

Services:

PARK
24-Hour secure bicycle parking for members
Free parking during staffed hours available for non-members

FIX
Tools available for members at no charge.
Non-members pay per hour
Professional mechanic services during regular business hours

PARTS/ACCESSORIES
Lights, locks, tubes, tires and all rider's basic needs
Members receive a 10% discount

FREE AIR

INFORMATION
A wide selection of bicycle transit and commuter information

SHOWERS/CHANGING ROOM
Private restrooms and showers for members

LOCKERS
Private, day use lockers available

BIKE TOURS & RENTALS
Call 562-436-BIKE (2453) to d
or stop in during business hours

Bikestation Long Beach
223 E 1st Street
Long Beach, CA 90802

OPERATORS

Bill Trimble

Downtown Los Angeles, circa 1905: Spring Street looking north from 4th Street.
Photo credit: Los Angeles Public Library.

WE ALL EXPECT TO ENJOY VEHICLES IN 2035 that are no more than a sketch today. We should also expect that those newly imagined vehicles will share the road with vehicles that even today seem old. Some people will keep old cars because they are affordable or because they want to make a statement. Old cars, operable only with the sentience of their human drivers, will be moving along next to the most advanced vehicles of 2035, vehicles that are sentient themselves and responsive to a sentient infrastructure.

The public space of vehicles, the space of our mobility system, is space we all share. Streets and sidewalks, highways, and transit lines are the public realm we use to get around, at least on the ground. How will we share that space in 2035?

Mobility has changed over time, of course, and it will keep changing. Trolleys, auto-mobiles, bicycles, and trucks all came with the promise of easier mobility. Walking was too slow and the horse too much trouble for most. The streets of downtown Los Angeles in 1905 accommodated every existing option: horse-drawn, engine-powered, or human-powered. Vehicles moved at speeds a pedestrian, at least a running pedestrian, could match. Even trucks and trolleys moved slowly enough for someone to jump on. Cyclists moved faster than the walkers, but

In 1905, vehicles moved at speeds a pedestrian, at least a running pedestrian, could match.

not so much faster in the crowded street. Deaths occurred, but few vehicles moved at speeds that were inherently life-threatening to a pedestrian.

People watched others in the public space in 1905, they do today, and they will in 2035, even when those others are in other vehicles. The way people "move"—how they walk, drive an automobile, ride a bicycle, how they take a seat on a bus or train—is revealing. The "gestures" of moving, the many decisions about what people do with themselves on the way, show what they think of themselves and those who share their space. Their gestures may be exuberant, aggressive, timid, competitive, fearful, gracious, angry, distracted. Even patient.

Speed matters. The public space of mobility today must accommodate disabled pedestrians moving at one mile per hour and motor vehicles capable of reaching sixty miles per hour in four seconds. Encounters can be deadly. How can travelers with so many different ways of moving share the same public space in 2035?

Speed matters. The public space of mobility today must accommodate disabled pedestrians moving at one mile per hour and motor vehicles capable of reaching sixty miles per hour in four seconds. Encounters can be deadly.

The mix of people in this public space will change by 2035. The chances of riding or walking next to someone who is past seventy years of age will double by 2035. The chances of encountering people older than eighty will nearly triple. The generation that will dominate the public space of mobility and the workplace—those between 35 and 55 years of age in 2035—will be the first generation to grow up digital and connected.

Patience with the journey may feel different in 2035, if "connectedness" continues to accelerate. Will travelers in the street shift the here-and-now of physical public space to the margins of attention, with instantaneous connections to everywhere else becoming the focus? The many generations of 2035 will not be traveling at the same speed, and not moving with equal patience.

Travelers in 1905 depended on their own human sentience, or on the sentience of a slow-moving animal, to get them safely where they were going. Vehicle sentience today protects some drivers from collisions. And it guides vehicles that are capable of autonomy, needing a human only as a passenger.

Technological sentience, and the other technologies that must accompany it, may be directed to three different roles, each representing a view of what can be expected of the human being in the vehicle, the severity of the risks, and whether the technology can be adopted universally. First, the technology may be used to *inform* the operator (i.e., provide *situational awareness*), so operation can be more responsive to the situation. Alternatively, it can be used to *require* proper behavior or to *block* dangerous behavior. Thirdly, sentient technology can be used to *encourage* safe behavior by conveying incentives and penalties to the operator, so decisions are more likely to benefit the public.

Every operator misses important information. The driving situation is more complex than the driver recognizes. Blind spots, changes down the road, the mental state or physical condition of the driver of the next vehicle— missing information limits the operator's

The chances of riding or walking next to someone who is past seventy years of age will double by 2035.

Sentient technology can be used to encourage safe behavior by conveying incentives and penalties to the operator, so decisions are more likely to benefit the public.

awareness and ability to respond. If the operator is attentive, additional information can make the difference between safety and collision. A commitment to technology that *informs* the operator, that enhances an operator's own sentience, places the responsibility on the operator, with considerable optimism.

Some are not so optimistic about the operators, or at least about *all* of the operators, so they choose another approach. Some operators today—whether inattentive or willful or inexperienced—have little regard for information that others consider crucial: traffic signals, the brake-lights of the next car, street signage, signals indicating trains are coming, speedometers showing excessive speed. If operators cannot be expected to adhere to safe practices, technology may be used to replace them, *blocking* the possibility of unsafe behavior. Of course, all technology can be hacked. And not all operators will want to operate vehicles that limit their control.

Incentives and penalties make a difference, and they are most powerful when linked quickly and clearly to a specific action. Immediate notification is more powerful than notification days later. Memories offer excuses. Not all operators will choose to operate responsibly. But when information about an action quickly results in the delivery of a penalty or an offer of an incentive, even before the end of the trip, drivers receive strong *encouragement* to operate safely. This third option for sentient technology does not control behavior; it pushes safe behavior.

The public space of mobility in 2035 will be even more mixed than a Los Angeles street of 1905. The range of possible speeds and the distribution of physical capabilities will require full attention and active sentience, if the space is to operate safely. The crucial question for the future of mobility is how technology will change the role of human attention and sentience.

CITIES FOR CARS: FUTURAMA AND THE CALIFORNIA ENVIRONMENTAL QUALITY ACT

Simon Pastucha

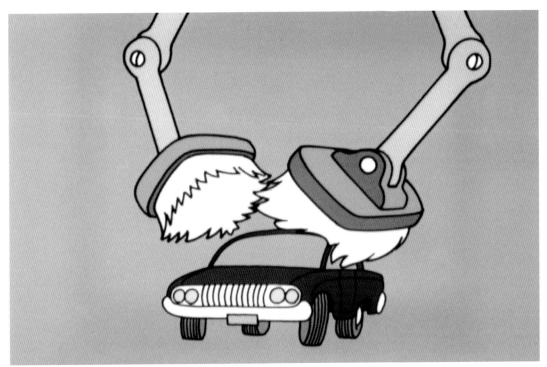

THE 1966 ANIMATION *WHAT ON EARTH!* BY THE NATIONAL FILM BOARD OF CANADA (NFB) was made before the environment was a widely shared concern. The film was prescient of a newly critical attitude towards auto-dependency. The film takes the perspective of aliens trying to understand our society. They observe that vehicles (Earthlings) are in charge of the planet and people (parasites) have a dependent relationship with cars. These machines are fed, cleaned and housed, and have ample roadways on which to move. They spend their time going between places where they can socialize. These roadways and social areas take up the vast majority of land, and the built environment is based on the automobile. The world is for the car and not for the less-significant creatures that rely on them. Cultural products like *What on Earth!* sparked awareness of the negative conse-quences of the relationship between cars and people, and by now, the issues are well understood. But despite longstanding efforts to make us less subservient to cars, our auto-dependency is a tough habit to shake, and in Southern California, it paves the way to our future.

Chances are strong that the Southern California city of 2035 will be very similar to the one we live in today. However, the current urban network of roadways is going to have to work with, and account for, many different types of vehicles, such as: autonomous vehicles, small and light vehicles ("city cars"), legacy vehicles made as early as the year 2020, three-wheeled and slow personal mobility scooters, and the very large number of bicycles, buses, and streetcars that will be on the road by 2035. Physically, the roadway network will not look very different from the roadway network of today, but we will rely on advancements in technology to create smoother traffic flow. New technology embedded in both vehicles and roadways will enable the individual vehicle to maintain an important role in our future lives. Onboard computer systems will ease decision-making and enable video conferencing and hands-free driving, among other activities. Today's popular and upbeat vision of the techno-car on the techno-roads of the future is a retread of ideas that were formed in the distant past and that produced the present.

The official 1939 New York World's Fair pamphlet's slogan was "Dawn of a New Day." The exhibition's stated goal was "allowing all visitors to glimpse the world of tomorrow." The fair had several different areas including a *Transportation Zone*, which featured a *Futurama* exhibit that moved visitors on a conveyor belt over a large model of the cities and freeways of tomorrow. The exhibit concluded with visitors exiting into a life-size model of an intersection in a city of the future, with multi-story buildings and stores on all sides. Exhibits of futuristic automobiles in storefronts and special pavilions were integrated throughout the *Transportation Zone* model urban environment. The connection between the automobile and progress was reiterated in an impressive display of a car being assembled, which echoed an earlier presentation in the Chicago World's Fair of 1933.

The *Transportation Zone* mindset, with its idealism and focus on automobiles as both making life easier and resulting in a better built environment, continues to this day. The relationship between the automobile and Southern California cities, especially the typical suburban city, is clear: The automobile is its very essence and integral to its survival. We know people are largely dependent on their private automobiles to function here. Private automobiles carry the vast majority of individuals on our roadways, while mass transit comes in at a distant second. Southern California cities could not exist without automobiles. If you live in Southern California, how would you get to your job or place of business if suddenly there were no cars? How would you get food and supplies? How could you live your current life? The region would not function if all automobiles stopped working tomorrow.

The automobile has woven the cities of Southern California together into a successful regional economy and it actively shapes our built environment. For example, the rules that govern building dictate every house must have a place to park a car, and every business must have a place for their patrons to park. Every employer must have parking for their employees, every religious,

The rules that govern building dictate every house must have a place to park a car, and every business must have a place for their patrons to park.

educational, and cultural institution and each medical entity must provide parking for staff, students, customers, and visitors. We have required city, state, and federal officials to create standards and laws that regulate the use, operation, and parking of automobiles.

We do this with the knowledge of the fact that automobiles require vast land area and infrastructure to be manufactured, sold, stored, moved, repaired, fueled, cleaned, and later scrapped, recycled, or trashed. Moreover, the estimate is that somewhere between 25 to 35 percent of the land area in cities is taken up by roadways. A roadway consists of all the elements you see in a street and everything along its edges: asphalt and the paint to identify parking spaces, travel lanes, crosswalks, the signs and lights for directing traffic, and the streetlights that provide visibility at night. Sidewalks, too, play their minor role. Also included in a "roadway" is the equipment that is out of sight, such as power systems, sensors, video cameras, and computer equipment to monitor and adjust traffic flows. In other words, beyond the land itself is a massive physical infrastructure that is required to support the street surface on which cars drive. And this is just the portion of land for automobiles devoted to public alleys, streets, and highways. Consider every paved surface on private property and every parking structure added to that.

We take for granted that the form of the city is shaped and governed by the necessity for all areas of the city to provide for the automobile. That mandate is so fundamental that the environmental law called the California Environmental Quality Act (CEQA), which was originally intended to protect the natural environment by requiring the disclosure of environmental impacts to endangered animal or plant species, has evolved to include the protection of automobiles. CEQA demands that for new developments in California, you must obtain a document called an Environmental Impact Report (EIR), disclosing environmental impacts based on a biological study of native plants and animals on the site. It must also cover impacts to the broader native species and suggest protection measures. The same document has another section containing a complicated traffic assessment detailing impacts of the new project on predicted traffic flow as measured in Levels of Service (LOS). It requires the recommendation of protective measures such as automated signalization, new travel lanes, left or right turn lanes, and signal timing adjustments that reduce traffic impacts to the movement of vehicles. In a context of continual population growth and increases in the number of vehicles on the road, CEQA leads the charge in codifying what has sadly become the most important and exhaustively considered question about any proposed change to the built environment: Is it going to cause traffic and congestion?

The reality is that alternative mobility options, improvements in vehicles themselves, and new roadway technology are the only viable measures to fight ever-increasing traffic.

This emphasis on traffic congestion leads to huge investment in its mitigation. But we are confronting the fact that the option of improving traffic flow through roadway widening and automated signals has already been exhausted—maxed-out—in most of our cities. These low-cost options for physical improvement to the streets, such as increasing capacity and efficiency, are no longer available as solutions. The reality is that alternative mobility options, improvements in vehicles themselves, and new roadway technology are the only viable measures to fight ever-increasing traffic.

Transportation agencies will regulate the flow of vehicles with increased efficiency by using a combination of sensors under the roadway, video cameras, and computerized signalization systems. Meanwhile, in individual vehicles, GPS technology will integrate real-time traffic congestion information that is reliable and accurate. We will have more detailed intelligence about traffic flow speeds, accidents and stalled vehicles in the roadways, road construction and closures, and other events that may affect travel time. The big leap will occur by connecting individual drivers' GPS routes or paths to desired destinations into transportation agencies' congestion monitoring systems. This will reduce traffic jams by re-routing traffic to other streets with more capacity and adjusting both vehicle speeds and traffic-light timing to enable smoother flow. It's very plausible that today's major traffic issues will be much less of a problem by 2035, and because of increasing social inequity and the rising price of fuel, the cost of owning and operating an automobile may eclipse traffic as the dominant threat to our mobility.

What would the aliens in *What on Earth 2* observe about a city like Los Angeles in 2035? They might see cars going about their business as before, but in many more shapes and sizes, and joined by human beings on bicycles and on foot. Having learned from their long and difficult experience since *Futurama*, would the humans in the sequel have succeeded in making driving and other forms of mobility safer and the environment cleaner?

HOW TO STOP DESIGNING THE TRANSPORTATION SYSTEM OF TOMORROW FOR THE CARS OF YESTERDAY

Christopher Gray

THERE ARE SIGNIFICANT CHANGES IN THE FIELD OF VEHICLE DESIGN AND TECHNOLOGY that will introduce a high level of differentiation in automobiles at a scale and form not seen previously in the history of transportation planning and engineering since the introduction of the automobile in the early 20th century. The main challenge will be how the transportation planning and engineering field adapts to these changes. If the current business-as-usual practices continue, adoption of new vehicle design and technologies will likely be limited or slowed. However, there are opportunities for changes to occur now that will ensure that these innovations in vehicles are not precluded or limited in the future and we can see their full benefits realized.

Any new paradigms for traffic planning and engineering would evolve from current practices. As transportation planners and engineers, one of our main tasks is designing transportation systems. This design process would remain a long-term and extensive one that incorporates the use of historical trend data, future projections, standardized design requirements, and modeling tools. The three major elements of transportation system development are travel demand modeling, traffic operations analysis, and roadway engineering. All of these could be carried out in a way that is more responsive to changes in vehicles.

Travel demand modeling applies demographic projections and data on the transportation system to determine the future roadway needs of a city, county, or larger region. It involves comparing the future projected volumes for a roadway against its capacity in order to identify roadways that need to be widened or extended. The decision for roadway narrowing, by the way, is based on other considerations. What seems to happen with a roadway narrowing is that people decide they want to do it and then make sure that it works operationally.

Travel demand modeling is often done far in advance of any transportation improvement project, with lead times of five to ten years being not uncommon.

Once travel demand forecasts are complete, detailed *traffic operations analysis* can commence. This analysis considers the roadway characteristics and the travel demand to determine the exact roadway configuration. For example, the traffic operations analysis will determine the length and width of freeway on-ramps and off-ramps or the presence of a traffic signal. This process often occurs subsequent to travel demand modeling and may precede construction by three to five years, or more.

The final step in the process, *roadway engineering*, employs the data produced by traffic operations analysis to produce construction drawings for any proposed improvements. In many instances, the persons preparing the construction drawings employ standardized design criteria established by reference manuals, which ensures a high level of standardization in geographically disparate locations. As a result, roadways in New York are designed very much like roadways in Texas or California. This process often occurs immediately prior to construction activities with less lead-time than the other steps require.

Currently, regardless of the location and the scale of analysis, traffic studies assume the future system will accommodate the same types of vehicles that we have today. However, we are looking at unprecedented

Currently, regardless of the location and the scale of analysis, traffic studies assume the future system will accommodate the same types of vehicles that we have today.

changes in vehicles in terms of, first, fuel and power systems, which will have a significant effect on the vehicle's performance. Secondly, differences in vehicle size, weight, construction methods, and shape will create a wider variety of vehicles than currently exist today. Thirdly, implementation of vehicle automation systems will create vehicle types different from what is on the market today. These developments could provide significant benefits in terms of reduced emissions, high roadway speed and capacity through automated control systems, and greater personal mobility choices. However, a number of factors inherent in our current transportation planning and engineering paradigm would likely result in limiting their adoption and reducing their benefits.

For example, in today's planning and engineering practices, one of the only levels of differentiation between vehicles occurs between light duty vehicles (passenger automobiles and light trucks) and heavier vehicles, including buses, delivery trucks, semi-trucks, and other similar vehicles.

The Federal Highway Administration (FHWA) currently has a standard classification system with 13 vehicle types. This system has one category for passenger cars, another category for light trucks (which are defined as pick-up trucks, vans, SUVs, and other similar vehicles), a separate bus category, and nine separate categories for various

types of trucks ranging from delivery trucks to multi-axle semi-trailers. This differentiation occurs for two main reasons. First, the emissions profiles of these light vehicles and heavy vehicles are very different. Trucks produce much higher levels of emissions on a per mile basis than passenger cars, and detailed emissions modeling requires information regarding the mix of vehicles to produce the most refined level of analysis. Second, larger vehicles generally require more space to turn from one roadway to another. To standardize the analysis process, transportation engineers have developed templates for various types of vehicles to verify whether a particularly sized vehicle is able to turn at a corner.

Despite the thirteen categories, the classifications are too reductive in practice, and they pervade the entire set of activities related to transportation planning and engineering. For example, travel demand models, which are used in the planning for future transportation facilities, often track only two categories: light and heavy vehicles. Standardized roadway design manuals devote a significant portion of their length on how best to accommodate larger vehicles. Even the thickness of roadway pavement is determined by flawed estimates of how many large vehicles will be driving on the roadway over its life span. Categories aside, trucks become the limit-case or lowest common denominator, in some cases resulting in overdesign and increased expenses.

A second level of differentiation important to transportation planners today occurs between highway lanes: those lanes that are toll facilities, requiring payment to travel on, and high-occupancy vehicle lanes (HOV), which are restricted to vehicles with one driver and at least one passenger. A combined facility, known as a high-occupancy toll lane (HOT), allows both HOV vehicles and single-occupant autos to travel on it. Nearly all other roadways are classified as mixed-flow roadways. The interstate highway system is a mixed-flow roadway except for selected portions that have HOV lanes.

Currently, there is no physical difference between a vehicle assumed to be travelling on an HOV lane, a toll vehicle, and mixed-flow vehicles. The main differentiation between the lanes is access. For example, HOV lanes are often physically separated from adjacent mixed-flow freeway lanes. Toll roadways are often even more restricted, with limited entry and exit points that are often where toll charges are collected. One recent development is the implementation of electronically collected tolls, in which drivers are issued transponders that are linked to a bank account or a credit card. A smaller number of toll facilities limit access to vehicles equipped with a transponder.

The fact that all types of lanes can accommodate the same vehicles makes it easy for drivers to use freeways, HOV lanes, and toll lanes interchangeably as they travel through metropolitan regions. This improves the efficiency of the system. However, HOV lanes, toll facilities, and mixed-flow freeways each perform differently in terms of traffic flow and capacity, impacting the results of travel demand models and traffic operations models. Current advances in vehicle design indicate that automated vehicles will perform most efficiently in dedicated lanes where they can drive faster and closer together in a convoy. This assumption already should be built into traffic demand models that segregate dedicated from mixed-flow highway lanes. The introduction of autonomous vehicles to the fleet is a realistic and imminent enough prospect now that the optimized use of autonomous vehicles needs to be included in scenarios and models for traffic demand and operations. And this would come into play especially vividly in the design and analysis of highways with differentiated lanes, skewing current results of travel demand and traffic operations models for highways that have dedicated lanes.

A third factor relevant to transportation planning and design is vehicle restrictions according to types of roadways and surrounding land use. For example, it is not uncommon for cities to restrict travel by large trucks on residential streets. Cities will often identify designated truck routes

that limit trucks to freeways and other major roadways. These restrictions affect the design of a roadway in that a different standard or criteria is applied during the roadway engineering process depending on whether trucks are allowed to travel on that roadway. As an example, it is common to prohibit large trucks on residential streets and to restrict their usage to major roadways and freeways. Outside of these restrictions, few others limit which vehicles can travel on roadways.

If we were to anticipate a wider variety of vehicle types, including those that only cover a small range, such as neighborhood electric vehicles and cars that are half the width as is currently typical—or if advances in design made trucks smaller or otherwise improved their performance—we would have to rethink the scenarios by which these vehicles could be used. We could partner with policymakers and designers to forecast hypothetical restrictions and design our transportation systems accordingly. The mismatch between the current planning paradigm and emerging vehicle trends is particularly problematic because it will likely limit or slow down the adoption of new vehicles and reduce certain aspects of their effectiveness.

HOV lanes, toll facilities, and mixed-flow freeways each perform differently in terms of traffic flow and capacity.

2035 NEW MASTER PLANNED COMMUNITY

Resulting from changes to number of cars, shaped by global factors.

SCENARIO 1: FEWER CARS

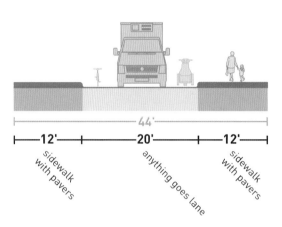

12' — sidewalk with pavers
20' — anything goes lane
12' — sidewalk with pavers
44'

Assumption: 1 car per house.

Vehicle Miles Traveled (VMT) taxes, tolled roads, scarcity of land, scarcity of fuel, lower standard of living, car sharing, pay-as-you-go insurance, more public transit, increased density, shorter trips, less need to travel for middle class.

Smaller roads in new developments, and wider, colored/textured sidewalks. Parking is not needed as much.

SCENARIO 2: MORE CARS

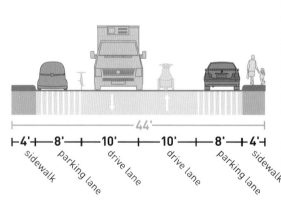

4' — sidewalk
8' — parking lane
10' — drive lane
10' — drive lane
8' — parking lane
4' — sidewalk
44'

Assumption: 5-6 cars per house.

More than one family living in some houses with vehicles at multiple sizes for different purposes because of affordability of vehicles due to economic resurgence, cars from India and China, advances in how cars are manufactured/marketed, new and cheaper fuel types, acceptance of Personal Mobility Devices.

Cars park on street, sidewalks sacrificed to parking.

Assumption for both: New master planned community, middle class.
Parking requirement: one car, in driveway.

All cross sections of 2035 streets designed by Christopher Gray, cars drawn by Rahi Zaland, sections drawn by Colleen Corcoran.

2035 SUBURBAN ARTERIALS

SCENARIO 1: NOTHING TO SLOW YOU DOWN
NO PARKING NEEDED

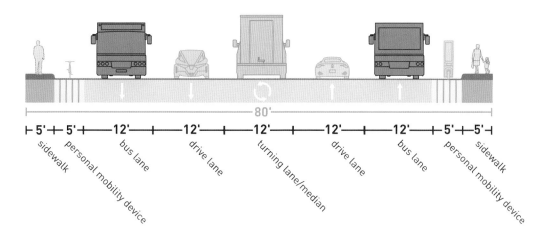

80'

⊢ 5' ⊦ 5' ⊦—12'—⊦—12'—⊦—12'—⊦—12'—⊦—12'—⊦ 5' ⊦ 5' ⊣

sidewalk   personal mobility device   bus lane   drive lane   turning lane/median   drive lane   bus lane   personal mobility device   sidewalk

SCENARIO 2: RETAIL ON BOTH SIDES OF STREET
PARKING NEEDED

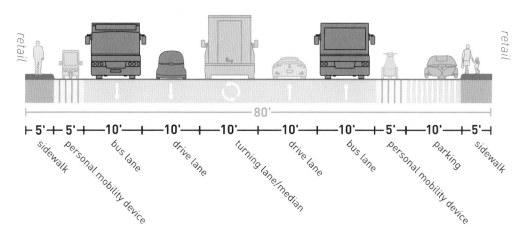

retail

retail

80'

⊢ 5' ⊦ 5' ⊦—10'—⊦—10'—⊦—10'—⊦—10'—⊦—10'—⊦ 5' ⊦—10'—⊦ 5' ⊣

sidewalk   personal mobility device   bus lane   drive lane   turning lane/median   drive lane   bus lane   personal mobility device   parking   sidewalk

Assumptions: Smaller delivery trucks, vehicles will need to mix, access for delivery trucks will be regulated. Both options allow buses and bikes to comingle.

2035 FREEWAYS

SCENARIO 1: BUSINESS AS USUAL

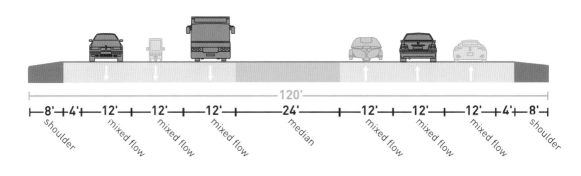

120'

| 8' | 4' | 12' | 12' | 12' | 24' | 12' | 12' | 12' | 4' | 8' |
| shoulder | | mixed flow | mixed flow | mixed flow | median | mixed flow | mixed flow | mixed flow | | shoulder |

SCENARIO 2: DEDICATED LANES FOR AUTOMATED VEHICLES

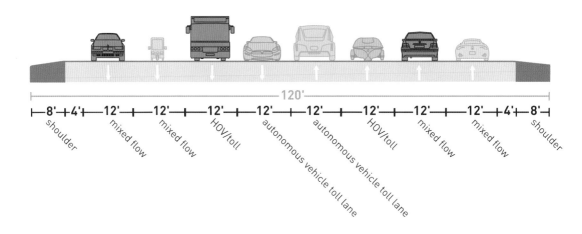

120'

| 8' | 4' | 12' | 12' | 12' | 12' | 12' | 12' | 12' | 12' | 4' | 8' |
| shoulder | | mixed flow | mixed flow | HOV/toll | autonomous vehicle toll lane | autonomous vehicle toll lane | HOV/toll | mixed flow | mixed flow | | shoulder |

2035 RESIDENTIAL

SCENARIO 1: SIDEWALKS HAVE A MIX OF BIKES AND PEDESTRIANS

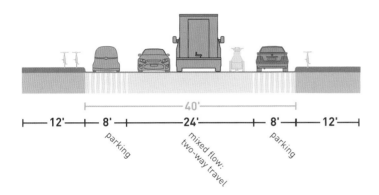

Same as existing roadway, except parking only allowed in dedicated parking lanes.

SCENARIO 2: PRIORITIZES LANES FOR HIGHLY REGULATED PERSONAL MOBILITY DEVICES (PMDs) AND BIKES

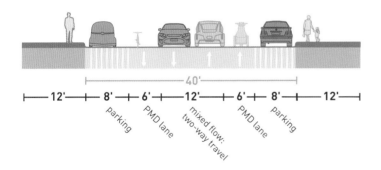

Only one lane for automobiles in scenarios 2 and 3.

SCENARIO 3: BI-DIRECTIONAL LANES FOR PERSONAL MOBILITY DEVICES (PMDs) AND CARS

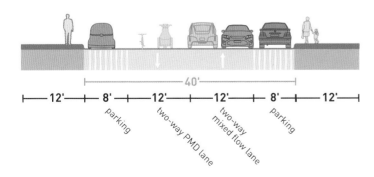

Automated vehicle control systems would perform differently from other passenger cars. These vehicles can travel much faster and at a much closer following distance than regular passenger cars.
As such, a roadway could provide a much higher capacity for cars with automated control systems.

The technology that is likely to be impacted the most is automated control systems. This negative impact can be anticipated based on how passenger cars are treated in current transportation planning, operational analysis, and roadway engineering. As we have seen, all passenger cars are essentially thought of as the same. However, automated vehicle control systems would perform differently from other passenger cars. These vehicles can travel much faster and at a much closer following distance than regular passenger cars. As such, a roadway could provide a much higher capacity for cars with automated control systems. However, none of the current HOV lanes or toll roads are being planned or studied to accommodate these types of vehicles. As these vehicles are deployed, it may be possible to retrofit a limited amount of HOV or toll lanes to accommodate them. However, this retrofit would be limited because much of the roadway network, in the form of regular surface streets, and most of the highways do not currently have lane differentiation. Therefore, it will be possible to dedicate lanes to automated vehicles only in the small subset of the overall transportation system that currently has physically distinct access-restricted lanes.

A similar lack of attention on the part of transportation planners and engineers to add specificity in the size and configuration of passenger cars results in lost opportunities for the public. The future will likely see the introduction of smaller vehicles, many of which will probably be powered by alternative fueled sources. Many of these smaller vehicles could potentially require dedicated facilities or may be difficult to operate within the larger transportation system if asked to comingle with buses, large trucks, and other larger vehicles. This lack of dedicated facilities for small vehicles could make it difficult for communities to allow their usage.

Two recent examples can be drawn from the introduction of neighborhood electric vehicles (NEVs) and Segways. NEVs have been widely implemented within select communities. However, current regulations in the state of California limit the roadways on which they can drive and have led several communities to incur the expense of creating separate roadway networks for their usage. While these vehicles are perfectly capable of driving on most roadways, their usage is excessively limited by regulations. As such, the adoption of NEVs has been severely constrained to select locations. The second instance relates to Segways, which are small, motorized, two-wheeled personal mobility devices. When first introduced, Segways were promoted as having the potential to revolutionize the transportation system. The difficultly is that Segways do not fit into the current transportation paradigm. Traveling at about 12 miles per hour, they are too slow to comingle with cars on most roadways, and they conflict with pedestrians on sidewalks. Currently, there is discussion over how best to accommodate Segways within the existing transportation system. As an example, the city of Boston initiated efforts to ban or limit the use of Segways in 2010, citing conflicts with pedestrians.

The transportation planning and engineering field can embrace new vehicle technologies in several ways. In many instances, these changes to vehicles are likely to occur without active participation from transportation professionals, but awareness of potential innovations in vehicle design should shift their focus to implementing changes now that will encourage, and not preclude, these future vehicle technologies.

First, given the long lead time for transportation improvements, current planning studies—particularly traffic modeling exercises for regional areas—should be taking into account informed research on potential changes in vehicle technologies. These discussions and this awareness early in the design process would engender new flexibility and adaptability in transportation planning and engineering paradigms, and lead to substantive improvements in the roadway systems of the future.

Second, any current roadway engineering efforts for limited access facilities, such as HOV lanes or toll lanes, should consider a potential future conversion to automated vehicle operation. It is likely that these facilities could be converted for efficient deployment of automated vehicles more easily than any other roadway facilities.

Lastly, engineering standards and, for that matter, the traffic planning process, should have the capacity to respond quickly to changes in vehicle technology, so new types of vehicles would have a fair chance of being accommodated within our existing roadways. A process that is designed to continually revisit and revise standards in light of ongoing innovation in vehicle design will ensure that the pioneering vehicles of tomorrow are not marginalized like NEVs or Segways are today.

Segways do not fit into the current transportation paradigm. Traveling at about 12 miles per hour, they are too slow to comingle with cars on most roadways, and they conflict with pedestrians on sidewalks.

THE OPEN ROAD

Jeremy Klop

THE APPEAL OF THE OPEN ROAD IS UNIVERSAL. The feeling of possibility, power, and control behind the wheel of a car or truck persists across generations and cultures. In the media, and in our imaginations, to drive with a full tank of gas with an open lane ahead means escape, unrealized potential, and freedom.

Up until the last decade, the vast majority of traffic engineers and transportation planners in the United States have focused on building and maintaining this freedom for drivers. Our mantra was speed, safety, and convenience, and our primary goal was to minimize delay wherever possible. To maintain this freedom, cities, states, and the federal government invested in roadway widening, new interchanges, and other types of "capacity improvements." The improvements were based on recommendations of transportation professionals using a unit of measure called Level of Service, or simply LOS. This small acronym, which is a measure of traffic flow (or congestion), has had far-reaching effects on the built environment and the way we travel.

LEVEL OF SERVICE

Level of service is a quality measure describing operational conditions with a traffic stream, generally in terms of such service measures as speed and travel time, freedom to maneuver, traffic interruptions, and comfort and convenience.

–Year 2000 Highway Capacity Manual, Transportation Research Board

While the profession describes LOS as a qualitative measure supported by decades of research of a variety of factors, it is most commonly expressed as the seconds of delay experienced by people driving, particularly at intersections, and at rush hour. Analyzed at the most congested point in the day, the Highway Capacity Manual (HCM) LOS method turns frustration into a precise engineering calculation. The resulting outputs are neatly packaged into an elegant scale, with letter grades from A to F, just like elementary school, with the amount of delay and related angst broken into six categories.

SIGNALIZED INTERSECTION LOS CRITERIA

LOS	Average Control Delay (seconds/vehicle)	Description
A	0-10.0	Operations with very slight delay, with no approach phase fully utilized.
B	10.1-20.0	Operations with slight delay, with occasional full utilization of approach phase.
C	20.1-35.0	Operations with moderate delay. Individual cycle failures begin to appear.
D	35.1-55.0	Operations with heavier, but frequently tolerable delay. Many vehicles stop and individual cycle failures are noticeable.
E	55.1-80.0	Operations with high delay, and frequent cycle failures. Long queues form upstream of intersection.
F	80.0+	Operations with very high delays and congestion. Volumes vary wideley depending on downstream queue conditions.

Source: Highway Capacity Manual, Transportation Research Board, 2000.

Analyzed at the most congested point in the day, the Highway Capacity Manual LOS method turns frustration into a precise engineering calculation.

Even as recently as the year 2000, transportation professionals have defined LOS in their working manual on the subject (HCM) almost exclusively in terms of roadway performance for people *driving*. This automobile-centric paradigm has been dominant in the profession for more than fifty years. It results, in part, from the powerful allure of the open road.

Billions of dollars of freeway, roadway, and intersection widening projects have been justified to the public and political leaders through F's on report cards resulting from LOS calculations. Such investments have been effective and the vast majority have served the purpose of maintaining our precious sense of freedom behind the wheel. But sustaining the open road is becoming less realistic.

CHANGING TRANSPORTATION VALUES AND METRICS

Numerous challenges of the LOS metric have come into focus over the last decade. For one, the cost associated with maintaining free-flowing roadways at all times of day, and especially in congested urban areas, has proven to be well beyond the taxing and spending appetites of all but the wealthiest states and communities. Even with the political will to take on roadway projects, heightened attention to air and environmental pollution, property impacts, community disruption, and competing local and regional interests often delay projects for years, if not decades.

Most challenging to the traditional LOS approach are the competing interests of other transportation system users. Also known as pedestrians, cyclists, or bus riders, they are the group of people using the roadways or sidewalks in ways that do not involve driving. Anyone with an elderly parent or small children knows that people walking want very different things from the local transportation system than the average driver does. Safe crossings, quiet streets without excessive traffic, cars traveling at low speeds, a tree canopy for shade in the day, and aesthetically pleasing and functional lights for a safe walk home after dark are much more important than waiting an extra 30 seconds at an intersection in your car. People riding their bikes also want different things. So do people riding transit. And all too often, choices that are advantageous to one group will penalize another.

Smart Growth (growth concentrated into compact, walkable, and livable urban centers to avoid sprawl) has been replaced by Complete Streets (streets that are safe and pleasant for all modes of mobility) as the planning concept *du jour*. Advocacy groups such as Streets for People are pushing for a more holistic treatment of transportation planning and engineering decisions. The number of people bicycling and riding transit are at all-time highs and growing rapidly. And fewer and fewer young people are even bothering to get their driver's license. In response, the transportation engineering and planning community has begun to shift their longstanding paradigm in response to changing customer demands. And slowly, the toolbox is being updated with new ways to measure performance.

In layman's terms, the industry has succeeded in turning a massive ship in the direction of measures that capture how people experience the entire system of transportation, whether they are driving, walking, riding a bike, or taking transit.

These changing values are reflected in the most recent 2010 edition of the Highway Capacity Manual. Now in its fifth iteration, the 2010 HCM has been hailed as an important step forward toward an integrated and multimodal approach. In layman's terms, the industry has succeeded in turning a massive ship in the direction of measures that capture how people experience the entire system of transportation, whether they are driving, walking, riding a bike, or taking transit. It has taken more than a decade of supporting research and countless hours of debate and discussion to recognize that our roadways need to be measured on more than just one set of performance criteria. Through a new series of complex formulas, you can now evaluate pedestrian level of service, bicycle level of service, and transit level of service for bus riders. And for any given project, you can now assess these factors at intersections, along roadway segments, and at multiple times of day. Nothing says progress to the engineering and planning community like more technical analysis!

While this new paradigm, built at the federal level, has resulted in new tools and metrics, many communities are finding the increased complexity and data required to analyze these concepts too costly and time consuming to be useful. What used to be a simple letter grade for roadways is now a series of grades with multiple sub-calculations, often highlighting difficult tradeoffs and the needs of competing interest groups. The increased complexity is also stretching the technical resources of engineering and planning staff and further extending the time it takes to deliver transportation improvements to the public. Unfortunately, this trend toward complexity is also running directly counter to rapidly diminishing transportation revenue sources at the local, state, and federal level. Despite these challenges, the next two decades of transportation projects will likely see unprecedented attention paid to the tradeoffs between conflicting community transportation needs and a new focus on moving all people—not just motorists.

THE IMPORTANCE OF PLACE

As the open road is less viable, and transportation professionals shift their attention toward serving competing needs (with shrinking funding), where will the road remain open? In the future, there will still be places where you can go as fast as you want whenever you want. However, this may be limited to the rich, the rural, and the renters.

Revenue-rich communities will be able to manage overall growth in demand for community services and roadway improvements and maintenance through high land values. They will pay for a technologically advanced infrastructure system with small, widespread, and long-term transportation utility charges. These elite communities will not only provide excellent schools, housing, commercial, and cultural amenities, but

Whether through congestion pricing and tolls, or through employer-based vehicle sharing and shuttle programs, many urban and rural communities will shift the burden of public infrastructure and transportation services to corporations and individual users.

their streets will have full tree canopies, detached sidewalks, safe crossings, bicycle and personal mobility device boulevards, and accessible transit mobility hubs with expensive grade-separated crossings and tunnels in sensitive areas. Specially approved delivery trucks that meet criteria for renewable-only energy use, minimal noise emissions, and remotely enforced low speeds to ensure safety will serve the community. Revenue collection systems will allow customized, variable transportation utility fees for everyone using the roadway infrastructure. These fees will be linked to actual trip generation and adjusted to reflect the mix of lower-cost walking and bicycling trips, and higher-cost single-occupant and freight-vehicle trips.

In rural communities, where distance and isolation demand a lot of travel by car or truck, twentieth-century patterns will persist. The planning, design, construction, and maintenance of dispersed and historically small, compact, and walkable downtowns will increasingly rely on external revenue sources. Limited local funds will be narrowly concentrated on critical downtown locations, and the surrounding long stretches of highway will deteriorate in all but the most scenic and attractive destinations. These communities will have to rely on long-distance transit services, similar to the National Parks Service, coupled with local car- and bike-sharing services, for community and regional mobility.

In states or cities where the appetite for collectively funding transportation services is limited, roadways will increasingly belong to *renters*. Whether through congestion pricing and tolls, or through employer-based vehicle sharing and shuttle programs, many urban and rural communities will shift the burden of public infrastructure and transportation services to corporations and individual users. Places with balanced employment mixes, a range of housing choices, robust transit systems, excellent schools, and urban design, will benefit from shorter travel distances and the associated lower energy use and costs. Other places that may have initially succeeded as bedroom communities will have to charge to access work or retail via costly tolled facilities. Land economics will be increasingly managed and influenced by powerful private sector transportation providers.

Technological innovations will play their part to preserve a sense (if illusory) of the open road. In the future, automated and metered travel, and more imminently, conflict avoidance systems, will ensure the feel of the uncongested open road, even while the volume of traffic and freight movement increases. Specific stretches of roadway, such as scenic byways, will be accessed like national parks, via day-use passes and e-ticketing.

FUTURE METRICS

In these new scenarios, performance metrics will continue to evolve. Unlike water, power, or telecommunications utilities, the experience of quality and design of the transportation system matters. Form affects value, both of the roadway, and the adjacent property. Accounting for these qualities with any accuracy will require another paradigm shift in transportation performance metrics. Context, value, quality, and maintenance of the user experience will become part of the new measurement paradigm that evolves out of LOS. The new metrics will go beyond understanding the movement of the number of vehicles, or even people, through space and time. The future metrics will be sensitive to multiple contexts, quantify the return on investment, describe the distribution of the benefits, and analyze outcomes in terms of quality of life and environment, not just mobility.

Life cycle costs and financially self-maintaining systems will be integrated into investment and environmental analyses. A shift will occur from assessing the need for capacity improvements toward a more holistic measure of population served per dollar of investment. Like McDonalds, our best transit and roadway projects will be measured in the billions, or even trillions served, and—importantly—by our customers' degree of satisfaction with those services.

Context, value, quality, and maintenance of the user experience will become part of the new measurement paradigm that evolves out of LOS.

Good measures are challenging to define and even more difficult to operationalize in an industry as large and unwieldy as transportation. The last century's emphasis on speed, safety, and convenience will continue to be relevant, and the research developed around these concepts will continue to provide value. In light of changing expectations, our energies would be best focused on finding terms—quantitative and qualitative—for describing what we require from transportation systems that promote health, economy, and quality of life. While the speed and freedom of the open road will always have a timeless allure, the future will demand much more from our transportation systems and our transportation professionals.

PEOPLE-MOVING CAPACITY

John Stutsman

IT IS CLEAR THAT WE ARE NEARING THE END OF THE FREEWAY ERA that was spawned by the Interstate Highway Program Act of 1956. Also waning is the notion that we can build our way out of urban-area congestion. Sprawl has hit the wall in Southern California. Very little developable land remains within the Los Angeles basin. Coupled with being at, or beyond, peak oil production, commuting costs are rendering far-flung housing developments economically infeasible, with the Great Recession delivering the final blow.

We have come to the realization that we must achieve better utilization of our scarce existing public rights-of-way to achieve our societal transportation objectives. Some recent public mass transit projects get around this problem by not involving the roadway network, which is "built out" in dense urban areas. For example, the Metro Green Line and the Exposition Light Rail Transit Project (Expo LRT) are largely making use of existing railroad rights-of-way, plus some street-running, elevated, or tunnel sections. The Westside Subway (Metro Purple Line) is all below-grade in twin-bore tunnels.

The Westside of Los Angeles is roughly defined by the I-405 on the east, the Pacific Ocean on the west, the Santa Monica Mountains on the north, and LAX on the south. As a result of the Expo LRT, Metro Purple Line, and Crenshaw/Green Line projects, the Westside will see bi-directional, peak-hour person-moving capacity increased by 30,000 people at the eastern and southern borders. These additional modes of transit represent a significant option for the 300,000 daily commuters either leaving or entering the Westside. This potential shift to mass transit may well facilitate substantial transit-related development. If so, the net result will

be that roadway congestion will remain at today's levels.

So, what are we to do? What tools will help us achieve our objective of improving personal mobility in Southern California? Several things are in the works. The city of Los Angeles has implemented an adaptive, computerized traffic signal control system for some 4,500 signals citywide. Metro has implemented congestion-pricing high-occupancy toll (HOT) lanes on the Harbor and San Bernardino freeways, and is implementing a bus rapid transit (BRT) project on Wilshire Boulevard from Western Avenue to Centinela Avenue at the Santa Monica border. This BRT project, which will be a peak-hour, curb-lane operation, has potential to substantially increase person-moving capacity in this corridor until the Purple Line subway opens to the West Los Angeles Veteran's Administration Hospital.

We have come to the realization that we must achieve better utilization of our scarce existing public rights-of-way to achieve our societal transportation objectives.

My Figueroa project. Image courtesy of Melendrez Landscape Architecture, Planning & Urban Design. Street by Valerie Watson, LADOT, cars by Yana Briggs, Art Center College of Design.

Microsimulation will help us work with this multi-modal complexity so that we can use our existing resources more efficiently. But having more responsive and more accurate traffic models is just one part of the solution.

BRT is only one example of the move toward a more systematic sharing of major arterials. Planners and engineers are now placing much more emphasis on the sharing of roadways by pedestrians, cyclists, and transit users. To address this new reality, development of a multimodal intersection "level of service" metric is underway. Other relevant factors are traffic-calming trends, such as road diets, where the available number of lanes on a road is reduced to make cars move more slowly, shifting local traffic to major arterials and increasing comfort and security for pedestrians. Regional travel demand models are ill equipped to discern the localized effects of such roadway sharing by multiple users. Fortunately, microsimulation models such as VISSIM (microscopic multi-modal traffic flow simulation software) are capable of performing such analysis and are increasingly becoming more cost-effective for addressing such problems. Driver behavior is one of the key analytics of such models. Further, some of the key output options are videos showing vehicular, pedestrian, and transit movements, which have proved to be very effective in demonstrating project effects, for both the public and technical staff.

The problems we face are indeed daunting as we confront the limited opportunity to increase roadway capacity and legitimate competing demands from pedestrians, cyclists, and bus transit patrons. Microsimulation will help us work with this multi-modal complexity so that we can use our existing resources more efficiently. But having more responsive and more accurate traffic models is just one part of the solution. Because the infrastructure we currently have in place is the one we will have for the foreseeable future, it will be up to the transportation industry, planners, developers, and the public sector to become more innovative as we face the need to do more with less.

HARTFORD'S IQUILT PLAN AND CONNECTICUT SQUARE

Doug Suisman

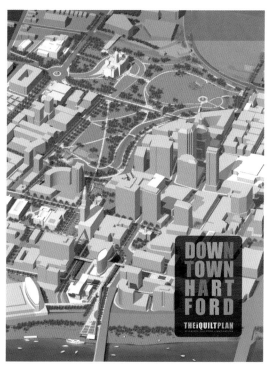

THE iQUILT PLAN BY SUISMAN URBAN

DESIGN *has a broader and deeper scope than is typical for urban design projects in the United States, where a chronic lack of funding and, more importantly, a lack of perceived value limit innovative approaches to urban design. In the iQuilt Plan, a varied pedestrian infrastructure is overlaid onto a large, heterogeneous area of both open and contained spaces. It links together parks, workplaces, and cultural amenities in a coherent network. The project offers an example of how a mobility-balanced urban district can work.*

–Kati Rubinyi

The iQuilt Plan is downtown Hartford's strategy for walkability and creative place-making. It capitalizes on two of Hartford's greatest strengths: its concentration of arts, cultural, and landscape assets and its compact downtown. The cultural assets are physically close, but the pedestrian links between them are often weak. The iQuilt Plan strengthens those links. It offers an array of physical and programmatic improvements to the pedestrian network of public space— parks, plazas, streets, and sidewalks.

BIOSWALE

TRANSIT

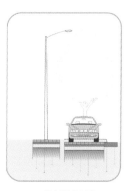

PARKING

PARKLET

Green Pockets: Streets in the iQuilt Plan are designed with special curb zones that can accommodate a variety of uses. Credit: Suisman Urban Design / iQuilt Partnership.

Downtown Hartford "minimap": The iQuilt project has installed more than 150 at nearly 50 intersections throughout the downtown district.

The iQuilt Plan is not a single large project but rather a strategic mix of small and large, immediate and long-term, and public and private endeavors to be implemented in stages. Each initiative contributes a patch to downtown's overall pattern, an irregular, quilt-like street grid dating back to 1636. The "i" in iQuilt stands for innovation, and each project incorporates innovative approaches to walkability and creative place-making. The goal is to bring vibrancy to downtown Hartford's streets in order to restore it as the region's central gathering place; as a magnet for residents, visitors, creative workers, and cultural innovators; as a driver of economic activity; and as a model of livable, sustainable urban design.

CONNECTICUT SQUARE

The iQuilt Plan connects new and existing public spaces in a walkable, mile-long chain called the GreenWalk. One of those spaces involves the transformation of a 6.3-acre, 700-car surface parking lot owned by the State of Connecticut into a sustainable, mixed-use public square. The space continues to serve much of the time as parking space for the state and for patrons of the Bushnell Performing Arts Center. But new electrical and lighting infrastructure allows the square to host festivals, markets, and performances on nights, weekends, and holidays. Its new perimeter landscaping enhances the surrounding streets and neighborhoods. And its green infrastructure for storm water—permeable paving, bioswales, and rain gardens—makes Connecticut Square a model of multi-use, sustainable public space.

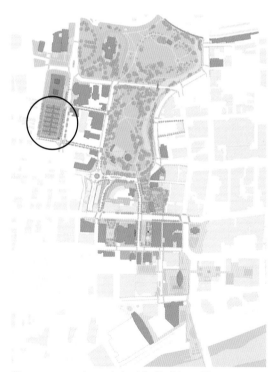

The green spine of the iQuilt Plan: The mile-long GreenWalk (Connecticut Square is indicated in the circle). Credit: Suisman Urban Design / iQuilt Partnership.

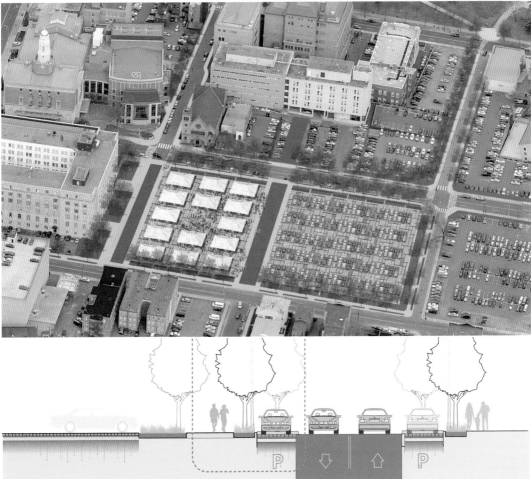

CONNECTICUT SQUARE   CAPITOL AVE.

THE EVOLUTION
OF PARKING

Shannon S. McDonald

Fiat Lingotto rooftop test track. Photo credit: Nicolas Nova.

CARS, CARS, FAST, FAST! *One is seized, filled with enthusiasm, with joy...the joy of power. The simple and naïve pleasure of being in the midst of power, of strength.*

–Le Corbusier, *The City of Tomorrow and Its Planning*, 1929

Le Corbusier stated in his book *The City of Tomorrow and Its Planning*: "A city made for speed is a city made for success." This concept continues to be a force in our culture, including our built environment. However, *the car-at-rest* has always been a necessary aspect of the quest for speed. Le Corbusier understood this, and he raised his buildings above the ground to free the ground plane for the open landscape and to accommodate hidden parking. For example, Le Corbusier's Villa Savoye, built in 1928 on the outskirts of Paris, is a country house made of reinforced concrete floating on stilts. The house is a manifesto for Le Corbusier's radically new principles of architecture. The ground floor is mostly open, with space for a car to be discreetly tucked underneath the

Twentieth-century design focused on speed and mobility as qualities and states of being. The flip side is that the car-at-rest has also significantly shaped our cities and towns.

building while the surrounding landscape appears to flow continuously under the hovering structure.

The Fiat Lingotto Plant (designed by engineer Giacomo Mattè-Trucco, completed in 1923), where the testing track for new cars was placed on the roof (speed in any location) is the architectural and programmatic expression of how a new kind of movement—of the car—could shape our built environment. Twentieth-century design focused on speed and mobility as qualities and states of being. The flip side is that the car-at-rest has also significantly shaped our cities and towns. It has caused buildings to be spread apart, forced us to enter our cities and buildings through empty, isolating parking lots and garages, and created zoning laws that are focused on the car, rather than people and places. Architecture and mobility (including parking) have always been intertwined, but as our ideas about cities and architecture evolved in the twentieth century, many unforeseen consequences came to light. After a long period of coming to terms with the negatives of parking, maybe we can have it all—mobility, rest, and freedom, intertwined—if we design for it.

HISTORY OF PARKING

The car was the savior of our environment at the turn of the century—it saved us from the illnesses created by coexisting with the horse in urban settings. Within a very short period of time, the car resulted in healthier cities and new town plans. It created a way of life desired by people in many parts of the world. However, because of the undisputable challenges parking creates for land use and the built environment, car designers, architects and planners now need to focus their imaginations on dealing with parking. It takes up so much space; it's everywhere! The actual amount of parking in the United States has never been documented and is almost impossible to determine, as it is under both public and private ownership, inside, outside, underground, and in stand-alone buildings. According to their web site, the Los Angeles Department of Transportation alone

The actual amount of parking in the United States has never been documented and is almost impossible to determine.

manages 11,000 parking spaces for public use, with 116 off-street parking facilities. Los Angeles is an interesting example, because it was designed to be auto-friendly. Some observers, including Clarence Dykstra, a former commissioner of water and power in Los Angeles, were not only untroubled by that city's outward spread, but reveled in it. In a 1926 article, he said:

Rapid transit—congestion-relief is a delusion and a snare as far as sound city planning is concerned. A population can be spread out without rapid transit or streetcar facilities. The private automobile and the bus turned the trick so far as transportation is concerned. The development of the motor truck and the availability of electric power for manufacturing will continue to decentralize the industrial district. There can be developed in the Los Angeles area a great city population which for the most part lives near work, has its individual lawns and gardens, finds its market and commercialized recreation facilities right around the corner, and which because of these things can develop a neighborhood with all that it means.

Under such conditions city life will not only be tolerable but delightful—infinitely more desirable and wholesome than the sort induced and super induced by the artificially stimulated population center which constantly must reach higher and higher into the air for light, air, and a chance to see the sun. It will be a city in which children will not be discriminated against.[1]

The vision worked for years, and still does for many. As long as you can stay in one job your entire life and live near your work, life in the Los Angeles area is as ideal as it gets. But our travel needs are generally more demanding. The result for cities is that the car-at-rest is at the center of the dilemma about the automobile. A study in Olympia, Washington, showed that 54% of land area for a commercial development is for parking. While we hate paying for it, there are also negative consequences when parking is free.

In the early 1900s, cars could not be left out in the weather because of the quality of their paint, surface treatments, and mechanical limitations. As a result, parking in the street was always short term. By 1905, parking garages in the United States proliferated in the thousands. As these technical issues were addressed, in the mid-1930s, the parking meter was invented and first installed in the streets of Oklahoma City. The issue of who has "the right to the street" emerged. The parking meter required that people *pay to use the street*. Those who had parked on the street for free loudly dissented; parking meters appearing one day were removed the next!

The first parking garages were enabled by the invention of central heat and ventilation, as in the Larkin building (1904–06) in Buffalo, New York, by Frank Lloyd Wright. Early parking garages were inspiring public edifices showcasing new visions for the future. Many of these parking structures are still in use today, converted into offices, housing, and retail. Early designs for parking structures had active retail street fronts and offices, or other combined uses. Similarly, the earliest parking lots were imagined as public spaces with multiple uses, such as in Country Club Plaza of Kansas City, Missouri.

In 1907, the Chicago Automobile Club had an interior, full-service parking garage, hotel rooms, ballroom, meeting rooms, and retail. It was based on the precedent of the most innovative parking garages for the Automobile Clubs in Cleveland, Boston, and New York.[2] Albert Kahn and Frank Lloyd Wright were just two of the early visionaries of the typology, creating the earliest continuous sloping floor ramp structures in the 1920s.[3] Even the current Smart Tower,

Nash Motors automobile elevator display, Century of Progress Exhibition, Chicago (Ill), ca. 1933. Chicago History Museum. Photo credit: Ken Hedrich, Hedrich Blessing, NB-00700.

a mechanical parking tower design for the Smart Car in France, was first imagined and built in 1932 as a marketing tool for Nash Motors, in Chicago. In the early twentieth century, designing a building for parking was designing for a cutting-edge program—a sought after opportunity to experiment with the latest technology.

In the 1950s, the parking garage was still a site for innovation. Theodore Osmundson, a California landscape architect, designed the Kaiser Center Garage in Oakland, a parking structure with a green roof built in 1961. T.Y Lin, a structural engineer, invented the concrete single tee just for the parking garage. Advances in architectural and structural precast were explored, resulting in several handsome garages, such as one for the Henry Ford Hospital in Detroit (1959). But as the twentieth century progressed, parking garages became bare-bones, multilevel fields of concrete, landscapes characterized by emptiness that separate and limit us in a sea of isolated spaces. The parking garage became renowned as a dark, alien, and dangerous place—a non-space of secrets, mystery, fear, and escape. As Isao Hosoe states in the book *Architecture & Mobility*, the parking facility "becomes the stage where backdrops are modified...where alienation happens, where surprise is born."[4]

The car-at-rest also created new patterns of mobility by becoming a link in a chain of different modes of travel. With the advent of the computer and new movement technologies in the mid-century, connections from parking garages to transit emerged. Paul Rudolph, Ulrich Franzen and Victor Gruen are just some of the designers who link personal rapid transit (PRT) to parking into their building projects. These systems are fragments of Rudolph, Franzen, and Gruen's visions of the modern city.[5] More recently, Herzog and de Meuron's inhabitable parking structure in the city of Miami Beach underscores the type's design potential. When a parking garage is understood as a design opportunity, magic can happen—soaring ceilings, triangular shaped columns, and dramatic lighting, with spaces for program tucked in between.

THE FUTURE OF PARKING FOR FUTURE MOBILITY

It is not only the automobile that must be revisited, but also the city, that must be organized to receive means of transport.[6]

Some ideas for the future of vehicles and modes of transportation call for minimizing the use of cars, or eliminating them entirely. Some perceive of cars as mass transit—leased, uniform, and driverless. Some are championing the automated vehicle or automated infrastructural systems. Others say Segways on the sidewalks of cities are the best transportation choice, while non-motorized transportation advocates want everyone to walk and bike. Advances in infrastructure, energy sources and automated movement

How can we turn parking into an asset, rather than a liability, and find a way to make parking engage with our lives and our cities? Our requirements for how to park well will need to encompass space, place, and uses beyond mobility.

will someday result in cars that provide entirely new ways to move and rest in space. The tiny folding City Car out of the MIT Media Lab, now in testing, could dramatically affect the way we design parking facilities, and the rest of our built environment.[7] Small spots of parking could be made available everywhere, among vehicles constantly in motion.

Motorized bikes, motorcycles, and bicycles are all clamoring for that closest parking spot, and spaces for them are now being included in street parking and in parking facilities. On one hand, our streets are becoming like the streets of San Francisco were in 1904, right before the great earthquake, with no form of management. They are naked streets with every mobility device managing to coexist in a self-regulated dance. In the opposite scenario, some of our streets could be completely controlled, as in Bologna, Italy, with bollards that block automobiles unless an approved transponder is in the car.

ULTra PRT at Heathrow International Airport Station.

Regardless of the type of vehicle or street, our currently most popular approach to parking strives to hide it, say, within the center of a building block shrouded in retail or greenery. New mobility options will provide flexibility and choice beyond those that existed in the twentieth century (but not the late 1900s). How can we turn parking into an asset, rather than a liability, and find a way to make parking engage with our lives and our cities? Our requirements for how to park well will need to encompass space, place, and uses beyond mobility. A more sophisticated, fluid understanding of vehicles as being both in motion and at rest alongside people will create a new infrastructure and culture. We need parking facilities that go *back to roots*: a multipurpose building type indistinguishable from other buildings that seamlessly integrates parking with the city.

The car-at-rest could be totally integrated into our buildings. This is an emergent trend that has the potential to change the dynamics of how we live. In Berlin and New York, and soon in Miami, you can drive your car into an elevator (the earliest garages used elevators for cars), and ride it up to your condo in the sky, into your own garage, even on the 27th floor. Also, fully automated machines that compactly park your car, standard in Asia, are now expanding in number in the United States, driven by the demand for more parking spaces in denser locations. This type of parking is highly sustainable and the simple building shape is easily adapted for new uses.

The long-term future of infrastructure will bring streets adapted to multiple scales of movement as well as *powerful new connections between movement and parking*. These connections will benefit from the development and adoption of technology that already exists. For one example, elevators will have the capacity to operate three dimensionally, challenging the traditional architectural/ engineering notion of the elevator shaft. No longer will the elevator only have vertical

The car-at-rest could be totally integrated into our buildings.

movement, it will also move horizontally without its passengers ever leaving the cab. (The prototype exists at the Otis Test Facility, and the technology is used on Disney's Tower of Terror theme park ride.) Second, transit pods in automated vehicle networks (recalling those mentioned previously, first seen in the 1950s) will rely on the integration of streets, buildings, movement, and parking. CityMobile; Masdar City, Abu Dhabi; and Heathrow airport are leading the way toward this integration, realizing the ideas of Archigram members Peter Cook (Plug-in City, 1964), Michael Webb (Sin Centre, 1961–63), and Ron Herron (Walking City, 1964), and New Urbanism, all rolled into one.

Our separation from an earlier personal movement device—the horse—has eliminated an element of nurturing from mobility (although some have a tendency to nurture their cars). In the distant future, vehicles may shrink, fold, and change their power sources, becoming car-as-womb—a blend of nature and technology that provides for our every need. But we will still "park." The only alternative will be to live in our cars, constantly moving. In "Gaia Fotovoltaica," in the Italian architecture and design magazine *Domus*, Ross Lovegrove foresees a technology "Maximizing Man, minimizing machine... Thus a scenario unfolds where we will see conceptual links between the nature of Architecture, Automotive, Product and Artificial Intelligence evolving into a seamless blend of coexistence."[8] In this scenario, parking garages are made of biological cells whose facades mediate the permeable boundary between inside and outside: the embryonic bubble where machine and man merge, both to be transformed.

In both its history and future, parking is not static, stultifying, reductive, or alienating, but rather the basis for experimentation— the connection between speed and rest.

[1] Clarence Dykstra, "And This From Los Angeles," *American City Magazine* (September 1926), 315.

[2] Shannon Sanders McDonald, *The Parking Garage: Design and Evolution of a Modern Urban Form* (Washington, D.C.: Urban Land Institute, 2007), 17.

[3] Ibid., 35–36.

[4] Gino Finizio, *Architecture & Mobility: Tradition and Innovation* (Milan: Skira, 2006), 200–201.

[5] Ulrich Franzen, Paul Rudolph, and Peter Wolf, *The Evolving City: Urban Design Proposals* (New York: The American Federation for the Arts, 1974), 74–75.

[6] Finizio.

[7] William J. Mitchell, Chris E. Borroni-Bird, and Lawrence D. Burns, *Reinventing the Automobile* (Cambridge, MA: MIT Press, 2010).

[8] Ross Lovegrove, "Gaia Fotovoltaica," *Domus* 800 (1988), 80.

TOP: 1111 Lincoln Road, Miami. Architects Herzog and de Meuron. Photo credit: Iwan Baan.

LEFT & ABOVE: Wedding at 1111 Lincoln Road. Photo credit: Maggie Steber.

PARKING STRUCTURES

Simon Henley

IF YOU'RE SHORT OF TIME, *use our Valet Parking service.... When you arrive in our exclusive Valet Lounge, you'll be given a hand-held Valet buzzer to take with you. Hand over your keys and relax in the luxury lounge whilst enjoying complimentary beverages and a wide selection of international reading material, or head straight to the shops!*

Ten minutes before you're ready to leave, simply buzz your hand-held device and your car will be waiting for you when you return. What could be simpler? [1]

This quotation is taken straight from a London shopping center website. While valet parking in the United States may be almost as old as parking itself, it is still rare in the United Kingdom, and unheard of in a shopping center. But things are changing. Tapping into an aspirational class by using a simple application of pager technology, businesses are creating an exclusive experience in a non-exclusive situation. This is *business class* parking for the leisure market. These people aren't in a rush. They just like the sound of the word *lounge* and being excused from the long haul through a *terminal* building (not an airport in this case, but the evidently second-rate space of a multistory parking structure). This changes the experience.

The parking structure is a kind of speculative space like the office, the house, the apartment, or the retail unit. But of them all, it is the one that changes hands most often (sometimes hourly), and for relatively small sums of money. Capitalism has a tendency to find every opportunity to differentiate within a service and to thereby open up new markets. It would be fair to say that parking as a service is more rudimentary than it could be, and one that has changed little since the 1950s in the United States and the 1960s in

The parking structure is a kind of speculative space like the office, the house, the apartment, or the retail unit. But of them all, it is the one that changes hands most often (sometimes hourly), and for relatively small sums of money.

Europe. Advances in computer connectivity between cars and parking garages will help owners differentiate within the service of parking. The airline industry and the hotel sector are two obvious places to look for how *service* in parking will develop between now and 2035. Both have developed a highly diversified offers at varying price points.

Parking is the first and last experience we have of a place, and it colors our view of the visit. Marketing teams recognize that the parking structure is a *foyer*—be it in a shopping center, hotel, or airport—and that there is money to be made from greater investment in parking services, parking environments, and parking management. Unless the future brings valet parking that effectively places the parking garage out of sight and the job of placing and retrieving the car from that environment entirely in the hands of the valet, the labyrinthine space of the parking structure ought to change.

Another familiar characteristic of the multi-story parking garage is the *light*—with its low levels and high contrast between peripheral daylight and the artificial gloom in the deep space of the interior. Minimum requirements for artificial light levels have increased significantly in many other kinds of buildings. More light and a more equally distributed light are physiologically better for the human eye. No doubt the health and safety lobby will demand this for parking garages.

Better floor treatments that introduce color and a finer grain—poured resin, carpet, or timber instead of exposed, tamped concrete or tarmac—raise the lowly parking structure from the status of mere infrastructure (such as a tunnel) to a public building. For developers, architects, regulators, and the market to make this shift happen on a large scale depends on their recognition that these reinforced concrete floor decks are as much for people as they are for motor vehicles. Sadly, normalizing the interior light levels and refining the finishes deprive the garage of many of the edgy, discernable qualities that distinguish it from other buildings.

Of course, technology will play a role in improving parking. Some garages are already equipped with technology that enables motorists to locate an available parking space in the maze, highlighting availability by floor, row, or individual bay using counters or a traffic-light system. It goes without saying that payment for parking will be electronic. Number plates will be read and the car will communicate directly with the garage's management system. The sudden emergence of the iPod, iPhone, and iPad in the last decade highlight just how difficult it is to predict the role of computing power and connectivity in this arena. Electronic connectivity between cars and the parking garage will eliminate the need for physical barriers like gates, and queues at the entrance to a parking structure will be a thing of the past. All of this will improve predictability in searching the city for parking and speed up actual arrival and departure times in the garage.

Mechanical parking systems offer space efficiencies, but they are inflexible in constrained urban sites because they conform to even stricter horizontal and vertical space-planning modules than traditional parking structures. Studies have demonstrated that, whatever parking and retrieval efficiencies they offer on paper, mechanical systems are not suited to circumstances where arrival and departure frequencies peak, because vehicles are retrieved in series, not in parallel, and this leads to significant backlogs. Mechanical parking is therefore not suited to multiple-occupancy residential and workplace parking, but may be fine for terminals (such as shopping centers and airports), where the load is distributed throughout the day.

In a capitalist sense, parking will evolve in an attempt to maximize returns. The rudimentary, primordial parking structures of reinforced concrete slabs and columns that we have grown so used to over the last 60 years (and that some of us find so fascinating) will go one of two ways. Most will be truly banal: not architecture—or even buildings—but simply infrastructure offered as a product by civil engineering construction companies. Facilities used for long stays (where revenues are minimal or where

> *Sadly, normalizing the interior light levels and refining the finishes deprive the garage of many of the edgy, discernable qualities that distinguish it from other buildings.*

Fundamentally, the problem of navigation and spatial legibility is one that that few, if any, garage designers address.

the parking experience does not offer a premium) will be as bare bones as possible. This is easy to see in parking facilities that do not reflect upon another service, such as in the hardnosed economic model of airport parking. It is not the airline that is offering the parking. Rather, it is the airport and the various off-site facilities trading on economy that effectively hold a monopoly.

But another strand is promising something new: parking garages as civic buildings offering their own unique *environments*. Fundamentally, the problem of navigation and spatial legibility is one that that few, if any, garage designers address. This is an area our studio, Henley Halrebrown Rorrison Architects, has begun to investigate using urban design principles to de-homogenize these environments. Parking structures can have recognizable features (such as a hall and staircase) that one would expect to find in a public building, courtyard, street, or bridge. Some aspects of parking-structure design are driven by technology and commerce. But this strand of research is driven by an intuition that success in achieving the identity shift from infrastructure to building depends not simply on surface finishes but also on the inclusion of more widely recognizable spatial systems.

The parking garage at 1111 Lincoln Road in Miami, known simply as *1111*, was designed by architects Herzog & de Meuron and completed in 2010. The 1111 Lincoln Road website describes the structure as creating "a unique shopping, dining, residential and parking experience." The architecture

website *Arcspace.com* describes how the structure's "ceiling heights vary between standard parking height and double or even triple height, in order to accommodate other programs, permanently as well as temporarily." It also notes that the structure "can be used for parties, photo or film shoots, fashion shows, concerts or other social or commercial activities, offering amazing views as the backdrop for the stage." According to Arcspace, not only are the uses varied, but moving about on foot also affords the same lyrical potential that a motorist enjoys inside the car on a helical ramp: "An unenclosed, sculptural stair in the center of the building makes pedestrian circulation in the garage a panoramic, ceremonial experience, as is moving through the building in a car."

This is not a one-off. Rather, it is the most recently built example of the spatially de-homogenized, hybrid-use car park that has been the subject of speculation by architects, in particular the Dutch, since the early 1990s. Unrealized projects include NL Architects' 1994 Parkhouse/Carstadt, a site in Amsterdam that envisaged a 1-kilometer knot of roadway into which commercial space was woven. Mike Webb, of Archigram fame, should probably be credited with the original idea of mimicking a parking structure in the conception of a public building with his unbuilt 1959 Sin Palace in London. However, it was Dutch architecture firm MVRDV (the practice that emerged from OMA in the early

Not only are the uses varied, but moving about on foot also affords the same lyrical potential that a motorist enjoys inside the car on a helical ramp.

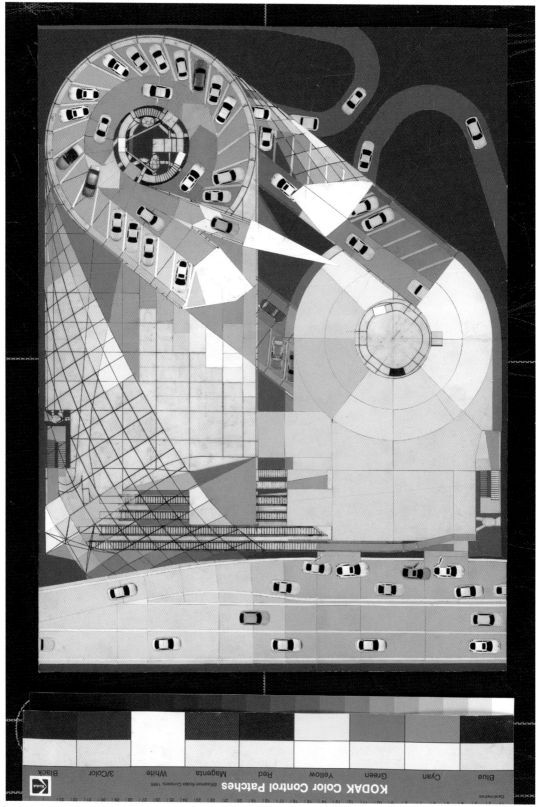

Sin Palace: Horizontal Section Cut. By Michael Webb. Project: 1962; this drawing begun: 1985. Private collection.

1990s) that built the first such building for VPRO in Hilversum, Netherlands, in 1993. They also sketched out a new town center in the form of a multistory parking structure for the Dutch town of Leidschenveen in 1997. Capitalism, fashion, land values, and branding are all likely to drive similar poetic developments in the future.

Our studio touched on the future of parking in our research project *Park&Jog*, which envisaged a sustainable commuting structure integrated into the wider urban area. The model foresees the replacement of major arterial roads with linear parks connecting out-of-town parking terminals with inner-city commuter *suit parks*. The model brings vital regeneration to areas blighted by freeways, which translates directly into increased land values and significant changes in commuter behavior. An even earlier example of an architect/master planner managing the car in the city was Louis Kahn, with his cylindrical harbors for 1950s Philadelphia. Kahn's unbuilt proposal for downtown Philadelphia envisages a city with a pedestrian center protected from the car by walls and a collar of cylindrical parking towers. His studies covered a fifteen-year period from 1947 to 1962. In his drawings, streets are called "rivers" and parking structures "harbors." The car parks are wrapped in an outer layer of shops, flats, or offices. Kahn separates the abstract building type, the car park, from the public realm.

Fuel technologies are changing, and new modes of refueling will change the *garage* (derived from the French word for warehouse) into a *station* or *fuel* station. The electric car and the hybrid fossil fuel/electric car are on the rise. Public transport is now utilizing hydrogen engines. Few engine types and fuel systems are likely to have the dramatic affect on the parking structure that the electric car will (or should). Battery technologies will develop, charging times will drop, and battery storage versus weight will improve, but, in the interim, refueling a stationary electric car is relatively slow. Other fuels, such as hydrogen, may have a similar impact. Large conglomerates in the oil industry diversifying into other forms of

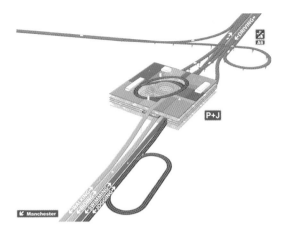

Car (P)Ark. This urban adaptor forms part of Henley Halebrown Rorrison's "Park&Jog" scheme for Salford, England (1998).

energy, and electricity generation and supply companies, may begin to develop multistory car parks in urban areas to serve as refueling centers. This will improve the feasibility and market for electric-powered cars in tandem with the development of battery technology.

Some of my students at Oxford Brookes University in the United Kingdom researched the impact of future car size on requirements for parking spaces. The research highlighted a prediction of a large *range* in length, width, and height, which would mean increasing the size of parking spaces (at least in Europe), if one were to attempt to accommodate all cars with a standard space.

New modes of refueling will change the garage (derived from the French word for warehouse) into a station or fuel station.

NL Architects' 1994 Parkhouse/Carstadt: commercial space is woven into a 1-km knot of roadways.

Car Park for 1000 Vehicles by James Renfrew, Henrietta Smart & Kate Ylioja (2007) explores how car parks may in future respond to vehicles of different sizes.

On the other end of the size spectrum, the proliferation of micro-vehicles in dense cities demands innovation and ingenuity to solve problems of miniaturization. The Smart Car can be perpendicular-parked on a street where only parallel parking would normally be permitted. The smart car is 2.7 meters long, the Toyota iQ is 3 meters, and the Fiat 500 is 3.5 meters.[2] A parking deck for these vehicles could be reduced in width from approximately 16 meters to 11 or 12 meters, resulting in a 30% smaller deck.

Audi launched an electric-powered car at the 2011 Frankfurt motor show. Their Audi Urban Concept has been described by *Esquire* magazine as "part roadster, part single-seat racer, part city car, part scooter." It seats 1 + 1 and is designed to "combat city congestion."[3] Renault has also produced the Twizy, which, at 2.4 meters long, establishes a new benchmark.[4] This electric vehicle has a turning circle of just 6.8 meters. A parking deck for vehicles of this size could be as little as 8.5 to 9 meters wide. Combine this with the reduced bay width, and the same number of vehicles cowuld be accommodated in 40% of the area. In a way, the precedent for this is the bicycle parking structure (or *fietsenstalling*) next to Amsterdam Centraal Station, designed by VMX Architects. The next generation of inner-city parking structures is likely to be miniaturized and designed to accommodate pedal bicycles, motorized scooters, and micro-cars.

Thus the parking structure will evolve, as will the scenarios in which we encounter it. Like all products and services, what's on offer inside a parking garage will continue to diversify, but progress in this area is more likely to diminish the architecture. Most parking garages will be predictably assembled: buildings made of normal materials that are nice to use. No accidents of brutality or refinement. No fear or surprise unless a work of art is intentionally commissioned. Dramatic potential lies in the multistory car park's capacity to house the proliferation of vehicles, the technology of retrieval and refueling, and in the emergence of the hybrid type predicted by Mike Webb's Sin Palace more than half a century ago.

[1] Westfield Centre London website.

[2] The Smart Car is 2695 mm long by 1752 mm wide by 1542 mm high. The Toyota iQ is 2985 mm long by 1680 mm wide by 1500 mm high. The Fiat 500 is 3546 mm long by 1627 mm wide by 1485 mm high.

[3] "The Future of City Cars," *Esquire* magazine website, September 2011.

[4] The Twizy is 2338 mm long by 1237 mm wide by 1454 mm high.

DRIVE-IN

Michael Webb

Hot Shot, Eastbound, at Iaeger, West Virginia, 1956. By O. Winston Link, 1956.
Image ©Conway Link, courtesy of O. Winston Link Museum.

1.

Westward look [for] the land is bright,[1] or so a précis of Reyner Banham's epochal 1965 article "A Home Is Not a House" might suggest. And he wasn't referring to the sort of corporate modern architecture purveyed in the United States by the likes of Paul Rudolph, SOM (Skidmore, Owings, and Merrill), and I. M. Pei. No, Banham wanted to bring to the attention of those of us back in the sceptr'd isle set in an azure sea[2] that the automobile-induced vernacular of mobile homes and drive-ins was far more interesting, that it represented a radical change in the basic program of a building,[3] and was quintessentially American in its seeming response to the needs of the restlessly mobile society we had all heard so much about.

Of the drive-in movie house (theater) Banham writes: "Only the word house is a manifest misnomer...just a flat piece of ground where the operating company provides visual images and piped sound, and the rest of the situation comes on wheels. You bring your own seat, heat and shelter as part of the car. You also bring Coke, cookies, Kleenex, Chesterfields, spare clothes, shoes, the Pill and god-wot [sic] else they don't provide at Radio City."[4]

And: "[T]he smoochy couple dancing to the music of the radio in their parked convertible have created a ballroom in the wilderness (dance floor courtesy of the Highway Dept., of course)..." This latter vision of rapture in the wilderness dissolves when the couple returns to their car and the dance floor turns back into a length of highway, and silence replaces the sound of music.

Dictum: When the event is over so is the building that housed it.

2

*Michigan Theater, 2001 © Lowell Boileau,
AtDetroit.com.*

But what about the following anomalous situation where an ornate palace substitutes for the flat piece of ground or length of highway? The auditorium is first eliminated because drive-in-erama has rendered it unnecessary, and then put back. You are looking at what once was the Michigan Theater. Let us pretend it is no longer just a rather sad parking garage in Detroit, but that the parked cars have rotated themselves through ninety degrees, affording the ghostly occupants, now dressed in tuxedoes and ballroom gowns, a view whereby the proscenium arch is now the perimeter of the windshield.

The implied exhortation to architects in this chapter is that attention should be paid not so much to the usual subjects like designs for fancy-pants art museums in city centers. For whatever museum directors and architectural critics may claim to the contrary, such projects are essentially conservative one-off jobs with totally conventional programs. Instead, the desperate need is for attention to be paid to the awfulness metastasizing between the cities: the strip malls, the vast acreages of parking, the hour-long commutes to work, the waste of natural resources, the despoliation of the Eden this land once was. And maybe, drive-ins, although usually considered part of the problem, might just suggest an answer. Consider the Webb special "multipurpose drive-in" as a first step: since the theatrical

spectacle of divine service is not far removed from that of a movie theater, could they not share the same equipment? Fold down crucifix. Altar boys, normally serving communion wine, could moonlight serving soft drinks. Result: one parking lot less.

It used to be that architects involved themselves with urban planning: the design of whole neighborhoods. Their training, based on the reliably socialist principles of their teachers, made such planning an essential part of their education. The one-off masterpiece was suspect.

To conclude this part of the chapter it can be said that a drive-in facility is a conventional building type—theater, church, drug store, bank, restaurant—where the square footage the facility offers is a case of *reductio ad absurdum*. But in order for the facility to function the car is necessary. To ponder what the drive-in might and should develop into, please consider the following:

3.

*Mobile Lounge, Dulles Airport.
Photo credit: John R. Harris.*

To get passengers from check-in directly to the gate, Washington's Dulles Airport used to employ mobile departure lounges.[5] Shown here is one of them, either disgorging passengers into a 747 or receiving them. Introduced in an era when passenger comfort was a consideration, the lounge would first position itself adjacent to check-in. Then, once loaded, drive out to the plane, elevating itself so that its floor lined up with that of the plane. The next step, so to speak, would be, with considerable modification of the lounge's skin, for it, along with other lounges, to be attached to the underside of a flying crane sort of airliner.

4.

Rudolf Schindler (the architect of the forward-looking Kings Road house in West Hollywood, California, c. 1922) is reputed to have said that a car should contain "removable cupboards and practical closets; a small, collapsible table with containers for records and papers. And a good reading light."

The head of a certain law firm in midtown Manhattan has a weekend house out in the Hamptons. On Friday afternoons he drives out there on the Long Island Expressway, infamous throughout the East Coast for being the world's longest parking lot. "Back in my midtown office my employees are bothering me all the time with stupid questions. Alone in my specially equipped SUV [with iPhone, printer, laptop and, presumably, a good reading light] I get so much more accomplished. Stuck in a traffic jam? No problem: my car is more my office than is my office."[6]

A map showing the total floor space of all the buildings in midtown might indicate, let us say, in yellow, those spaces given over to office accommodation. But, based on what the lawyer has told us, would not therefore the floor plan of his car interior need to be included on the map as well...and colored yellow to boot? And, since our lawyer is far from alone in his use of space and time, should not Friday's map show a veritable diaspora of small yellow rectangles exploding outward from midtown, only to be reversed on Sunday's map?

5.

This is Giacomo Vignola's Villa Farnese (1559–1573) at Caprarola, Italy. It makes the cut because it eloquently talks about the journey between one's vehicle and one's home. According to the late Professor Dennis

Villa Farnese, Caprarola, G.B. Vignola, 1573.

Broodbank of the onetime Regent Street Polytechnic School of Architecture, the signor and signora would arrive in their horse and carriage, from which they would alight. The four horses would be led into the stables to be watered and rested, and two sedan chairs carried by flunkies would transport the couple to the next level. Finally they would walk up the remaining ramp, presumably the signor on the left ramp and the signora on the right ramp, and enter in through the main portal.

6.

In this ex-urban development, the homeward car—now powered not by Signor Farnese's four horses, but by the resident's likely three hundred and twenty seven—is confronted by a wall of garages with the houses—sorry, "homes"—hidden behind. Ah! So much for the neighborly stoop! Upon arrival, the clicker on the dashboard first reconfigures the form of the two car garage by raising the "Up and Over Door." Then, once inside, the kitchen becomes the distributor from which the remaining rooms of the home can be accessed. There may be a vestigial front door that no one ever uses.

The resident would likely be offended by the suggestion that he or she is living in a drive-in house—in which the car is now within the building envelope—but it's not far off. If you imagine applying the principles of drive-ins to a home, then it's true.

I wrote back in '72: "Wasteful and sad, though, that out there in the 'burbs the mobile component of *vita domestica* sits out on the driveway or in a parking lot unused for most of the day. Luxuriously appointed interior with crushed velour seats, surround radio, hi-fi, TV and cocktail cabinet, the car is swankier than the house interior to which it is supposedly ancillary."

The inference here is that the car should enter or attach itself to the house—should become additional floor space. Then the home, when everyone is out, is the "empty piece of land." The car, when it arrives back, becomes the energizer.

7.

Today's homes are no more than a place to sleep next to your car.

–George Bernard Shaw

The first attempt at designing a true drive-in house was the Skyrise project, begun in 1969. Residents, returning home in their specially designed electric runabout cars, arrive at the foot of the building where chassis and body become separated. The chassis are then stored in underground racks and the bodies hoisted vertically or diagonally upwards, cradled by a crawling crane that deposits them at the appropriate apartment in the sky—or more naughtily, the inappropriate apartment. Once detached from the crane, the body blooms, opening out to form additional living space. At the foot of the building on the right, stored room sets await

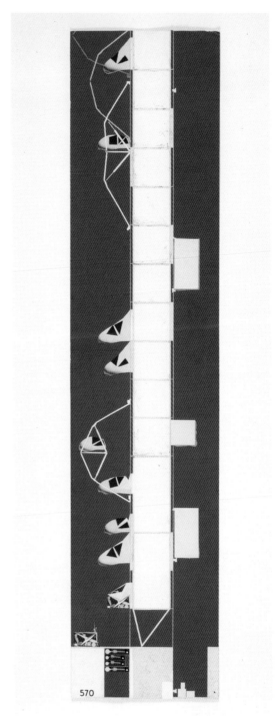

570

Skyrise: Vertical Section Cut. By Michael Webb. Project: 1969; drawing: 1974. Courtesy of Archigram Archive.

a summons from a resident planning, let us say, a party necessitating additional living space.

8.

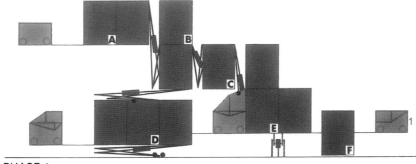

PHASE 1

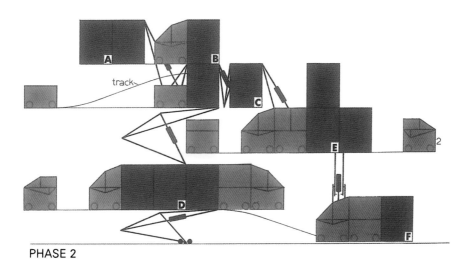

track

PHASE 2

Variable Volume: Housing that expands or contracts according to the number of people in it at a given time. Elevation. By Michael Webb. Original drawing: 1970. Animation by Dennis Crompton. Courtesy of Archigram Archive.

A variant of this was a hypothetical building structure where the fixed, permanent parts of the home—family heirloom, king-size bed, gas oven—would be motherly relative to the suckling cars nestling around them. As car babies returned to their mothers, the building would need to expand to allow them access. During the workweek, the building envelope would be small. But on Saturday, party night, the envelope would expand outward to many times its previous size.

"The motor bus rushes into the houses which it passes, and in their turn, the houses throw themselves upon the motor bus and are blended with it."[7] Whatever are the Futurist painters getting at here? Are the noise, vibrations, and smell of the approaching motor bus impacting both the fabric of the houses and their occupants, such that the occupants see in their mind's eye an image of the bus and its passengers? Likewise the passengers: Do they not imagine the lives lived behind the lit windows of the houses the bus is passing? Or is the meaning more literal? Does the bus physically merge with the houses and the houses with the bus? If so, then there you have the drive-in house.

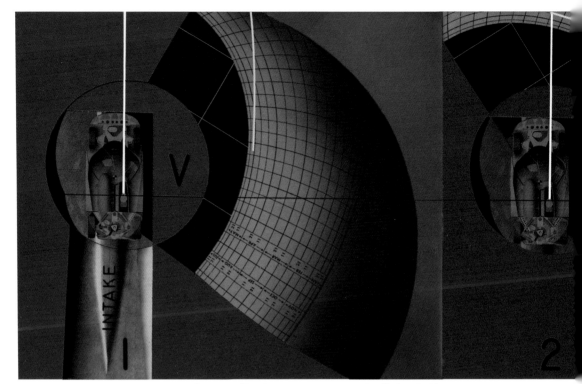

9

Three stages in the movement of parts allowing a car to enter the Drive-in House.
By Michael Webb. Original drawing: 1987; digital reworking: 2005. Courtesy of Archigram Archive.

A convention of architectural projection drawing is that, when depicting the plan (a.k.a. horizontal section) of a building, the main entrance facade should be placed along the bottom edge of the drawing so that, in effect, you enter and penetrate the interior by moving your eye upward. In frame 1, the car has entered through an intake tube placed vertically on the page so as to obey the convention. Its forward motion has been arrested within a circular drum. The driver's center of vision is also vertical (see white line).

In frame 2, the drum bearing the car has rotated clockwise so that its interior is now sealed off from any cold air in the intake tube. Nevertheless, in order to follow the rules, the driver's center of vision remains vertical. This means the rotating drum is graphically inert, while the inert house rotates graphically around the drum. The car's doors begin to open.

In frame 3, the drum has rotated further such that the car shares the same space as the schematic living area. Graphically, however, its position is such that the driver's steadfast center of vision is yet vertical. The car's doors are now fully open. As the car rotates about the house, so does the sun (see the yellow line in each frame), a statement pleasing, surely, to the Holy Inquisition.

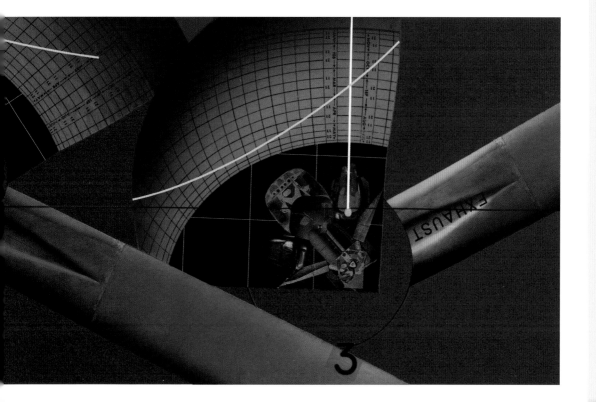

[1] This line is from the 1849 poem "Say not the Struggle Naught Availeth" by Arthur Hugh Clough that Winston Churchill used in a wartime speech from 1940. Intended for American ears, it expressed the hope that help would soon be coming in the fight against Hitler. For us young Archigrammers a decade and a half later, the light was more architectural in nature. There was Konrad "Turning Point of Building" Wachsmann and Buckminster Fuller, of course, and now there was Reyner Banham to interpret for us what was going on there. America did seem just the place to be.

[2] A certain irony is intended in the use of this quotation from the speech of Henry V before Agincourt. Between the end of World War II and the advent of the Beatles/Carnaby Street era, the mood of England was decidedly gray.

[3] The program is a list of all the proposed rooms and spaces, internal and external, that will comprise the building once completed. Regarding a drive-in movie theater, the absence of the theater part does suggest a remarkably unconventional program.

[4] Reyner Banham, "A Home Is Not a House," *Art in America* 2 (April 1965).

[5] Worthy of study might be just why Dulles Airport abandoned the idea.

[6] Words in brackets are author's addition.

[7] From the *Technical Manifesto of Futurist Painting*, launched March 18, 1910, in the limelight of the Chiarella Theater in Turin, Italy.

PART 3

POLICY:

POLICY:

TRANSPORTATION, PLANNING, HEALTH, AND CAR CULTURE IN THE INLAND EMPIRE

Mark Hoffman and Kati Rubinyi

URBAN PLANNERS ASPIRE TO CREATE UTOPIAS—cities, towns, or neighborhoods that offer healthy, prosperous, safe, and vibrant places to work and live. In that pursuit, planners break the complexity of community down into broad themes—the built environment, transportation, the economy, health and safety, housing, parks, and land uses. This focus may extend to the social institutions that reduce conflict and enhance personal development, education, health, and wellbeing. The end goal is no less than to understand, predict, and ultimately shape urban form, coupled with the human institutions and processes that empower people to achieve their fullest potential.

The Inland Empire, a vast 27,000-square-mile region in Southern California, includes the city centers of San Bernardino, Riverside, and Ontario. It's an expansive area of bedroom communities, suburbs, towns, and tracts that extends to the Arizona border. Although some communities have a viable job base and are working toward a more independent economic future, the major employment centers are in faraway cities in Los Angeles and Orange Counties. Because of the relative affordability of housing and way of life, Inland Empire residents live far from their places of employment, and endure the tenth longest commute of 366 metropolitan regions in the nation. Out of these patterns, however, a unique Inland Empire car culture is thriving.[1]

The urban form and transportation patterns that have emerged over time in the Inland Empire have had unintended consequences, predominantly concerning health and quality of life. In a survey of 190 metropolitan regions across the nation, the Inland Empire ranks the 133rd lowest in health and wellbeing.[2] This is due in part to pollution and lack of access to basic services—for which the region ranks near the bottom nationwide. Reliance on the car, and a roadway system that was once the envy of the nation, means long commutes, air and noise pollution, asthma, lack of physical activity, stress, obesity, and other issues relating to poor health.[3]

Theories about the challenges facing the Inland Empire are many. Urban geographer Waldo Tobler's theory of distance decay, which explains how the interaction between two places declines as the distance increases, has application to the region. Distance decay holds that city centers have more businesses, public transit, sanitation services, health services, and better quality roads. Farther from the center, services begin to break down—public transit runs less frequently, septic tanks and wells replace sewage systems and municipal water, and the road network is less complete.[4] Health care facilities tend to be fewer and farther between, and amenities may be lacking. Distance decay has multiple direct and indirect implications for public health. In the Inland Empire, the effects are evident and become most obvious in the sparsely populated desert areas.

Public urban planning policy is often directed at decreasing the distance or travel time between towns, suburbs, and central cities or at creating more compact, self-sustaining communities with housing, jobs, services, and infrastructure.[5] In both cases, there are no easy fixes, just multiple challenges for planners who are tasked with designing communities in regions that are increasingly complex, polycentric, and interdependent. In the Inland Empire, a key denominator in both scenarios is economic development. An increase in living-wage jobs within communities would allow residents to work closer to home and forego the long commute to neighboring cities or employment centers.

Often lost in the equation is culture—a subjective and complex phenomenon that takes a back seat to traditional land planning. Contrary to some perceptions, the Inland Empire has produced a number of distinctive cultures, relationships, events, and artifacts that are different from those created elsewhere. No one culture is dominant or ubiquitous in the region. For many in the Inland Empire, a unique culture of community and ingenuity based on cars has emerged—a vibrant and creative culture of car shows, car clubs, and competing styles and ideologies for modified cars and trucks. This car culture would not exist if the urban form were different.

According to some planning perspectives, this culture of the car has emerged out of the dysfunction of sprawling urban form and interregional imbalances in housing and employment. It nonetheless presents an important challenge to urban planning. If the utopian demands of urban planning extend beyond simply "urban form" to "how community is experienced," culture cannot be bracketed out of the discussion. Culture must be embraced as an integral part of the planning equation. And, despite the often-heard claims of the dysfunction of urban form in the Inland Empire, its car culture continues to connect families and friends, as well as people of different ethnicities, income levels, and political viewpoints.

The solutions that would help the Inland Empire address crucial issues like the balance of jobs and housing might imply a different way of life and result in a different culture. But an implication arises from a conclusion based on research and hard data—that a specific form of low-rise urban culture (not really urban, but rather small town), made up of small mixed-use districts—is the most virtuous. While best practices point to all people living in denser communities, with all the attendant benefits and drawbacks, the Inland Empire's culture would not exist as such if the region was not sprawling, suburban, and ex-urban.

The following conversation with the Parranderos Car Club touches on a number of themes—examining at close range the issues urban planners wrestle with at an elevation of 20,000 feet. One of these is chronic disease—specifically diabetes, one of the most prevalent serious health conditions in the region. Another is the long commute required to get to low-paying jobs. The economy forces extended families from far-flung suburbs to move in together, and friends and family need to travel large distances to socialize. Car clubs, like the Parranderos, are social support networks. In addition, they are part of a vibrant network of car clubs that span not only regions and nations but also generations.

How could planning reconcile the car culture that has grown for over a century in the Inland Empire? No one would argue that the struggles faced by residents because of the lack of job opportunities and poor health, and the hardships and stress faced by recent immigrants and underserved communities, should be perpetuated or romanticized. But dispersed land uses, an interregional imbalance of land uses, and a focus on the car have all made the Inland Empire what it is—for good and bad.

[1] "Public Transportation Usage Among U.S. Workers: 2008 and 2009," *American Community Survey Briefs, ACSBR/09-5* (October 2010), accessed at http://www.census.gov/hhes/commuting/.

[2] *Healthways Quality of Living Index*, Gallup (2011).

[3] "At the Intersection of Public Health and Transportation: Promoting Healthy Transportation Policy," *American Public Health Association* (2010).

[4] "Distance Decay and its use in GIS", accessed at http://gislounge.com/distance-decay-and-its-use-in-gis/

[5] U.S. Environmental Protection Agency http://www.epa.gov/dced/index.htm.

INTERVIEW WITH PARRANDEROS CAR CLUB

Kati Rubinyi

Salvador Gurrola, left, and Alex Ruiz in Alex's truck at Cruisin' the Galaxy, Ontario, California.

I MET ALEX RUIZ *and the Parranderos Car Club on June 11, 2011 at an event called Cruisin' the Galaxy, which took place in the parking lot of Galaxy Hamburgers in the warehouse district of Ontario, California. Approachable, enthusiastic, and articulate, Alex was an ideal person to talk to, so I got his contact information in order to learn more about his club, Parranderos, and his amazing labor of love—a rough, unpainted Dub-style mini truck made up of a Chevrolet body with a Cadillac front end and Cadillac rear headlights (see pp.224–25). I received an e-mail from Alex on July 15 about the Mini Trucks for Troops cruise night that was to take place a few weeks later at Toro Sushi restaurant on Mountain Avenue in Ontario. Looking forward to talking with him further, I arrived at the event and was shocked to find out that Alex had died of diabetes complications a week after he sent me that e-mail. He was 34 years old.*

The Parranderos Car Club consists of the two Gurrola brothers, their sister (who was Alex Ruiz's wife), and a few of their friends. The Gurrolas—Salvador (Chava), Octavio, and

Cecilia—are from Zacatecas, Mexico. Junior Lopez is from Tijuana, Mexico; Bola Marin is from Michoacán, Mexico; and Tony Rosales is from Colima, Mexico. Alex Ruiz was from Los Angeles, but he grew up in Michoacán. He spent 15 years in Michoacán and then moved back to California for high school and college.

Interviewed August 13th, 2011, at Mini Trucks for Troops in the parking lot of Toro Sushi on Mountain Avenue in Ontario.

CLUB MEMBERS:

Salvador "Chava" Gurrola, President
Alex "El Peke" Ruiz (1976–2011), Vice President
Octavio Gurrola
Antonio "Tony" Lorenzo Rosales
Jose "Bola" Marin
Roger "Junior" Lopez
Cecilia Ruiz (maiden name, Gurrola)
Wendy Gurrola
Iris Graciano

Alex's truck is an amazing labor of love—a rough, unpainted Dub-style mini truck made up of a Chevrolet body with a Cadillac front end and Cadillac rear headlights.

THE RIDES

JUNIOR: I have a 2000 Honda Civic DX but it's down right now. The motor got messed up and I have to put another motor in it. So far the car is stock, but I put Lambo doors on it. I put on 17-inch rims and tires, neon lights, LEDs underneath the car—on the undercarriage. I put a box in it. I have two kicker amps—one for the highs and one for the bass. I have two TVs on the headrest. I put an LED light in the hood and the trunk. It lights up the trunk. We customized the trunk where it opens up a different way. I have pedals with glow lights. I'm trying to hook it up to the best of my ability. Not only me, but all the members are helping me accomplish what I'm trying to do to my vehicle.

LORENZO (TONY): My name is Lorenzo Rosales, and I have a 1994 Chevy Suburban. Me and the president, Salvador, we do suspension, we do front air bags, we do hydraulics, we do suicide doors, we do Lamborghini doors, we do paint, we do fiberglass—we do pretty much everything. We do TVs. We do everything from scratch. Nothing from shops, everything from the backyard— Backyard Boogie, you know. I'm about to put on ramps, a paint job, suspension, and TVs. Right now, the car's not here because we're still working on it. The suspension is air

bags. With the air-ride suspension, it drops slow and smooth.

CHAVA: I have a 1995 Chevy Tahoe four-door. Right now, I've put on Lambo doors, butterfly doors on the back, full suede and Coach interior upholstery with fiberglass door panels. I have twelve TVs. The new paint job is Laguna Seca Blue, BMW edition. I'm about to put in a new air ride suspension and my hood is custom. The gas tank has a custom cover. In the back, we have a custom box for audio, neon lights, and suede. We also have custom painted taillights. They're black—sometimes the cops give you a ticket for that. They still glow red, but they're dimmer. The front end of this truck is factory, but we want to modify it in the future. My friend Tony and I have a lot of projects for my truck. Little by little, I will add all the details until it is perfect. We're trying to make it work.

TONY: [*talking about Alex's truck, which is now Cecilia's*] This white truck is a '96 Chevy Tahoe with full custom systems—a custom trunk, with shade doors in the back, shade doors in the front, custom intake on the engine, custom paint on the dash, custom steering wheels, air bag suspension, intake headers, custom hood. It has a Cadillac front end with a 2005 GMC Sierra front bumper. The truck is a Chevy but the front end is Cadillac, and the bumper is GMC. So it's three different cars mixed into one. The back has Cadillac taillights. Whatever the front end is, the taillights are the same. But here, the front is a Cadillac Escalade, and the back has Cadillac Fleetwood taillights. It's a Cadillac car in the back and a Cadillac truck in the front. So we're not driving the same truck as what the dealer sells. We upgraded it and made it our own style. It has a custom-built front grille. Another friend made the grille. We cut the Cadillac front grille out and stuck the new grille in and it fit perfectly. We have strobe lights inside the front lights, like a cop—they flash, neon all the way around, even under the hood. We have suspension, 20-inch wheels in the front and 22-inch in the back. We have offset wheels, and the whole truck can lay flat on the floor. We're trying to get together to work on the truck to get it the way Alex wanted. We're going to do the paint job the way he wanted as well as some air-brushing, the interior, and a couple of details. We will pitch in with his wife and brother-in-law and get it the way he wanted it to be.

BOLA: This is an '89 Nissan hard-body mini truck. The president and his brother did the airbag setup and they also did the speaker box. [*Bola indicates the air compressors in the truck bed.*] This is your valve and your tank and compressor to fill up the airbags. The truck goes up and down and side to side. This aluminum box with switches controls everything. Those are '05 stock Chevy Silverado wheels. This is a Nissan but we're putting Chevy stuff on it. The headlights will be 2008 Silverado headlights. Same with the rear headlights. I want a top-of-the-line car—get the code and then paint it like that. I don't know yet what color it will be. It will also have remote control doors. The one on the passenger side is going to be a sliding door. It takes a long time and a lot of money. We have to pay bills, and this takes extra money. We can't take it to a shop. Everything

In this car club, we have rules. We can't be drinking, doing drugs, smoking, racing. We can't have trouble with members of other clubs. If anything happens, if something gets out of hand, the president takes care of it with the president of the other car club.

is me, Chava, and his brother. His brother does welding cutting, chopping, painting. Salvador's dad, back in the day in Mexico, would paint Pepsi trucks as a job. So he's an expert.

THE CLUB

TONY: Parranderos was Chava's and Alex's idea, and we only started about three months ago. We all belonged to different car clubs before, but we decided we wanted our own. Chava had been with a car club that is really established, but they had a lot of drama, a lot of fighting—situations where he was uncomfortable. And they would discriminate against people with simpler cars. We wanted to start a club where we don't care if you want to start at the bottom, with whatever car or truck. We'll give you a chance. A car club is about family—creating a second family. So we got our closest friends together—Chava, Bola, Junior, and Octavio. Most of us were born in Mexico and raised here, but Alex was born here and then he went to Mexico and came back.

Before we started this car club, we had another car club, back in the day, about five years ago. It was called Neighborhood Riders, but now we're back with a different name. I started it with Chava and Alex and Octavio, in Moreno Valley. We all live in different places now, but we all used to live in Moreno Valley. Later, Alex moved to Riverside, but we stuck together. Now we live spread out between Moreno Valley, Riverside, and Perris, but we still meet in Riverside twice a month, at Arlington and Van Buren, in the K-Mart parking lot. At the meetings we talk about what car show or cruise night we're going to go to, and what we're going to do on our cars and trucks. Some of us got married, some of us are still single; but this club, now that we're older, is more about family. We're more mature. Our wives help and support us. And yes, the wives are members, a part of the club. You see we're just chilling, joking around, having fun, snacking. That's what the car club is about—just being together.

For example, Junior used to race, but he doesn't anymore. Plus, you can't race with these cars—you can't get very far. [*Everyone laughs.*] And in this car club, we have rules. We can't be drinking, doing drugs, smoking, racing. We can't have trouble with members of other clubs. If anything happens, if something gets out of hand, the president takes care of it with the president of the other car club. If we have a problem with another person, we tell the president and he will talk to the leader of that other club and he talks to his members. We don't get crazy with anybody. We just come, cruise, chill, show our cars, get ideas for how to improve our cars. That's what we do.

CECILIA: Alex was so excited about the car club. When I first met him, he loved new cars with no problems—just make the payments and drive the car. But then he met my brothers, and he started to learn to fix cars from our family. He became so excited about his cars—his new toys. He was like a kid. He sold his Monte Carlo and he bought the Chevy truck on Craigslist. The Monte Carlo was big but low, and so he felt more comfortable in an SUV because he was a big guy. He was so responsible, and would always plan so carefully to make things perfect. The rest of us have to make his dreams happen. There was a cruise night three weeks ago in Fontana in his memory. We had a lot of support from three car clubs: Sunset, Concrete Deep, and Regulators. They each really helped us out so much; it was amazing. California Sound helped us with the location. People were crying at the cruise night. Alex had so many friends. He was so outgoing, not shy at all. There were 35 cars at the cruise night, and we were not expecting that many cars. At his funeral, we were expecting 200 people, but there were 500 people. It was at Rose Hills, in Whittier. There were a lot of people there from cruise nights.

We still don't know exactly why he died. It was probably a heart attack, but we're still waiting to find out. He was diabetic and had high blood pressure. He'd been diabetic since he was 13, but we only found that out two years ago. He had a lot of health problems, especially with his eyes. He had had four surgeries on each eye to recover his vision, so we were always fighting back with surgeries, but they never really worked very well.

Alex was a good student, and had graduated with honors from Cal State L.A. in East L.A. As a job, he did loss prevention and security. He worked at the Big Lots warehouse in Rancho Cucamonga. He took care of the warehouse at night. He checked the cameras. He checked the trucks coming into the warehouse to make sure the merchandise was logged. The night before he died, he worked 18 hours. Three years ago, we bought our first house in Hesperia, near Victorville. We also bought new cars, but when the economy started going down, I lost my job and he lost his second job and we started to lose everything. So then we moved to Moreno Valley, into a small apartment. My parents also had an apartment there, and we all had a lot of bills. So then we all moved to Riverside together, into a house, to help everybody reduce the bills. And then, just a couple of months ago, we started to talk about moving out and having kids. So, I still live with my parents. We're going to fix up Alex's truck. I told my brothers that I don't care if I spend too much money on it. I have to fix it and drive it and have it the way Alex wanted it. We're going to accomplish it all in our house, garage, and backyard—none of it in a shop.

TONY: I used to go to Alex's house all the time. We were best friends. I used to look for Alex. Even if he was asleep after working the nightshift, he'd come down and we'd be chill and talk about things. He lived in Riverside. I live in Perris. A car club like ours is a second family. You have a family, but a car club is a family that you communicate better with. They understand you. They know what you're going through and if you're struggling. Sometimes your car club can help you more than your family. It's a fraternity where we understand where we came from, what we've been through, and what we're going through. You help each other. And all of these things that happened to us, like about Alex, make us closer and more united. We know we need to take care of each other.

CECILIA: Alex helped me a lot. He helped me with my citizenship and he helped my parents; my brother's is in process. If anyone asked him for help, he would never say no.

A car club like ours is a second family. You have a family, but a car club is a family that you communicate better with. They understand you.

He would say, "You never know when you'll need help. You never say no." He taught me that. I've changed my mind totally to where I see you need to help each other. I've had so much help from his friends, and we've all now had to help each other so much. I think totally differently now. You can't choose your family, but can choose another, second family. We're close and we can make it work. We started this car club, and I hope you will see it grow bigger, and we will recruit more family and more friends. The cars will get fixed up.

TONY: We have Alex's, mine, Junior's, my wife's, and his wife's car. We have a lot of projects, a lot of cars. Salvador has two cars. We have a lot to do, and we have to make it work with our paychecks.

CECILIA: My dad does the paint and mechanics, and I'm a seamstress.

CHAVA: I do the upholstery. I learned how to do it. It's a lot of work.

TONY: If we see something and we like it, we're going to try to do it.

OCTAVIO: I work in a mechanics shop. My family had a shop in Zacatecas, and I'd love to have my own shop here—that's the idea. But there's a lot regulation and insurance, so it's complicated. It would be great to have a shop in the future. It would be great to call the shop Parranderos.

LEGACY VEHICLES AND SUSTAINABLE NEIGHBORHOODS

Terry A. Hayes

NEIGHBORHOODS ARE THE BUILDING BLOCKS OF A CITY. A neighborhood defines the physical urban space and provides residents with a comprehensible framework within which to go about their daily routines of work, school, shopping, and leisure/entertainment. The collection of neighborhood variety in any given city defines that city's character. However, not all neighborhoods are equal. There are socioeconomic, racial, and cultural differences, as well as differences in home ownership, housing types, availability of amenities, housing density, etc.

The geographic location and spatial relationship between neighborhoods also plays an important role in defining the quality of life in urban neighborhoods. The distance traveled to school, work, or church and the accessibility of services all figure in to the equation. Neighborhood mobility and accessibility are key factors in establishing the relative desirability of one neighborhood versus another. Most importantly, mobility and accessibility set the groundwork for the relative sustainability of a neighborhood. Are there convenient exit routes during a natural or man-made disaster (earthquake, wildfire, riot, etc.)? Can residents get to grocery stores, emergency centers, or food banks when they need to? Overall, does the neighborhood represent a convenient spatial relationship to jobs, services, and community facilities?

In Los Angeles, neighborhood growth and distribution has been stimulated in large part by the access afforded by the private automobile. While it is true that older neighborhoods evolved around the mobility afforded by the red and yellow car transit lines that once sprawled across the region, the real thrust of suburban growth was fueled by the accessibility of the private automobile

and the expansion of the freeway system. For many years, the freeway and highway system expanded and flourished, while the transit system was allowed to atrophy into an inefficient, infrequent, and inconvenient collection of bus routes. Since the 1980s, the pendulum has been swinging back, with a massive public policy emphasis on re-creating the public transportation system. As expanding highways has become cost prohibitive—and politically unpopular—an environmentally based view has emerged that the Los Angeles region must reverse 60-plus years of transit neglect. Los Angeles County voters' support for sales tax Measure R in November 2008 confirms the popularity of this view.

Los Angeles neighborhoods are caught in the middle of the evolving tide of transportation investment policy. As we look 20 or so years into the future, the implicit ideal planning

As expanding highways has become cost prohibitive—and politically unpopular—an environmentally based view has emerged that the Los Angeles region must reverse 60-plus years of transit neglect.

Used car lots in Mid-City, Los Angeles.

vision for our urban area now seems to entail nodes of high-density, transit-oriented land use developments linked by efficient and high-capacity fixed guideway transit systems, such as bus rapid transit, light rail, and heavy rail. California state legislation on greenhouse gases (e.g., the Global Warming Solutions Act of 2006 and Senate Bill 375) seems to mirror this vision that transit and land uses conforming to transit will cure the region's environmental quality and traffic congestion issues.

It is interesting that the passenger car is strikingly omitted as a positive element of this vision. Like the dinosaurs that fuel it, the passenger car is assumed to become extinct or on the verge of extinction as a viable transportation mode, as if a region that has been built up around the car will simply cast it aside in the face of economic and environmental imperatives. Our current transportation policy fiction leads us to believe that new neighborhoods will be clustered around hierarchies of urban centers that will be linked via all varieties of transit guideways and networks. But the expected extinction of the passenger car is greatly exaggerated. The California Air Resources Board expects that in the year 2035 there will be 6.4 million light-duty cars and trucks operating in Los Angeles County and making approximately 38 million daily trips. This would represent a 2.1-million-vehicle increase from today's 4.3 million light-duty vehicles. The accessibility and mobility of neighborhoods will continue to be linked in large part by the car and its roadway infrastructure. On average, a one-square-mile neighborhood will be served by more than 30 miles of major arterials and collector roadways. With the premium placed on mobility, it is extremely doubtful that this neighborhood space will be left dormant

The expected extinction of the passenger car is greatly exaggerated.

and unused. Without the major catastrophic effects of a peak oil shortage, transit travel demand models show automobile trip reduction of one to two percent at best. The vast majority of travel in and out of Los Angeles neighborhoods will continue to be by car.

The survival or sustainability potential of all urban neighborhoods, however, is not the same. In a 1970 study, the U.S. Department of Housing and Urban Development describes the life cycle of a neighborhood, stating that, within a given urban area, neighborhoods are in various stages of evolution—from initial formation to decay and disinvestment. Similarly, neighborhoods are cast along a continuum of sustainability. Electric car charging stations and community gardens may be an important objective for one type of neighborhood, while another neighborhood's focus may be on adequate jobs and convenient grocery stores with fresh produce. Any particular, unforeseen event intersecting these neighborhood life cycles could create unusual opportunities, or possibly have devastating results. Witness the effects of Hurricane Katrina on the Ninth Ward of New Orleans, where disinvestment—compounded with scarce emergency preparedness and few elements of sustainable infrastructure—led to the near-obliteration of the neighborhood.

Using census tracts as a rough surrogate for neighborhood boundaries, the 2000 Census for Los Angeles County showed a wide separation of median incomes. Fifty-one percent of the 2,054 census tracts in the county were below the median income. These socioeconomic differences create strong implications for future mobility. As incomes rise, neighborhoods with higher incomes will likely generate more discretionary trips to schools, shopping, and other non-work destinations. These trips will likely be shorter because of the white-collar nature of many of these neighborhoods and a more even geographic balance between jobs and housing. Even the need to travel will be diminished by future advancements in telecommuting and remote access to the Internet and corporate intranets. For all other neighborhoods, however, future mobility will be more

Higher turnover rates for replacing older vehicles are more likely in higher income areas than in lower income areas. As a result, those areas least able to invest in advancements in automobile technology will have both the greatest access needs and the greatest proportion of legacy vehicles on the road.

challenging. In places like South and East Los Angeles, the imbalance between jobs, housing, and basic services is likely to be exacerbated. There will be longer commutes and discretionary trips to job centers in West Los Angeles or the South Bay. Similar to today, socioeconomics will figure into differences in auto retention. Higher turnover rates for replacing older vehicles are more likely in higher income areas than in lower income areas. As a result, those areas least able to invest in advancements in automobile technology will have both the greatest access needs and the greatest proportion of legacy vehicles on the road. In the year 2035, current vehicle models (2011 to 2015) will still be on the road, and it is highly likely that these vehicles will be concentrated in lower income areas of the county.

COMPARATIVE AGE OF AUTOMOBILES BY NEIGHBORHOOD

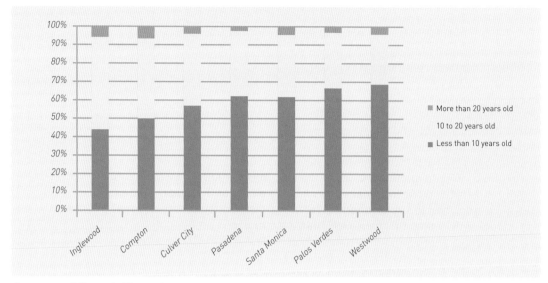

Courtesy of Terry A. Hayes Associates.

Even in an expanded capacity, it is doubtful that the transit system will be able to adequately fill the mobility gaps for neighborhoods cast over such a wide spatial landscape. The passenger car will continue to be the backbone of the transportation system. It remains to be determined how older vehicles with more primitive technologies will be integrated into intelligent highways, or how these vehicles will be segregated from more advanced vehicles.

So far, few have peered into this mobility looking-glass with any clarity. Advancements in roadway and automobile technology are taken as givens that are assumed to magically wash across the region through "market acceptance." The socioeconomic differences in the city are becoming more starkly contrasted. There is no reason to believe that the divide between the "haves" and the "have-nots" will not increase.

Because the concept of an economic divide is subjective, I decided to look closer at the notion of neighborhood differences in automobile choices and the model-age of cars. Though the study was not set up to meet a specific statistical test, my team used census data to select seven neighborhoods with contrasting socioeconomic differences (i.e., Inglewood, Compton, Culver City, Pasadena,

Santa Monica, Palos Verdes, Westwood). We surveyed grocery store parking lots in each of these communities as the best indicator of local automobile choice. The range of differences was not surprising. In Inglewood and Compton, the proportion of cars less than 10 years old was 45% and 50%, respectively. In comparison, the proportion in Westwood and Palos Verdes was 67% and 68%, respectively. For the oldest vehicles (those over 20 years), the proportion in Inglewood and Compton was almost twice as high as the proportion in Westwood and Palos Verdes. It is these differences that will likely be the baseline for the future. In 2035, 70% of the vehicles in affluent communities will be manufactured after model-year 2025; in less affluent areas, well over 50% of the vehicles will be manufactured prior to 2025, possibly with a significant proportion manufactured before 2015. We strongly suspect that the number of model-year 2015 vehicles will be even higher than the existing baseline, given the persistent economic woes that currently beset the region and will undoubtedly retard new automobile sales and increase automobile retention for some time.

COMPARATIVE AGE OF AUTOMOBILES BY NEIGHBORHOOD

While vehicle age points to one difference that may carry into the future, vehicle features and accessory packages also hold clues. Perhaps a critical factor in determining accessibility and mobility is determining what type and extent of automotive technology is within reach for differing neighborhood communities. For example, in our informal survey it was not uncommon to see an abundance of Chevrolets and Toyotas that were less than ten years old in the South Los Angeles region. It was equally common to see Toyotas and BMWs in the Pasadena area that were also less than ten years old. But when looking at the spectrum of models, model levels, equipment packages, and additional options, it becomes apparent that there are significant differences between entry-level models and those that are feature-rich. Thus, even amongst new cars, important differences in feature technology will likely accentuate access differences to advanced transportation infrastructure in the future.

Aside from purely economic determinants, the changing demographics of city neighborhoods also figure into the future role of the car. For decades, the car has served as symbol of economic mobility and independence. This type of symbol has not been lost on minority neighborhoods as they strive for economic advancement. The car is the quintessential symbol of making it into the middle class. The car represents independence and self-worth that may not be realized in other aspects of minority life in America. In Chester Himes's 1947 novel, *If He Hollers Let Him Go*, Bob Jones (an African American shipyard foreman) seems to find self-worth in racing his 1942 Buick against white workers along Alameda Street on his way to work in San Pedro. Similarly, the roots of the low riders in East and South Los Angeles can be traced directly to the parity and positive recognition that can be achieved with a car in relation to the larger society. Tracy Chapman, in the lyrics to "Fast Car," observes:

...You got a fast car
And we go cruising to entertain ourselves
You still ain't got a job
And I work in a market as a checkout girl
I know things will get better
You'll find work and I'll get promoted
We'll move out of the shelter
Buy a big house and live in the suburbs
You got a fast car...

While we, as planners and policy makers, place great emphasis on public-transit investment as a way to enhance the sustainability of the urban area, even the equitable distribution of transit service throughout the region is problematic, and the allocation of this vital mobility resource is often a function of the relative political power and savvy of neighborhoods within the region. The reality in Southern California is that transit will be, at best, a last-resort backstop and safeguard against the automobile's catastrophic failure to perform. Maybe that failure will be the scarcity of fossil fuel, or maybe the failure will be unbearable gridlock and congestion. Should public policy focus on how to ensure that there is no such failure and should it support the automobile's continued adaptation to changing circumstances? Or will market forces do the trick? The automobile (along with its emergent design and technology) is not an end in itself. It is a means to an end. It is the central support element

Thus, even amongst new cars, important differences in feature technology will likely accentuate access differences to advanced transportation infrastructure in the future.

Our challenge as policy makers is that automobile technology has not and may not ever be equitably dispersed throughout the consumer market, given vehicle price and the wide variety of makes, models, and ages of vehicles on the road.

necessary to realizing the mobility and accessibility that support quality of life in neighborhoods throughout the city. Our challenge as policy makers is that automobile technology has not and may not ever be equitably dispersed throughout the consumer market, given vehicle price and the wide variety of makes, models, and ages of vehicles on the road. Likewise, the rollout of "smart streets" and "intelligent highways" has historically been spotty. Priority is typically given to the areas of greatest congestion, or where transportation infrastructure systems receive the greatest political visibility. There are still portions of Los Angeles that have yet to see the City of Los Angeles Automated Traffic Surveillance and Control/Adaptive Traffic Control System at local intersections, or where the system has not been fully activated (good examples of this are intersections along Slauson Avenue, east of the Harbor Freeway, in South Los Angeles).

Undoubtedly, if the past provides us any clue, some neighborhoods will be better positioned to take advantage of improvements in automobile technology than others. With our love and attachment to the car in Southern California, as well as our dependence on it given our sprawled spatial landscape, it is naïve to assume that transit will be the great equalizer. The "haves" will have their smart cars, and the "have-nots" will have buses and light rail. But, they may not even have that. Transit may not reach the far corners of the city, where lower-income households (regardless of race) may be pushed by rising housing prices. Nor will transit satisfy the mobility independence that a car has historically provided to otherwise disenfranchised areas. It will be ironic that those neighborhoods with the longest journeys to work and services may have the most outmoded automobile technology and transportation infrastructure. Under these circumstances, the relative sustainability of neighborhoods in the city will be greatly strained.

It will be left to public transportation policy makers to achieve some level of acceptable parity between neighborhoods from a sustainable mobility perspective. This is a much-needed role in order to achieve social justice, but one simultaneously facing down both the dynamic and powerful forces of consumer automobile economics and the hardball politics of how infrastructure improvements are allocated within the city.

ROAD AND CONGESTION PRICING: TEN QUESTIONS ON THE PATH TO SUCCESS (OR FAILURE)

Steve Finnegan

DIRECT ROAD PRICING is increasingly being considered both as a way to manage the finite resource of road capacity at peak travel times and as a way to generate revenues that will pay for a variety of transportation projects and services. Direct road pricing proposals range from simple toll facilities (bridges and roads financed by toll revenues) that charge a set price for all users to more complex arrangements that vary the toll (or price paid) based on any number of factors, including time, day, congestion levels, number of occupants in the vehicle, or even type of vehicle.

People view road pricing in many different ways. Some see road pricing simply as a way to raise money—a de facto tax. Some see it as a way to inject market forces into travel decisions, thereby improving traffic flow when some motorists—in an effort to avoid tolls or peak congestion charges—choose other travel times, routes, or modes (or don't travel at all). Others see pricing as a way to charge more for driving in an effort to increase its relative cost compared to other modes, or to cover "externalities"—the real or perceived costs of driving not currently paid by motorists. And still others see road

pricing as unfair to low-income households, a threat to personal privacy, or wrong because motorists and taxpayers have already paid to build the roads.

Legitimate points can be made across the spectrum of thought and motivation in support of road pricing. However, despite substantial backing from planners and some policy makers, road pricing remains a controversial topic with many skeptics.

For road pricing to be implemented on a broad scale in the United States it will have to be supported by most people and elected officials. The following ten questions are the mile markers on possible paths to road pricing. The success—or failure—of road pricing proposals rides on how these questions are answered and how the issues raised in the questions are addressed. The outcome is in the hands of policy makers.

1. WHAT ARE THE OBJECTIVES?

This is the most important question. Objectives often discussed include less congestion and better mobility, new or increased revenues, and less driving (or vehicle miles traveled).

Using road pricing to improve mobility is perhaps the most understandable motivation for road pricing. Improved mobility, less congestion, faster travel speeds, and more predictable travel times are all widely supported objectives. If increased mobility is the core objective, then policy decisions need to be made and carried out to support and deliver this outcome.

If increased mobility is the core objective, then policy decisions need to be made and carried out to support and deliver this outcome.

Another primary motivator for road pricing proposals is revenue generation. Although this may be the most inherent and assured result of road pricing, it can only be achieved if the pricing proposal is accepted and implemented, and if there are enough drivers using the priced facility to generate expected revenues.

Reduced driving (and reduced personal mobility in most cases) is another motivation for road pricing. Reduced driving—in and of itself—is not likely to be accepted as a reasonable or beneficial goal if it reduces mobility, access to employment, commercial activity, services, recreation, or economic and social opportunities. These negative outcomes are a risk across broad swaths of many urbanized areas where convenient alternatives are not available for many trips, travel patterns, and needs.

2. WHAT'S IN IT FOR ME?

This is the essential, bottom-line question for most people: What value will motorists paying the charge receive? New lanes or capacity projects (such as the construction of the SR-91 express lanes in Orange County) have inherent value for those paying to use the lanes—the lanes would not exist without the toll revenue to pay for them. For conversion of existing lanes, the value question is more challenging. Some conversions can be relatively easy, like when the grossly under-utilized carpool lanes on I-15 in San Diego County were changed to high-occupancy toll (HOT) lanes. But adding tolls to existing, non-priced, general-purpose lanes is much harder for most people to accept. For any road-pricing proposal to be successful, there must be direct, recognizable benefits for motorists paying the toll and no adverse effects on those who are unwilling or unable to pay.

For any road-pricing proposal to be successful, there must be direct, recognizable benefits for motorists paying the toll and no adverse effects on those who are unwilling or unable to pay.

3. HOW WILL THE MONEY BE USED?

Despite other objectives, ultimately it's always about the money. Revenues derived from tolling should be used to improve mobility and benefit users within the corridor where the charges are collected. This can include paying for the capital costs of new priced lanes or routes, operating and maintaining the priced lanes, improving and expanding priced and parallel lanes and routes, and providing effective transit services.

4. WHAT ARE THE OPPORTUNITY COSTS OF ROAD PRICING?

The money paid by drivers for priced road facilities will no longer be available to be spent or invested elsewhere in the economy. This is the opportunity cost of redirecting these resources from other potential uses to tolls or congestion charges. In short, "there is no free lunch." For pricing to be successful and for society to benefit, the individual and societal value derived from imposing prices on roads (primarily in terms of better mobility) must meet or exceed the total value that could have been derived from other uses of those funds.

5. HOW AND WHAT ARE PROPONENTS OF ROAD PRICING COMMUNICATING?

Positive and negative impacts need to be realistically assessed and explained up-front, honestly, and in terms both policy makers and the public can understand. If the objective is to improve traffic flow by changing behavior (route, time, or mode of travel), then people need to understand the level of change that would be needed to accomplish the objective. That level of change needs to be realistic and still meet people's travel needs. Real, meaningful input needs to be obtained from current and future users—those who will be paying the charges—and incorporated into plans. Failure to do so will set pricing proposals back many years, as happened in the early development of carpool lanes: The public widely rejected the first high-occupancy vehicle (HOV) lanes, which had been converted from existing lanes.

6. WHAT ARE THE EQUITY IMPACTS?

How pricing affects people of varying incomes is an important issue that should not be swept aside. Oftentimes, equity concerns are addressed by overly simplistic assurances that even low-income drivers will pay for faster lanes when they really need to be someplace on time and that revenue from pricing will be used to pay for public transit, which is predominantly used by people with less money. We effectively have a two-tiered transportation system in most cases now—those who can afford to drive and those who can't. Pricing should not result in a three-tiered system based on wealth or income.

7. HOW MUCH SHOULD DRIVERS PAY, AND FOR WHAT?

This question has two parts. The first involves the amount and uses of taxes and fees currently and previously paid by motorists. The second involves how much motorists should pay in the future, and for what purposes.

Some argue that adding tolls to existing "free" lanes is essentially double taxation, because motorists have already paid taxes to build the roads. The issue is clearly more complicated than that, because the money used for transportation comes from multiple sources and because the United States has chronically underinvested in infrastructure for years. However, addressing this basic concern about an additional charge to motorists will have to be part of any serious pricing proposal.

There are many views regarding how much money motorists should pay in the future and how those funds should be used. For pricing proposals to be successful, the amounts and uses need to be reasonable, proportionate, and politically realistic. In addition, pricing cannot be used as a reason to allow existing transportation funds to be redirected to non-transportation uses.

For pricing proposals to be successful, the amounts and uses need to be reasonable, proportionate, and politically realistic.

8. DOES PRICING MEAN WE STOP BUILDING ROADS? IF NOT, HOW WILL WE STILL BUILD ROAD CAPACITY WHERE IT IS NEEDED AND POSSIBLE?

New road capacity for private and commercial passenger vehicles and the movement of goods will still be needed, and new roads can be built in some places. Pricing cannot be used as an excuse for not building needed and viable highway improvements, such as adding truck lanes to serve busy ports, widening two-lane rural roads to improve safety, addressing long-standing bottlenecks, and completing carpool-lane networks.

Pricing cannot be used as an excuse for not building needed and viable highway improvements.

9. CAN PRICING IMPROVE TRANSPORTATION PROJECT DECISION MAKING?

Some argue that pricing will result in better project selections because market forces and investment analysis will be used to choose projects. But how can this happen if the agencies and boards now charged with making transportation investment and policy decisions retain and continue to exercise their authority? Without more fundamental changes, transportation decisions will continue to be made by local, state, and federal elected and appointed officials who will continue to be influenced by myriad political pressures to build or not to build various projects. Pricing alone will not change this dynamic.

10. IS CONGESTION A TRUE "EXTERNALITY"?

Time wasted in congestion is often labeled an "externality" that needs to be internalized through pricing. However, during congestion, those imposing the costs of wasted time on others are also those paying the price of sitting in traffic. The time-value of congestion is already internalized to all users, although it is not monetized. Therefore, there may be limited or no external congestion time-cost to be captured by pricing.

However, economic theory and the "tragedy of the commons"[1] tell us that under-priced or under-controlled public resources can be over-consumed to the detriment of all. This was certainly the case when overgrazing by farm animals on the public common land of communities resulted in the over-consumption of edible resources and the ultimate starvation and death of livestock. The analogy has been extended to driving, with motorists over-consuming a limited amount of road capacity at any given time and place. But there are important differences. The "commons," in the case of driving, is road space that may be insufficient at any point, but that is never consumed in a way that eliminates it for future users. Although congestion is harmful and frustrating, ultimately people do get to their destinations.

Moreover, society has a big toolbox with many tools that can be used to maintain and improve mobility over time. These tools include building and improving roads (essentially expanding the commons), providing effective transit services, facilitating non-motorized travel, and using technology to both increase system performance and—in the near future, I hope—leap-frog over many of our problems. For example, the use of automated or semi-automated vehicles, such as the Google Car now on the road, can both substantially reduce congestion and, more importantly, dramatically improve safety.

The question now lies before us: Is road pricing a tool that will be employed to further mobility, and, if so, in what forms will it be acceptable for most people and their representative governments?

[1] G. Hardin, "The Tragedy of the Commons," *Science* 162: 1243–48 (1968).

HOW WE PRICE AUTOMOBILITY

Marco Anderson

OUR AUTOMOBILE TRANSPORTATION SYSTEM CONTAINS TWO MAIN COMPONENTS: individual vehicles and the infrastructure upon which those vehicles are driven. Beginning 60 years ago with the passage of the 1936 Federal Highways Act and culminating with the 1956 Federal Highways Bill, a social contract was developed by which roadways would be partly paid for through taxes on gasoline. This accomplished two goals: providing a proxy for a user fee that would be more comprehensive and easier to manage than locally collected, roadway-specific tolls, and linking operating costs to payment for the infrastructure system.[1] While most local roads have largely been paid for by local property and sales taxes, revenue from the fixed gasoline tax has diminished over the last 30 years due to inflation and increased fuel efficiency.[2] An increase in the complication and expense of road planning and construction, and in the cost of vehicle licensing, has led to a complicated and diffuse system for paying for the total cost of driving. Policy conversations are already taking place at metropolitan planning organizations, and at the federal and state levels, to radically reform the system. However, changing a paradigm that has evolved over 80 years will be challenging.

From the individual's perspective, the total cost of driving, or automobility, is the cumulative amount spent yearly on the lease or purchase of a car, plus fuel, insurance, registration fees, parking, tolls, repairs, and depreciation. From a region-wide perspective, the total cost of automobility is the cumulative amount spent over the lifetime of the system on planning, design, construction, safety, administration, and maintenance. Private sector forces, influenced by an underlying framework of public policies, determine the total amount of money available to pay for our cars and roads.

In Southern California today, the cost of automobility has been defined independently of alternative forms of transportation. Therefore, the stated price of the entire system of cars and roads does not reflect the fact that cars and their infrastructure diminish the viability of other forms of transit and cost us time and stress spent in traffic. Any alternatives to cars have been rendered irrelevant in Southern California over the course of the past 50 years. However, significant investment in alternatives to the automobile beginning over the past 25 years have begun to change that. The increased relevance of all modes of mobility (and their interplay) will upend the hegemony of the car and car infrastructure over the next 50 years in the denser areas of our region. How we determine the cost—and how we pay for all the various modes, cars included—will have a bearing on how attractive non-automotive modes will be to future users.

The stated price of the entire system of cars and roads does not reflect the fact that cars and their infrastructure diminish the viability of other forms of transit and cost us time and stress spent in traffic.

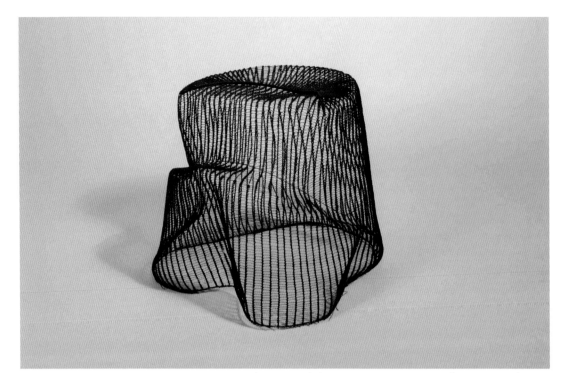

The Hat of a Bureaucrat: Gentleman's Hat (tanggeon) / Korea, Joseon dynasty (1392—1910), 20th century. Horse hair and bamboo. Pacific Asia Museum Collection, 1972.30.6.

The pricing strategies that have evolved over the past 50 years will continue to evolve in the future. Looking at how we paid for mobility 50 years ago, and again 25 years ago, certain assumptions and best guesses can lead us to see at least a hazy picture of the pricing strategies of the near future of 2035. One certainty emerges: The trend has been towards the privatization of the determining prices of automobility. In other words, automobiles depend almost entirely on public-policy structure (and public roadways), but private markets determine most of the prices we pay.

Automobiles depend almost entirely on public-policy structure... but private markets determine most of the prices we pay.

THE HISTORY OF USER COSTS

The full picture of how we pay for mobility (automobility and other modes) is much more complicated than other consumer products, because there are so many components that are all priced and paid for in different ways. For example, in the case of automobility, there are the sunk costs of purchasing a vehicle; ongoing finance costs for purchasing the vehicle; various operating costs, including insurance, maintenance, and fuel; and, finally, the hidden cost of depreciation. In the future, technology will influence each of these pricing mechanisms in a number of ways. The questions are: Will the new pricing strategies support adequate access to mobility for a broad enough range of the population? Will they ensure a distribution of cost for mobility that is equitable? And will they make other modes of transportation viable?

In the last 50 years we have seen dramatic changes not only in automobility, but also in its pricing strategy and structure. In 1962, car ownership in the United States was significant at 41% per capita, and obviously on the rise, but hardly universal. Ownership seems to have peaked in 2007 at 82% per capita.[3] In Los Angeles, the Pacific Electric Streetcar system ceased operation in 1961 due to declining ridership. Bus ridership served a sizeable proportion of the public, especially among low-income and minority populations. Car loans were not as common as they are today. It could be said that General Motors used to be a car company that sometimes helped its customers buy cars, but that now (when measured by profit sectors) GM is a bank that manufactures and distributes cars in order to produce loans.[4] In 1962, drivers paid for their gas and insurance with cash. Twenty-five years later, in 1987, drivers paid with checks. In 2012, drivers generally pay with credit or debit cards. First invented in 1932, parking meters have changed from individual, coin-operated mechanical devices to electronic, wired, smart-payment stations that access online accounts.

Major changes in pricing strategy occur when the private sector sees an opportunity to make more profit out of a new method of payment. In the case of financing automobility, banks and lenders are able to make more profit over time on a car loan than they are by letting the consumer drive out the door with the capital. New methods of payment are attractive to those setting prices because they make purchasing easier and more appealing to the consumer, resulting in more sales. They can also result in lower administrative costs for the producer. For example, in the past 30 years there has been a steady progression in the availability of, first, fuel company credit cards (Exxon, Gulf, Shell) that were run by hand, then general credit cards, and finally ATM cards read at the pump as methods of payment for gas. In Southern California, low-cost ARCO stations impose a $.45-per-transaction charge for using any method other than cash—a rare reminder of a time when the cost of the transaction and the cost of the product where not bundled.

Major changes in pricing strategy occur when the private sector sees an opportunity to make more profit out of a new method of payment.

The result of adding cost to the *method* of paying for fuel, as opposed to the fuel itself, is that it prevents the user from grasping the per-mile costs of automobility. Many people may factor their insurance and fuel costs into their vehicle purchase decisions. They probably also calculate the fuel and parking costs of their commutes, or compare usage costs for a long trip against an alternative like flying. However, I would argue that fewer people think about fuel costs for short trips, and fewer still are able to factor all of the costs, such as depreciation, into all general travel decisions. There are too many moving parts to understand.

THE FUTURE OF PRICING

The technological ability to break down each small transaction required for individual mobility into smaller and smaller increments will have a significant impact on mobility choice at large. For example, advances in the technology of paying for private, on-demand mobility (such as summoning a car by pressing a button on a phone) has the potential to stimulate a significant increase in the number of customers for taxis and short-term rental cars. But technological barriers have made it difficult to get the vehicles in the fleet to the customers who need them as quickly as they would like them. Providers are also faced with the challenge of collecting payment quickly enough to provide timely service without incurring excessive risk. Most car-sharing systems require registration and membership. Renting a car to an individual requires establishing trust between the consumer and the car-sharing company, and a membership registration allows the company to establish the credit and risk-worthiness of the driver. But universal on-demand mobility requires a much more streamlined process of establishing that relationship in real time.

One scenario for widespread car sharing envisioned cars with credit card swiping capabilities. This seems entirely within the realm of possibility, since many stores and restaurants no longer require a signature when paying by credit card. This demonstrates that the ease of payment on the part of the consumer is worth a risk to the seller, overriding the prior model under which providing your signature made it harder for someone to steal your credit card. However, card-swiping machines need maintenance so another technology may supersede card swiping over the next 25 to 50 years—cellular phone banking and other digital moneys.

Being able to order up a driverless car (or a bicycle, for that matter) and pay for it using a smartphone is a wonderful image for 2035, but it won't really help a person who doesn't have a bank account.

GM's OnStar recently entered this market by partnering with a peer-to-peer car-sharing service.[5] This shift raises important equity concerns as payment methods become predicated on having access to technology investments and credit. Being able to order up a driverless car (or a bicycle, for that matter) and pay for it using a smartphone is a wonderful image for 2035, but it won't really help a person who doesn't have a bank account.

Again, the social contract is being redefined. At some point, enough of "us" have access to a technology that it becomes accepted as the norm. At that point those who do not have that access are considered marginal, and society only expects basic accommodation to be made for their needs. Paying income taxes is becoming more enabled by technology every year, as well as registering and paying for your car on the Internet. Some people will still line up at the Department of Motor Vehicles to renew their car registration with cash and checks, but using a phone to pay for products at the point of sale will become ubiquitous even if debit cards, credit cards, and cash do not entirely disappear. When that happens, one answer will be to provide public-access computers at public libraries and to offer limited government assistance that enables people to obtain enough financial literacy to marginally engage in the digital economy.

Another major innovation currently being discussed is pay-as-you-drive (PAYD) insurance. The common concern with PAYD insurance is that consumers are worried about a Big Brother effect, since insurers will be able to record data about drivers' whereabouts and could potentially provide that information to the state. However, experience has shown that consumer concerns are trumped by significant ease of use or savings gains.[6] But at least for now, there is little incentive for insurance providers to push pay-as-you-drive insurance (and its attendant collecting of personal data) because the insurance companies are limited by statute from making any profit from the extra data reaped from pay-as-you-drive technology. Regulation in California states that the only factors that

For many years in our region, driving an automobile has become an economic necessity and therefore can be argued to be a right.

companies can consider for setting insurance rates are your zip code, your years driving, and your credit rating. These factors are really proxies for other actuarial data that are still strictly regulated. The intent behind such regulation is to avoid punishing individuals for their driving habits, but in effect this is a deeply flawed model. For example, the zip code where you live is a signifier for the risk of theft, but it says nothing about where you do most of your driving. If regulations were changed, the pay-as-you-go model would result in "fairer" rates that were customized to individual consumers' driving.

With the rise of plug-in hybrids and electric vehicles, fuel prices are also poised to change dramatically. Utility companies are already offering special pricing plans to encourage nighttime charging, in order to avoid overloading the grid. Now, attention has turned to developing a business model that will facilitate owners charging their vehicles at work, at shopping malls, and at home—even if they live in multi-tenant buildings. Smartphones, smart meters, and the smart grid will all need to communicate with each other in order for this system to work. The most promising model is that of a subscription fee for using a particular charging network, but this raises issues of inconvenience if different charging stations are exclusive. Work-based charging requires businesses to grapple with a business model that will allow employers to recoup energy costs and avoid being accused of subsidizing some employees' fuel costs and not others'.[7]

PUBLIC POLICY AND PRICING

Pricing strategies all have consequences to the fairness of cost, as it is manifest across different income groups. This gets to the issue that, for many years in our region, driving an automobile has become an economic necessity and therefore can be argued to be a right. Any impediments to universal access to driving, be it roadway pricing or more stringent licensing standards, are seen as a regressive tax on the poor, on minority communities, and on undocumented immigrants. Therefore, public policy has an important role to play in how we price mobility.

Public policy has resisted roadway pricing in Southern California, as well as pay-as-you-drive insurance in the state. However, challenges to the status quo on these issues have come from both the left and the right. First, there is agreement on the part of both liberal and conservative transportation policy makers on the efficacy and fairness of pricing as a policy lever. Moreover, there is agreement from all sides that the process of funding mobility is completely broken, and that future enhancement and maintenance is dependent on new sources of financing. The locally approved Southern California Association of Governments 2012–2035 Regional Transportation Plan includes the eventual introduction of vehicle-miles-traveled financing, called user fees. This language was heavily discussed for over a year, with many economic, social equity, and public funding issues brought up at the regional council meetings. It was adopted as a necessary solution for ensuring a good state of repair for regional roads.[8]

The distribution of local tax-based funding for local streets has also resulted in the strikingly uneven quality of roadway surface conditions across our region, according to the economy of the area. In essence, the social contract in some parts of the region results in the implication that you get the road conditions you deserve, meaning the locally maintained road conditions that you pay for.[9] In the ultimate example of privatization, the comfort of your journey is a function of not only where you drive—such as, in wealthy neighborhoods with smooth roads—but also how much you have paid for the suspension of your vehicle. Countless advertisements for SUVs over the past 20 years have shown them conquering the urban jungle, rolling through potholes and over speed bumps. With wealth, you can drive comfortably over smooth road surfaces and, with a large suspension system, over bumpy ones too.[10]

One complication among many is that both social equity advocates and anti-tax advocates believe that charging people to use existing infrastructure is unfair. As noted above, taxing fuel (even if indexed) is also problematic because, due to the increased fuel efficiency of vehicles, the linkage between fuel tax and system usage is largely disconnected. In other words, the driver of an efficient vehicle does not necessarily pay more fuel tax, despite inflicting more wear and tear on road infrastructure. On the other hand, a person with an old, inefficient car may end up, by economic necessity, contributing more pollution, purchasing more fuel, and paying more fuel tax than he or she can afford. For the sake of argument, if it can be agreed that driving (at least in

The low-income individual driver who cannot bear his or her own share of the trip cost becomes an economic liability (consuming infrastructure while not paying for it) instead of an asset.

In the case of pricing, the usual order of things is reshuffled: It is the rare case where new technology leads to policy and market acceptance follows from there.

Southern California) is a right on the grounds of economic necessity, then the low-income individual driver who cannot bear his or her own share of the trip cost becomes an economic liability (consuming infrastructure while not paying for it) instead of an asset. Rather, that cost should be spread as equitably as possible throughout the region. But this goes against the reality presented by new technologies for metering and paying for driving. Because of the potential of smart technology to be a powerful tool for designing pricing strategy and influencing driver behavior, the opportunity to extract money from tolls and roadway pricing may simply be too compelling for policymakers desperate to find revenue for road maintenance and construction. Much of this book operates under the theory that design innovations precede market acceptance, and that policies and regulations follow from use. However, in the case of pricing, the usual order of things is reshuffled: It is the rare case where new technology leads to policy and market acceptance follows from there.

Some researchers see converging forces pushing the automobility market toward a service-based model.[11] If fully automated, autonomous shared vehicles become widely available. And if the trend continues for young drivers to be disinterested in vehicle ownership, then it is easy to imagine a future scenario in which people pay for mobility-as-a-service, paying a monthly fee for access and per-mile charges for usage. The transitional pricing and payment schemes that will lead us down that path are currently under development.

[1] Brian D. Taylor, "When Finance Leads Planning: Urban Planning, Highway Planning, and Metropolitan Freeways in California," *Journal of Planning Education and Research* 20(2), 2000: 196–214.

[2] Southern California Association of Governments, "2012–2035 Regional Transportation Plan / Sustainable Communities Strategy," 2012.

[3] Joyce Dargay, Dermot Gately and Martin Sommer, "Vehicle ownership and income growth, worldwide: 1960–2030." Institute for Transport Studies, University of Leeds, 2007.

[4] Kai Ryssdal and Jeremy Hobson, *Marketplace Morning Report*, 2011.

[5] Andrew G. Simpson, "GM's OnStar Car Owners Now Able to Rent Out Their Vehicles," *Insurance Journal* (July 17, 2012), retrieved September 15, 2012.

[6] "We're just going to market with a type of telematic device for people who want pay-by-mile insurance. But if they get into a collision, the Auto Club—whom they trust—is keeping track of them, so people are flocking to it" (Steve Mazor, Auto Club of Southern California, in conversation with the author, winter 2011).

[7] Brett Williams, JR. DeShazo, and Ayala Ben-Yehuda, "Early Plug-in Electric Vehicle Sales: Trends, Forecasts, and Determinants," prepared for the Southern California Association of Governments, d04, University of California, Los Angeles, Luskin Center for Innovation, 2012, www.luskin.edu/ev.

[8] Southern California Association of Governments, "2012–2035 Regional Transportation Plan / Sustainable Communities Strategy," 2012.

[9] Todd Litman, "Evaluating Bicyclists' and Pedestrians' Right to Use Public Roadways," Victoria Transport Policy Institute, 2012.

[10] Any car or truck commercial from the 1990s shows this focus on the urban warrior theme, complete with fine print "Driver on closed course, do not attempt." Even before, European automakers Audi, BMW, Volvo, and Volkswagen had experience building weather-resistant features into sedans and station wagons in the 1970s. They used the sport of rally car racing as their test bed for suspension improvements. Only later did they enter the SUV market with full-sized models. U.S. auto designers, on the other hand, opted to introduce those features into their trucks and vans instead, creating the sport utility vehicle market of the 1980s to present day. One recent trend is toward "crossovers," with the look of a more rugged vehicle on a car chassis.

[11] Transportation Research Board, "Proceedings of the 2012 Road Vehicle Automation Workshop," Irvine, California, 2012.

THE IMPACT OF AUTONOMOUS VEHICLES ON CAR INSURANCE

Alan Dobbins

THE PERSONAL AUTO INSURANCE MARKET has benefitted from a long stream of vehicle technology advances, including safety features, driver monitoring/recording, event recorders, and location tracking. The next generation of technological innovation is at a different level, however, with emerging technology potentially coming between the driver and actual driving decisions. Advancing technology and the advent of semi-autonomous vehicles—and even fully autonomous vehicles ("driverless cars")—have the potential to change not only driving, but also the nature of liability coverage, confusing first-party liability issues with product-liability issues.

ADVANCES IN ONBOARD VEHICLE INFORMATION GATHERING

Over the last decade, information-gathering technology has been an area of rapid development for both vehicle manufacturers and technology companies. The use of onboard information-gathering technology has evolved considerably since its introduction in the early 1980s, with simple malfunction indicator lights. An array of technologies is now available, from onboard black box and global positioning system (GPS) devices to video monitoring.

+ Progressive's Snapshot technology is an onboard monitoring device that plugs into the vehicle's onboard diagnostics (OBD) port, capturing the number of miles driven, time of day, rates of acceleration and braking, and vehicle speed. Customers load the device for 30 days, after which the company reviews the data to assess eligibility for insurance discounts and assigns an initial discount.

+ The DriveCam technology from American Family is a video event recorder mounted on the windshield. Hard braking, swerving, and other unexpected behaviors cause the recorder to save 20 seconds of audio and video footage—the ten seconds immediately before and after the triggered event. Recorded information can be used to identify patterns of behavior and to analyze which patterns represent higher-risk driving.

+ 21st Century's Mobile Teen GPS program allows parents of teen drivers to monitor the youthful driver's location and driving via telephone or Internet. Using a small GPS unit in the insured's vehicle, parents can instantly determine its exact location. According to the company, the Mobile Teen GPS program will alert the parent with an e-mail or text message if the teen's car exceeds predefined speed or mileage limitations.

All of these technologies—onboard data collection devices, cameras, and GPS units—can provide significant advantages to both the insured and the insurer, in that they deliver the ability to identify and correct risky driving habits and thus potentially lower claim costs for the company and premiums for the consumer.

FUTURE OPPORTUNITIES FOR INSURERS

People are becoming increasingly comfortable with technology inserting itself into all aspects of their lives—including driving. They are also becoming increasingly comfortable with this technology gathering and using their personal data. Perhaps Facebook and Twitter have made consumers more at ease with sharing information, but it extends beyond that to store reward cards, GPS monitoring, and sharing of Internet search histories.

The increasing comfort with which consumers are surrendering private information is creating opportunities for insurers. One area opening up is the usage-based/pay-as-you-drive insurance model. Usage-based insurance is not new, but it gathered steam when Progressive began to pursue the concept aggressively in the mid-1990s. Usage-based insurance started as a basic concept with simple odometer readings, but with a significant push from Progressive it has ballooned into a number of different technologies that provide information to insurers. While several versions of this concept exist—from odometer readings to telematics to video monitoring—these approaches all lead toward greater insight into actual driving behaviors, moving from proxy data to actual driving-risk data.

Acceptance of the usage-based/pay-as-you-drive model is improving driver safety as well as providing exponential growth in both the amount and specificity of data available to insurers. Using telematics-based, pay-as-you-drive approaches pushes this forward several steps. Progressive describes the jump as follows: Traditional rating variables provide perhaps 50 data points for risk

The increasing comfort with which consumers are surrendering private information is creating opportunities for insurers.

These approaches all lead toward greater insight into actual driving behaviors, moving from proxy data to actual driving-risk data.

analysis and pricing. The introduction of credit-based insurance scores expanded the rating data set by about two orders of magnitude—from 50 data points to perhaps an additional 2,000 data elements. Now, however, with the company's onboard monitoring device, Progressive collects about 1,000 data points per trip:

So we're at 2,000 today on our current model. One trip, we have 1,000 new data points. Over a single term of driving that equates to about 750,000 data points. There's a vast, rich source of data that, instead of being closer to proxies for how you drive, like how old you are, is actually measuring the driving behavior we are interested in. That is a great new source of data.

As indicated in the figure at right, each of these advances moves the insurer further along the rating-variable sophistication continuum, increasing the specificity of the rating-variable content and the speed of regularity with which that information is delivered.

The traditional application-based underwriting information provided a snapshot of the risk under consideration. The next evolution in risk assessment, including credit-based information and other predictive analytics, provided additional data and greater insight into the policyholder's (or potential policyholder's) risk profile, and provided it as updatable data—a series of snapshots over time. Telematics and other forms of onboard information-gathering

AUTO INSURANCE RATING SOPHISTICATION CONTINUUM

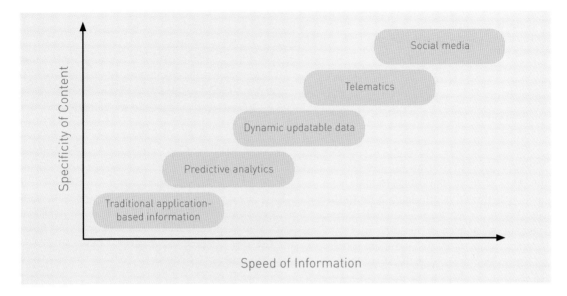

technologies take a step beyond regularly updatable risk-assessment variables to a real-time data set—moving from "more data" to "more access" to "real-time" insight.

Telematics and other forms of onboard information-gathering technologies take a step beyond regularly updatable risk-assessment variables to a real-time data set—moving from "more data" to "more access" to "real-time" insight.

THE DRIVERLESS CAR

Advances noted thus far focus on information being gathered about the car and the driver. Automakers and technology companies are now moving the information-gathering targets from inside the vehicle (car and driver) to outside the vehicle (traffic, hazards, roads, and other vehicles).

In February 2012, Ford Motor Company Executive Chairman Bill Ford outlined his vision for an interconnected transportation network in which pedestrians, bicycles, cars, and buses would be connected, with benefits for traffic congestion and safety. The vision is to create a global transportation network that utilizes communication between vehicles, transport infrastructure, and individual mobile devices.

The Ford vision includes:

+ The development of intuitive, in-car mobile communications that proactively alert drivers to traffic jams and accidents (estimated availability: 2017–19)

+ Increased capability for vehicle-to-vehicle warning systems and intelligent speed-control features (estimated availability: 2015–17).

+ The introduction of semi-autonomous driving technology, including driver-initiated "auto pilot" capabilities providing driver assistance features but still allowing the driver to take control, if needed (estimated availability: 2017–25).[1]

Ford, however, is not even the leader in pursuing this vision. Volvo, BMW, and Mercedes-Benz are already publicizing computer-aided vehicle control, introducing accident-avoidance technologies that allow the car's computer systems to take over control of the vehicle in certain emergency situations.

Volvo has deployed its City Safety technology as a standard feature in the Volvo S60, S80, XC70, and XC90. The European auto manufacturer notes that 75% of all reported collisions occur at speeds less than 20 mph, and that half of these occur in city traffic. To help reduce the consequences of low-speed collisions, Volvo's City Safety infrared laser sensor can determine whether the driver is approaching a vehicle too fast from behind. If the driver fails to react in time, the City Safety will automatically apply the brakes in order to slow down the car and avoid a collision.

Volvo has also developed pedestrian detection with full auto-brake capabilities. This feature can detect pedestrians and automatically avoid collisions at speeds up to 22 mph. The driver is alerted by a sound signal together with a flashing light in the windshield's head-up display. In order to prompt an immediate, intuitive reaction, the visual warning is designed to look like a brake light coming on. If the driver does not respond to the warning and the system assesses that a collision is about to happen, the car's brakes are applied with full force. The car only brakes if it is too late to steer away and applies the brakes less than a second before the calculated impact time.[2]

The Volvo technologies are designed to reduce both the frequency of collisions, by avoiding crashes, and the severity of collisions, through decreased impact speeds.

This creates the potential to involve technology in the car to predict adverse driving behavior and either correct for the behavior or create an alert—preventing dangerous driving and accidents.

BMW ConnectedDrive offers similar assistance, with a collision warning that is activated when a lead vehicle stops short. The car reacts immediately: In stage 1, it sends the driver an optical warning, and in stage 2 (if the driver has not reacted), an acoustic signal calls attention to the situation. If the driver still does not react and brake, the ConnectedDrive takes over and initiates braking. BMW ConnectedDrive only takes control of your driving at the decisive moment, when accident prevention is the issue.[3] Mercedes Benz expects its new S-Class to provide similar functionality, with autonomous driving capabilities, by 2013.

A few car companies have experimented with facial recognition technology—tracking the driver's facial movements in the vehicle. This technology is actually quite evolved and is developing the ability to identify a "pre-crash face"—the nonverbal pattern that occurs seconds before the driver exhibits bad behavior, including swerving, lane violations, and collisions. This creates the potential to involve technology in the car to predict adverse driving behavior and either correct for the behavior or create an alert— preventing dangerous driving and accidents.

The company that is perhaps closest to accelerating the future of driverless technology is not even a car company: Google has developed a fully self-driving Prius, which has already been tested at speeds up to 75 mph in traffic. It is estimated that human error accounts for upwards of 90% of all vehicle crashes, and the Google Prius removes the human element from the equation: The robot car can think faster, process more information, and react more quickly and with less emotion than any human driver.[4]

THE IMPACT ON AUTOMOBILE INSURANCE

Autonomous-vehicle, driver-assistance, and vehicle-to-vehicle technologies have the potential to radically improve transportation safety and efficiency, with tremendous social and economic benefits. The impact on automobile insurance is less clear.

Brian Sullivan's *Auto Insurance Report* has been sounding the alarm for a couple of years that improving claims frequency will limit growth in the personal auto insurance market. The logic is that fewer claims limit the ability of insurers to raise prices—and therefore limit growth.

A Rand Corporation study on the impacts of the more advanced vehicle safety technologies takes this argument one step further, noting that if these technologies are particularly effective at reducing crashes, they may obviate the need for specialized auto insurance and allow other policies to pick up coverage—perhaps a health policy or a homeowners policy—as one would for a bicycle accident.

Another impact on the auto insurance market is that these advances toward autonomous vehicles will dramatically reduce first-party liability and increase the subrogation opportunities against the manufacturer for product liability—shifting responsibility for driving from the driver to the vehicle itself. Under current law, the driver is assigned exclusive responsibility for control of the vehicle.

Autonomous vehicle technologies will likely dilute the sense that drivers are directly and solely responsible for their automobiles. By shifting responsibility for the automobile from the human driver to the car or its manufacturer, these systems are likely to undermine the conventional social attribution of blame for automobile crashes.

—Nidhi Kalra, James Anderson, and Martin Wachs, "Liability and Regulation of Autonomous Vehicle Technologies," Rand Study, 2009

The reduction in crashes caused by human error (which is the proximate cause of the vast majority of crashes, be it from recognition error, decision error, or performance error) should drive adoption of these technologies. But, according to the Rand Corporation, the prospect of increasing liability now facing manufacturers may stall the integration of this technology into automobiles. A manufacturer facing a decision as to whether to employ such a technology in its vehicles might very well decide not to, purely on the basis of expected liability costs.

Autonomous vehicles will shift responsibility for driving from the driver to the vehicle itself.

[1] Ford Media.

[2] Volvo website for the S60 features.

[3] BMW ConnectedDrive [CDC system website].

[4] *Wired* magazine.

EPILOGUE:

THE CAR OF THE FUTURE DRAWN FROM MEMORY

AND A TRAFFIC UTOPIA THAT NEVER HAPPENED

John Chris Jones

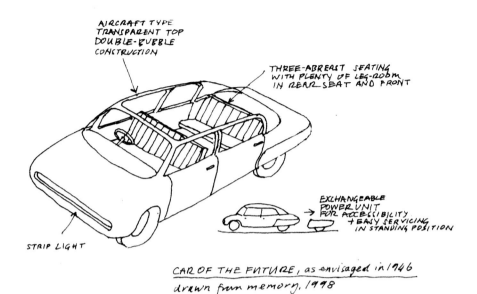

AIRCRAFT TYPE
TRANSPARENT TOP
DOUBLE-BUBBLE
CONSTRUCTION

THREE-ABREAST SEATING
WITH PLENTY OF LEG-ROOM
IN REAR SEAT AND FRONT

EXCHANGEABLE
POWER UNIT
FOR ACCESSIBILITY
+ EASY SERVICING
IN STANDING POSITION

STRIP LIGHT

CAR OF THE FUTURE, as envisaged in 1946
drawn from memory, 1998

A car of the future, as envisaged in 1946 (drawn from memory in 1998).

Jonathan encouraged me to make a drawing of the "car of the future"... This is the first time I've drawn it—what I sent to the competition in 1946 was a balsa wood model.

PART 1: THE CAR OF THE FUTURE

OVER THE YEARS SINCE 1946, I've been watching car design to see if it has followed my prediction, and by now it very nearly has (apart from the adequate leg room for passengers and the detachable power unit capable of being serviced by a mechanic in a comfortable posture while the car owner drives off with a newly serviced one).

Does this mean that the future forms of cars and similar hardware can easily be inferred from their present forms, fifty years ahead? I guess it does. And it also means, I suppose, that improvements proposed for people without economic power (in this case the backseat passengers and the motor mechanics) are far less likely to be realized.

Looking now at this attempt of 1946 I realize that it lacks any trace of the traffic automation (in which cars and buses are replaced by automatic taxis and minibuses finding their own way through a city without congestion) that took hold of my thinking once I'd experienced some of the early computers, around 1957. Nor does this 1946 vision take account of the traffic accidents, parking problems, noise, air pollution, etc. which by now are turning many people against the car, though as yet there is no good alternative. My car of the future doesn't even have seat belts, and I had no conception of urban motorways, parking meters, or multistory car parks!

*I conclude from this that, while it is easy to extrapolate existing designs and trends, it is difficult or even inherently impossible to anticipate how future people will react to misuses and side effects. It seems to me now that determinism is a fact for as long as existing forms and attitudes can be stretched to accommodate the effects of increased numbers. But eventually, when the whole situation becomes so negative that people actually change their minds and motivations, the future becomes indeterminate and unpredictable (as perhaps it is at present). Especially when the rigid technology of wheels is supplemented by the flexible micro-technology of electronics. For "all things become possible" if we are willing to change habits.

—jcj march 1998 (slightly edited 2011)

PART 2: TRAFFIC AUTOMATION: A UTOPIA THAT NEVER HAPPENED

The central point of this proposal was to reject the present mixture of cars, buses, taxis, roads, traffic lights, traffic police, car parks, traffic meters, etc. as a hopeless failure, with its notorious "insoluble" problems of congestion, parking and traffic accidents, not to mention pollution, etc., and the attempts to solve the problem by adding the urban highways and the multistory car parks that create "the concrete jungle." I took the first three of these problems of high-density traffic and asked myself if there were other kinds of crowded movements in which such problems do not occur. What came to mind were the movements of swarms of bees, flights of migrating birds, and the complex movements of people walking in all directions across a railway station plaza without slowing down, without colliding with each other, and without clogging the space with empty vehicles!

Why, I asked myself, are people in road vehicles so unable to travel smoothly and safely in high density when birds, insects, and people on their feet can do so easily? The answer, I thought, is "information." Because the professions then responsible for city traffic (civil engineers, police, lawmakers, and vehicle designers—this was in 1959) were each trying to solve the problem piecemeal by the inappropriate methods of pouring concrete, enforcing laws, and making feeble attempts to reduce the size and parkability, but not the number, of cars. The right solution, I felt sure, was to give to each driver and vehicle sufficient information and freedom of action to be able to steer clear of congestion before it became excessive, and to free everyone from parking difficulties by making each vehicle automatic enough to find its own way to the next people wanting to move, once its present occupants had got out. The automatic control of vehicles, through a magnetic

What came to mind were the movements of swarms of bees, flights of migrating birds, and the complex movements of people walking in all directions across a railway station plaza without slowing down.

tape embedded in the road, would remove the need for traffic lights and would make traffic collisions almost impossible. Car parks could be eliminated and the utilization of vehicles could rise from, say, five percent, as at present, to perhaps ninety percent, as each vehicle would be moving most of the time, thus freeing up most of the curb space for getting in and out wherever you wish and perhaps reducing the need to manufacture so many cars in the first place.

The result of this thinking was a scheme for complete traffic automation, which could be introduced in easy stages over the twenty years from about 1960 to 1980, and would gradually reduce the main features of the traffic problem to nearly nil provided that the users of cars, taxis, and buses could be persuaded to abandon their present vehicles for small automatic cars and minibuses that could be called to any phone or (transformed) parking meter from which the traveler indicated his or her position and destination. Each traveler would be given an expected arrival time at the destination, depending on the density of traffic, and if this was excessive would have the choice of cancelling the request until a quicker journey became possible. In this way, I proposed to provide each of the millions of minds presently immobilized by information

scarcity the means to use its own intelligence, as in the case of birds, bees, and people walking on a plaza. This is what I call true decentralization, or constructive anarchy. I think control from the center is barbaric. It's useful only in emergencies.

*There's more to this scheme but I think I've said enough to show why I reject altogether the "bad design" of city traffic, and indeed of industrial life as we know it, and why the kinds of solutions I seek, though so beautifully fitting in theory, are so very difficult to realize. They cut against the vested interest of each of us in our specialized, paid, or sanctified roles as car owner, investor, car worker, civil engineer, policeman, lawyer, parking attendant, taxi driver, bus driver, etc., and they call for a scale of thinking, and of collective responsibility, that is far beyond what is encouraged in the culture as it is. Yes, it's courage we need, the courage to "tackle the whole," but without imposing our preconceptions, and to live out the probably amazing consequences of doing so decentrally and without control. "I made it without an idea," said Marcel Duchamp, referring to *The Large Glass*, his central work. What I'm describing is I think art, the art of technology, unthreatening and free, the spirit of the time. Why not?

**However, all is not hopeless. Since about 1960, when the scheme became technically feasible (using the kind of electronics which were then being developed for the space program) many electronic fragments of the scheme have appeared piecemeal: the linking of traffic lights permitting tidal flow, automatic control of the distance between vehicles, electronic maps in cars to show congestion, parking places, etc. Unfortunately, these bits and pieces are being allied with ideas, such as road pricing, automatic surveillance, and central control, that show none of the equality and trust that are possible if these sub-solutions are linked together in a cybernetic and democratic anti-plan for collective intelligence, such as "true" traffic automation allows. Again: the need to change our minds. When will it happen? And where is the selfless kind of non-directive leadership that could make

Many electronic fragments of the scheme have appeared piecemeal: the linking of traffic lights permitting tidal flow, automatic control of the distance between vehicles, electronic maps in cars to show congestion, parking places, etc.

it possible? I believe they're to be found in the work of socially minded artists like John Cage and Joseph Beuys and in the unspoken thoughts of many.

PART 3: CREATIVE DEMOCRACY

My website "softopia" (www.publicwriting.net) includes longer and more fictional versions of these thoughts in which I am exploring the possibility that such utopias as traffic automation are attainable only if we simulta-neously tackle what is wrong with the whole of industrial life, with its many "insoluble" problems... and if at the same time we de-specialize and accept new and wider roles shared with intelligent software, and begin to practice what I call *creative democracy*. A semi-fictional work-in-progress at http://www.publicwriting.net/2.2/creative_democracy.html (or search words "public writing" "creative democracy").

REFERENCES

J. Christopher Jones, "A Credible Future for City Traffic," in *Technological Forecasting*, Edinburgh University Press, Edinburgh, 1969, 369–88. A detailed analysis of the functions of road traffic, and this proposal for traffic automation, as submitted to the New Roads for London competition in 1959.

John Chris Jones, "the future of breathing," in *designing designing*, Architecture Design and Technology Press, London, 1991, xvii–xlv. Copyright has reverted to the author. This is an essay on "my life with the car," and a correspondence with Edwin Schlossberg and Erwin van Handenhoven, in wide-ranging discussions of traffic automation, with extensive references.

John Chris Jones, *the internet and everyone*, ellipsis, London, 2000. Copyright has reverted to the author from whom copies may be obtained by writing to jcj @ public-writing.net. The preceding text and drawing are edited and shortened versions of pages 210–211 and 46–50.

FLEET TRANSFORMATION TIME LINE

HISTORY & PROJECTIONS

The Car Future Group

THIS TIME LINE of interrelated facts, figures, dates, and events delineates changes to the car and its context over the past 150 years. This time line is by no means exhaustive or comprehensive, but it provides a springboard for speculating about the future of the car in the next 25 to 40 years.

One notion for how cars change is as follows: Advances in technology push forward the design of cars and their accessories. Next, purchasing decisions about new products inform subsequent phases of manufacturing and design. Meanwhile, policy and regulations moderate these forces. But how the automobile has changed in the past and will change in the future depends not only on advances in technology, but also on a broader range of forces that shape the entire transportation system. Thus the time line is organized according to the three broad categories that comprise this book as a whole: The Car, The Street, and Policy.

One of the highly anticipated innovations of the future is the self-driving vehicle. Designers, engineers, business managers, policy makers, and consumers all have a stake in speculating about the shifts that might occur as a result of autonomous technologies. Their assumptions for how quickly and radically transportation might change are based on the revolutionary precedent of smart phones and tablets. However, cars and computers develop in entirely different cycles.[1] Adapting the fast-paced development cycle of communications technology to the slow and painstaking development of new cars can be a challenge for technology companies used to cannibalizing their own products every two to three years.[2]

In trying to anticipate the future of cars, streets, and policy, it's important to note that in 2012 the average automobile was 16 years old. At that rate, it will take decades for the fleet to turn over in a meaningful way. Meanwhile, policy decisions about infrastructure and public space that will shape the transportation system for the next 50 to 100 years are being made today.

—Marco Anderson

[1] In *Innovator's Dilemma*, Clayton Christensen posits a difference between *sustaining innovation* and *disruptive innovation*. The former occurs when technology is employed to improve the performance characteristics of an existing product. The latter occurs when a technology that initially has poorer performance and potentially higher costs eventually displaces an existing product due to some other beneficial characteristic, such as size, reliability, or interoperability. Christensen chronicles this process taking place over a matter of years in the case of computer hardware, but taking decades in the case of construction equipment. With some new technology, buyer patterns ("the market") can move quickly and we see major paradigm shifts. In other cases, a technology may not find a market application for decades. See Clayton M. Christensen, *The Innovator's Dilemma: The Revolutionary Book That Will Change the Way You Do Business* (Boston: Harvard Business School Press, 1997).

[2] At the 2012 Meeting of the Minds conference in San Francisco, Paul Hedtke, the senior director of business development at Qualcomm, stated that the company had to devise a new business model in order to support telematics for the car industry. Qualcomm has to freeze the development of chips for eight years while a car model is in development. And they have to continue to support their products for years after that, as the cars go into production. Meeting of the Minds 2012, http://cityminded.org/events/sanfrancisco/agenda.

FLEET TURNOVER

DESIGN

INDUSTRY

REGULATORY

TECHNOLOGY

ROADS   **1869**

First bicycle appears
on the streets of
Los Angeles

TOLL ROADS

HIGHWAYS

TRANSIT   **1869**

**FIRST RAILWAY
IN SOUTHERN
CALIFORNIA OPENS**

PARKING

California admitted to the
Union as the 31st state

FEDERAL

1850

LOCAL

PLANNING

REGULATORY

L.A. County
population: 1,610

L.A. County
population: 4,385

DEMOGRAPHICS

1850   **1860**

1896 | DESIGN

GOTTLIEB DAIMLER BUILDS THE FIRST MOTOR TRUCK WITH A FOUR-HORSEPOWER ENGINE AND A BELT DRIVE WITH TWO FORWARD SPEEDS AND ONE REVERSE

1897 | INDUSTRY

First known automobile in Los Angeles

REGULATORY

William Morrison of Des Moines, Iowa, builds the first successful electric automobile in the United States

Henry Gaylord Wilshire builds Wilshire Blvd. to service newly developed residential tracts near present-day MacArthur Park

TECHNOLOGY

1891

1880   **1890**   ROADS

MAIN STREET OPENS, FIRST PAVED ROAD IN LOS ANGELES

Bicyclist   **1895**
organizations successfully lobby local and state agencies for paved streets and roads

TOLL ROADS

HIGHWAYS

1880   **1885**   **1895**   TRANSIT

Rail line extended between Los Angeles and San Pedro

Santa Fe Railroad completes a second transcontinental rail line into Los Angeles

HENRY HUNTINGTON DEVELOPS THE FIRST SEGMENT OF THE LOS ANGELES INTERURBAN RAILWAY

PARKING

FEDERAL

LOCAL

PLANNING

REGULATORY

FIRST MASSIVE MIGRATION OF MIDWESTERNERS INTO SOUTHERN CALIFORNIA

L.A. County population: 12,394

DEMOGRAPHICS

1880   **1885**

FLEET TURNOVER

DESIGN

INDUSTRY

1908

Taxicabs appear for
the first time in
Los Angeles

1914

Ford Motor Co. opens
the first automobile
assembly plant in Los
Angeles for Model T's

REGULATORY

1900

TECHNOLOGY

Of the 4,192 cars
produced in the United
States, 28% are
powered by electricity

1912

**CHARLES KETTERING
INVENTS THE FIRST
PRACTICAL ELECTRIC
AUTOMOBILE STARTER**

1913

Peerless introduces a centrifugal
governor, advertising "maintain speed
whether up hill or down"

California
State
Legislature
authorizes the
painting of
center lines on
highways

ROADS

1912

First appearance of manually
operated traffic signals
(Salt Lake City, Utah)

1924

First national conference
on street and highway
safety recommends white
on red background for
stop signs

TOLL ROADS

HIGHWAYS

Henry Huntington
forms the Pacific
Electric Railway Co.

1902

TRANSIT

1901

First Pacific Electric "red car" begins
operation along Long Beach Avenue
and Willowbrook Avenue

1924

Major Street Traffic Plan proposes
first parkways across Los Angeles

Downtown
Los Angeles
parking ban
(established,
then lifted)

1924

**PEAK MILEAGE
& RIDESHIP
OF PACIFIC
ELECTRIC
STREETCAR
SYSTEM**

PARKING

1917

A downtown entrepreneur
leases an empty lot and
advertises off-street
parking for 5 cents

1920

Reinforced
concrete
becomes the
cheap, global
standard
building
material
for parking
structures

FEDERAL

LOCAL

1924

Los Angeles begins annexation
of neighboring cities

ZONING FIRST
UTILIZED IN THE CITY
OF LOS ANGELES

1909

1922

County Board of
Supervisors creates
Los Angeles County
Regional Planning
Commission

PLANNING

REGULATORY

**U.S. AUTO
REGISTRATIONS: 8,000**

DEMOGRAPHICS

L.A. County
population: 500,000

1910

**U.S. AUTO
REGISTRATIONS:
8,000,000**

L.A. County
population: 936,000

1920

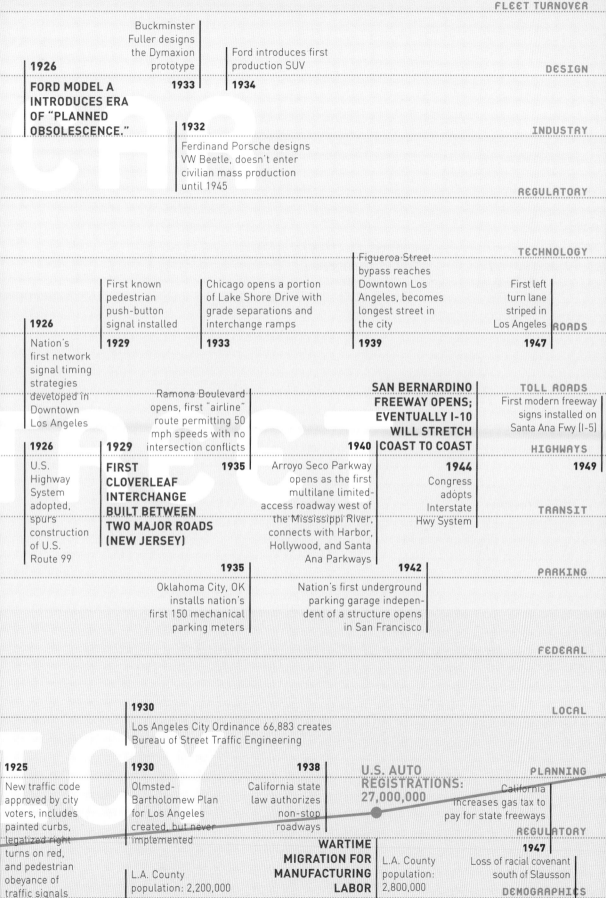

FLEET TURNOVER

Buckminster
Fuller designs
the Dymaxion
prototype

Ford introduces first
production SUV

1933

1934

DESIGN

1926

**FORD MODEL A
INTRODUCES ERA
OF "PLANNED
OBSOLESCENCE."**

1932

INDUSTRY

Ferdinand Porsche designs
VW Beetle, doesn't enter
civilian mass production
until 1945

REGULATORY

TECHNOLOGY

Figueroa Street
bypass reaches
Downtown Los
Angeles, becomes
longest street in
the city

First known
pedestrian
push-button
signal installed

Chicago opens a portion
of Lake Shore Drive with
grade separations and
interchange ramps

First left
turn lane
striped in
Los Angeles

1926

1929

1933

1939

1947

ROADS

Nation's
first network
signal timing
strategies
developed in
Downtown
Los Angeles

Ramona Boulevard
opens, first "airline"
route permitting 50
mph speeds with no
intersection conflicts

**SAN BERNARDINO
FREEWAY OPENS;
EVENTUALLY I-10
WILL STRETCH
COAST TO COAST**

First modern freeway
signs installed on
Santa Ana Fwy (I-5)

TOLL ROADS

1926

1929

1940

HIGHWAYS

U.S.
Highway
System
adopted,
spurs
construction
of U.S.
Route 99

**FIRST
CLOVERLEAF
INTERCHANGE
BUILT BETWEEN
TWO MAJOR ROADS
(NEW JERSEY)**

1935

Arroyo Seco Parkway
opens as the first
multilane limited-
access roadway west of
the Mississippi River;
connects with Harbor,
Hollywood, and Santa
Ana Parkways

1944

Congress
adopts
Interstate
Hwy System

1949

TRANSIT

1935

1942

PARKING

Oklahoma City, OK
installs nation's
first 150 mechanical
parking meters

Nation's first underground
parking garage indepen-
dent of a structure opens
in San Francisco

FEDERAL

1930

LOCAL

Los Angeles City Ordinance 66,883 creates
Bureau of Street Traffic Engineering

1925

1930

1938

U.S. AUTO
REGISTRATIONS:
27,000,000

PLANNING

New traffic code
approved by city
voters, includes
painted curbs,
legalized right
turns on red,
and pedestrian
obeyance of
traffic signals

Olmsted-
Bartholomew Plan
for Los Angeles
created, but never
implemented

California state
law authorizes
non-stop
roadways

California
increases gas tax to
pay for state freeways

REGULATORY

1947

Loss of racial covenant
south of Slausson

**WARTIME
MIGRATION FOR
MANUFACTURING
LABOR**

L.A. County
population:
2,800,000

L.A. County
population: 2,200,000

DEMOGRAPHICS

1930

1940

1948

FLEET TURNOVER

DESIGN

INDUSTRY

**FORD INTRODUCES SAFETY BELTS
AND PADDED DASH BOARDS**

1956

1964

Ford introduces
the Mustang

REGULATORY

1963

U.S. mandates lap
seat belts in cars

1965

UNSAFE AT ANY SPEED
BY RALPH NADER

TECHNOLOGY

1958

Chrysler introduces
the first modern cruise
control on the Imperial

1971

Chrysler
introduces
computerized
anti-lock
braking
system
(ABS) on
the Imperial

ROADS

Sepulveda Boulevard
underpass running
beneath LAX becomes
first tunnel of its kind

1953

1970

First speed bumps
installed as traffic
calming device (Delft,
the Netherlands)

TOLL ROADS

**CITY OF
L.A. BEGINS
INSTALLING
OVERHEAD
FREEWAY
GUIDE
SIGNS**

Embarcadero
Fwy opens in
San Francisco

1974

First HOV facility
in L.A. County

HIGHWAYS

1955

1958

1973

First Southern California
HOV lane (I-10 Busway
between El Monte and
Downtown L.A.), opened to
3 or more persons

TRANSIT

1953

Metropolitan Coach Lines acquires
Pacific Electric's passenger
service franchise

1961

Last Red Car
trolley lines
cease operation

PARKING

**INTERSTATE HIGHWAY ACT
PASSES, ESTABLISHING
INTRA-URBAN SEGMENTS,
HWY TRUST FUND, AND 9:1
FEDERAL/STATE FUNDING**

Congress passes Urban
Mass Transit Act, providing
capital grants for up to
two-thirds of transit
capital improvements

FEDERAL

1955

Congress fails to pass an
interstate highway act

1956

1964

U.S. AUTO
REGISTRATIONS:
62,000,000

LOCAL

1958

MTA begins operation
as the first public
transit agency to serve
Los Angeles County

1964

Southern California Rapid
Transit District established,
operating arm of Los Angeles
County bus transit system

PLANNING

1959

DMV sends out
2.8 million travel
surveys in L.A.,
Orange, and
Ventura counties

NEPA signed
into federal law

REGULATORY

1967

California
establishes
the Air
Resources
Board (ARB)

1969

CEQA
signed
into law

1970

L.A. County
population: 4,000,000

DEMOGRAPHICS

1950

L.A. County
population: 6,000,000

1960

L.A. County pop.:
7,000,000

1970

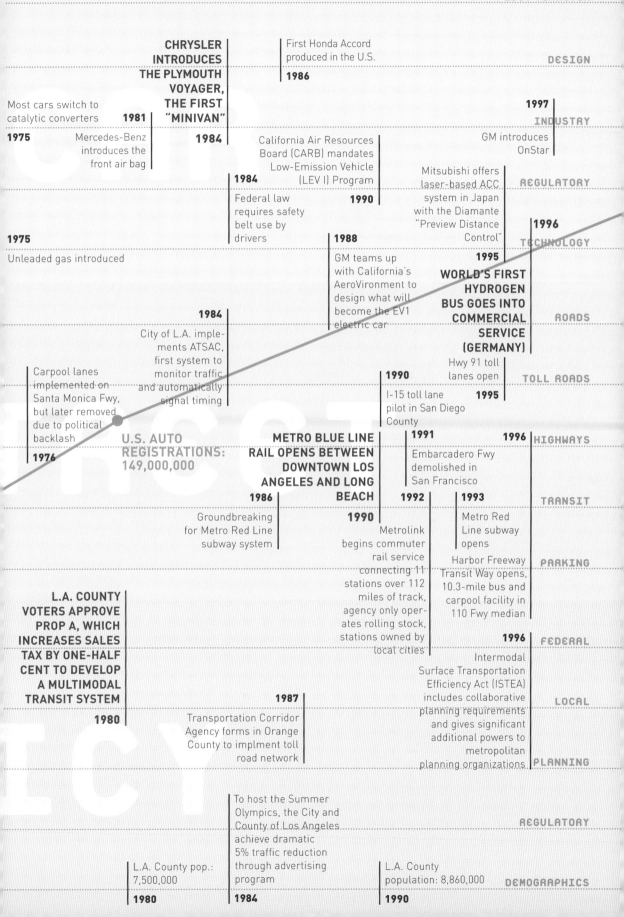

CHRYSLER INTRODUCES THE PLYMOUTH VOYAGER, THE FIRST "MINIVAN"

First Honda Accord produced in the U.S.
1986

DESIGN

Most cars switch to catalytic converters   **1981**

1997

INDUSTRY

1975

Mercedes-Benz introduces the front air bag   **1984**

GM introduces OnStar

California Air Resources Board (CARB) mandates Low-Emission Vehicle (LEV I) Program
1984

Mitsubishi offers laser-based ACC system in Japan with the Diamante "Preview Distance Control"

REGULATORY

Federal law requires safety belt use by drivers   **1990**

1996

TECHNOLOGY

1975

Unleaded gas introduced

1988

GM teams up with California's AeroVironment to design what will become the EV1 electric car

1995

WORLD'S FIRST HYDROGEN BUS GOES INTO COMMERCIAL SERVICE (GERMANY)

ROADS

1984

City of L.A. implements ATSAC, first system to monitor traffic and automatically signal timing

Hwy 91 toll lanes open
1990

TOLL ROADS

Carpool lanes implemented on Santa Monica Fwy, but later removed due to political backlash

I-15 toll lane pilot in San Diego County
1995

1976

U.S. AUTO REGISTRATIONS: 149,000,000

METRO BLUE LINE RAIL OPENS BETWEEN DOWNTOWN LOS ANGELES AND LONG BEACH
1990

1991

Embarcadero Fwy demolished in San Francisco
1993

1996

HIGHWAYS

Groundbreaking for Metro Red Line subway system
1986

1992

Metrolink begins commuter rail service connecting 11 stations over 112 miles of track, agency only operates rolling stock, stations owned by local cities

Metro Red Line subway opens

Harbor Freeway Transit Way opens, 10.3-mile bus and carpool facility in 110 Fwy median

TRANSIT

PARKING

L.A. COUNTY VOTERS APPROVE PROP A, WHICH INCREASES SALES TAX BY ONE-HALF CENT TO DEVELOP A MULTIMODAL TRANSIT SYSTEM

1996

Intermodal Surface Transportation Efficiency Act (ISTEA) includes collaborative planning requirements and gives significant additional powers to metropolitan planning organizations

FEDERAL

1980

1987

Transportation Corridor Agency forms in Orange County to implement toll road network

LOCAL

PLANNING

To host the Summer Olympics, the City and County of Los Angeles achieve dramatic 5% traffic reduction through advertising program

REGULATORY

L.A. County pop.: 7,500,000
1980

L.A. County population: 8,860,000
1990

1984

DEMOGRAPHICS

2000   **2013**   **2024**

FLEET TURNOVER

Widespread application of
autonomous technology to
transit vehicles in urban areas

DESIGN

| | | Nissan Leaf and Chevy Volt introduced | | Mercedes-Benz introduces Jam Assist semi-automated adaptive cruise control | Manufacturers encourage acceptance of onboard "black box" systems |

Decade-long trend: long term reliability improving and engines being sealed by manufacturers | 11.4 million natural gas vehicles worldwide | Nissan Leaf and Chevy Volt introduced |

INDUSTRY

2000   **2009**   **2011**   **2012** Prius plug-in introduced   **2017**   **2018**   **2022**

REGULATORY

• U.S. AUTO REGISTRATIONS: 213,000,000

Acura introduces the first adaptive cruise control in the U.S. with a collision mitigation braking system.

Transition from hybrids to plug-in hybrids

Widespread deployment of CNG home fueling technology

2012 PZEV Standards are the least stringent standards for vehicles by 2020

TECHNOLOGY

2004   **2006**   **2008**   **2011**   **2015**   **2019**   **2020**   **2022**

First retail-style hydrogen fueling station, supporting publicly leased Honda fuel cell vehicles

Ports of L.A. & Long Beach introduce emissions-free, 30-ton container hauler

First fuel cell vehicles commercially available in California and other select markets

Hands off/feet off test vehicles deployed in select markets

ROADS

2010
Gerald Diamond Bridge ends structural life

TOLL ROADS

2009   **2012**   **2013**

I-15 variable toll lane opens | San Diego I-15 toll lane completion | I-10 and I-110 HOT lanes operational in L.A. County

HIGHWAYS

2009   **2010**   **2018**

210 extension, last new freeway segment in So Cal | L.A. County has 512 miles of HOV lanes and 132.2 HOV lane miles currently in construction | I-5 improvement project from L.A. County line to I-605, and from SR-134 to the mountains. Last major traditional interstate widening project in L.A. County

2000   **2022**

TRANSIT

2005   **2012**

Last three stations of the 15-year $4.7 billion Metro subway project open | Metro Orange Line opens as the first grade-separated Bus Rapid Transit line in the Metro system | Metro Expo Line opens to Culver City | Metro Westside Purple Line opens to V.A. Center at 405 Fwy

PARKING

FEDERAL

2005

"Watch the Road" safety campaign launched in Los Angeles | SAFETEA-LU | Measure M passes in L.A. County, refocusing on transit investment

Majority of U.S. states pass enabling legislation for autonomous vehicles similar to Nevada, Florida, and California

LOCAL

2004   **2008**

SCAG adopts 2012 RTP/SCS

Widespread deployment of "black box" recording systems in new cars

PLANNING

2006   **2010**   **2012**   **2020**

Ports of L.A. & Long Beach adopt San Pedro Bay Ports Clean Air Action Plan | Nevada State DMV approves autonomous vehicles

REGULATORY

2016   **2019**   **2021**

L.A. County population: 9,500,000 | L.A. County population: 9,819,000 | Lawsuit against doctor who allowed elderly woman to drive | CAFÉ Standards require 35.5 mpg | Auto manufacturers fail to achieve strict interpretation of CAFÉ Standards mid-review

DEMOGRAPHICS

2000   **2010**   **2012**

FLEET TURNOVER

U.S. AUTO REGISTRATIONS: 285,000,000

Numerous reports of auto drive feature malfunction, auto makers face major liability test

2025

Many reports of auto drive malfunction prove to be false, similar to the Toyota acceleration issues of 2011

2029

DESIGN

INDUSTRY

REGULATORY

Fully autonomous self-navigating car for sale to the public

2029

Significant decline in number of traditional gas-only fueling stations

2030

2035

Fully autonomous vehicles comprise 5-10% of all new vehicles sold

TECHNOLOGY

I-10 potential HOT lanes completed from Downtown Los Angeles to Redlands

2025

Widespread deployment of congestion pricing and cordon pricing throughout United States

I-15 HOT lane open from Hwy 395 in San Bernardino all the way to San Diego

2035

SCAG HOT lane network completed

ROADS

TOLL ROADS

4 existing light rail lines reconfigured: Azusa to Long Beach and East L.A. to Santa Monica

2025

2028

Metro Green Line opens to LAX airport

Metro Green Line extended from Redondo Beach to South Bay Transit Center

2035

Metro Westside Purple Line subway opens to V.A. Center at 405 Fwy

2036

2039

Metro San Fernando Valley I-405 transit corridor connects San Fernando Valley transit to Metro Westside Purple Line subway and Metro Expo Line

HIGHWAYS

TRANSIT

PARKING

FEDERAL

LOCAL

Most states change licensing language from driver to operator

2027

U.S. implements recommended Federal VMT Tax

2025

CAFÉ standards require 54.5 mpg fleetwide average

Planning horizon for SCAG 2012-2035 RTP/SCS and for SB375 goals

2035

Advocacy groups question current (circa 2012) seatbelt regulations

2035

L.A. County population: 11,000,000

2035

PLANNING

REGULATORY

DEMOGRAPHICS

CRUISE NITE
Galaxy Hamburger
5-9pm

1st Saturday of every month

No Cruise in July

Aug 6th
Sept 3rd
Oct 1st
Nov 5th
Dec 3rd

Trophies
50/50
Raffle

All Custom vehicles & bikes welcome

All Car Clubs & Solo's welcome

Roll in 5-7pm

$5 per Ride
To Show

2150 S. Archibald Ave
Ontario, Ca

XTREME LOWE
O.C. Chapter
909-636-7198

D&G Kustoms
951-522-3933

FURTHER READING

CARS AND PLACES

Funaro, G.H., and B. Baker. *Parking*. New York: Reinhold, 1958.

Henley, Simon. *The Architecture of Parking*. London: Thames & Hudson, 2007.

Klose, Dietrich. *Multi-Storey Car Parks and Garages*. London: Architectural Press, 1965

McAvey, Maureen, Uwe Brandes, and Matthew Johnston. *The City in 2050: Creating Blueprints for Change*. Washington: Urban Land Institute, 2008.

McDonald, Shannon Sanders. *The Parking Garage: Design and Evolution of a Modern Urban Form*. Washington: Urban Land Institute, 2007.

Mitchell, William J., Chris E. Borroni-Bird, and Lawrence D. Burns. *Reinventing the Automobile*. Cambridge: MIT Press, 2010.

Shoup, Donald C. *The High Cost of Free Parking, Updated Edition*. Chicago: American Planning Association, 2011.

Sperling, Daniel, and Deborah Gordon. *Two Billion Cars: Driving Toward Sustainability*. New York: Oxford University Press, 2009.

Vanderbilt, Tom. *Traffic: Why We Drive the Way We Do (and What It Says About Us)*. New York: Random House, 2008.

Vollman, William T. *Imperial*. New York: Penguin, 2009.

ART AND DESIGN

Ferguson, Francis. *Architecture, Cities and the Systems Approach*. New York: George Braziller, 1975.

Finizio, Gino. *Architecture and Mobility: Tradition and Innovation*. Milan: Skira, 2006.

Gans, Deborah, *The Le Corbusier Guide*. Princeton: Princeton Architectural Press, 1987.

Gilbert-Rolfe, Jeremy. *Beauty and the Contemporary Sublime*. New York: Allworth Press, 1999.

Jones, John Christopher. *Design Methods: Seeds of Human Futures*. New York and Chichester: John Wiley and Sons, 1970. 3rd edition, 1992.

Sadler, Simon. *Archigram: Architecture without Architects*. Cambridge: MIT Press, 2005.

Schnapp, Jeffrey T., ed., *Speed Limits*. Milan: Skira Editore, CCA, and Miami: Florida International University, 1999.

Thackara, John. *In the Bubble: Designing in a Complex World*. Cambridge: MIT Press, 2005.

Parking Lot Dance by Anita Pace.
Photo by Warren Neidich.

CONTRIBUTORS

MARCO ANDERSON is a senior regional planner with the Southern California Association of Governments (SCAG). He currently works in the Sustainability division integrating land use and transportation policy. Anderson is currently the project manager for SCAG-funded local land use plans and studies, the EV Readiness Program, and the Toolbox Tuesdays program of training sessions for planners from the SCAG region. Anderson lived car-lite in Orange County for eight months, but was tempted back into two-car ownership with the arrival of the 2011 Kia Soul and the commuting needs of a toddler in suburbia. He still can be seen riding to the train station on his modified 1988 Schwinn Circuit with a steel-lugged frame.

COLLEEN CORCORAN is a graphic designer and design educator in Los Angeles. Her design and advocacy work focuses on ways to use design as a tool for education and positive change within the urban environment. She has collaborated on projects with a variety of public agencies and community organizations around Los Angeles, including Los Angeles Metro's in-house Design Studio, the City of Santa Monica Bike Program, Museum of Contemporary Art, Center for the Arts Eagle Rock, and the Green LA Coalition. Her graphic design work has been published in *GOOD*, *Print* magazine, Design Mind, and other print and online publications. She is a co-founder and board member of CicLAvia, an organization that opens several miles of streets in Los Angeles as a temporary park space on Sunday mornings.

ALAN DOBBINS is a vice president and senior research analyst with Conning Research and Consulting, focused on the automobile and homeowners insurance markets. Prior to joining Conning, Dobbins was a management consultant with both BearingPoint and IBM Business Consulting Services. As a management consultant, he worked with insurers and other financial services clients on issues of strategy, performance measurement, management information, and cost management. Dobbins began his career as a commercial lines underwriter and has worked in finance, marketing, and product development. He holds a master of business administration degree from the University of Rochester and a bachelor of arts degree from Colgate University.

STEVE FINNEGAN has over 20 years of experience in transportation, finance, business, and advocacy. His career includes work as a financial analyst with Bank of America, positions in planning and operations with the Los Angeles County Metropolitan Transportation Authority, serving as a management consultant to public agencies and nonprofit organizations, and leading government affairs, community relations, traffic safety, advocacy, and public policy work for the Automobile Club of Southern California. Finnegan received a master of arts degree in urban planning from the University of California at Los Angeles and a bachelor of arts from Claremont McKenna College. Finnegan loves to walk and takes transit and bikes when he can, but he treasures the freedom and opportunities that come with driving his own car—a 2008 Prius.

JEREMY GILBERT-ROLFE is a painter who also writes about art and related topics. His paintings are part of several public collections, including the Museum of Contemporary Art, Los Angeles, and his written works include *Immanence and Contradiction* (1985), *Beyond Piety* (1995), *Frank Gehry: The City and Music* (2000), and

Beauty and the Contemporary Sublime (2000). Born in England in 1945, he has lived in America since 1968, and in Los Angeles since 1980. He is chair of Graduate Studies in Art at Art Center College of Design and visiting tutor at the (British) Royal Academy.

CHRISTOPHER GRAY, AICP, is a senior associate with Fehr & Peers Transportation Consultants working out of their Irvine and Riverside offices. He has 15 years experience in multi-modal transportation planning, corridor studies, travel demand forecasting, parking studies, transit studies, and Smart Growth. His work includes projects in California, other states in the United States, and even international locations. He is a member of many professional organizations related to land use and transportation planning, including APA, CNU, ULI, and AEP. Gray enjoys planning and using all modes of transportation, ranging from automobiles, trains, and cruise ships to underwater modes, such as scuba diving.

A native of South Los Angles, **TERRY A. HAYES** grew up with a strong affinity for cars, which was encouraged by both his parents. His excitement about cars led to an epic drive in a small Fiat from Los Angeles to Boston, where he began his professional planning studies at the Harvard Graduate School of Design. With a master's degree in city planning, Hayes continued with his interest in cars and his training in community impact in his work with Alan Voorhees, Skidmore Owings and Merrill, and Gruen Associates. This focus has continued with Hayes's own firm, which he founded in 1984. His interest has broadened to include the assessment of the community and environmental justice impacts of most forms of transportation infrastructure (highways, railroads, buses, and rail transit). Outside

of work, Hayes has restored a classic 1967 Mini. And for fun he races his Ferrari P3 in a computer simulation of the historic 400-mile Sicilian Targa Florio.

SIMON HENLEY is an architect and director of Henley Halebrown Rorrison in London. He studied at the University of Liverpool and in Eugene at the University of Oregon. Henley combines practice with writing and research, and is the author of *The Architecture of Parking* (2007). He teaches at the University of Southampton School of Engineering and is a Fellow of the Royal Society of Arts. In 1991, he traveled 13,500 miles around the United States in five weeks, in search of the finest structures on the continent: the great multi-story car park. These days he is addicted to his bicycle, a fold-up Brompton, on which he goes everywhere. Henley has combined these two interests in leading cycle tours of multistory car parks in London.

MARK HOFFMAN is a Senior Planner in community planning, housing, and health for the Ontario, California office of The Planning Center|DC&E, an urban planning and environmental consulting firm. Hoffman has been working for more than 20 years with local government, hospitals, and nonprofit organizations on a wide variety of community projects. These include comprehensive planning, housing and community development, municipal service reviews, and strategic plans. His recent work has focused on integrating public health and comprehensive planning to create healthier communities. Hoffman's work has received multiple awards from sections of the American Planning Association, the Southern California Public Health Association, and other organizations. Hoffman completed his undergraduate work in public administration at Biola University, and holds two masters degrees in public policy and in planning and development studies from the University of Southern California. As a resident of the Inland Empire, he could not imagine a day without a car.

JIHA HWANG is a visual interaction designer currently living in Chicago. She grew up in Korea but decided to move to the United States to fulfill her dream of studying art. In her work, she often combines several different disciplines, such as art, psychology, biology, and computer science. Her interest is in researching the inner relationship between physical objects and human beings and imagining how technologies can play an important role between them to create provocative designs for the near future. She graduated from School of the Art Institute of Chicago with a major in visual communication, and studied media design at Art Center College of Design in Pasadena. She owns a car but has a horrible sense of direction; she cannot drive without her best friend—GPS.

JOHN CHRIS JONES was born in Wales in 1927. He lives in London without a car but with a free pass on buses and trains throughout the city. He was formally educated in engineering, art, and ergonomics and self-educated in design through childhood projects such as building a hut, an air raid shelter, a canoe, and a primitive cinema in the attic. His car of the future that appears in this book was a balsawood model that won a prize in a public competition in 1946. His design for the automation of road traffic was entered in another competition in the early 1960s. It has yet to be realized as a complete system but is appearing in bits and pieces. His best-known book, *Design Methods* (1970/1980/1992) is still in print and has appeared in Japanese, Spanish, Polish, Romanian, Russian, and Chinese. His latest book, *the internet and everyone*, and his newsletter, *Daffodil*, can be obtained via his website: www.softopia.demon.co.uk.

JEREMY KLOP is a Principal with Fehr & Peers transportation consultants in Los Angeles, CA. He has advised decision makers throughout the western U.S., seeking to improve communities through careful stewardship of transportation systems. His work with leaders in both Denver and Los Angeles contributed to major changes in roadway classification and performance measurement systems. He has published articles in the *Transportation Research Record* and co-authored the Pedestrian and Bicycle Planning chapter of the *Transportation Planning Handbook* for the Institute of Transportation Engineers. He grew up on two wheels, riding BMX bikes, dirt bikes, and an enduro motorcycle during his high school years in Chino, CA (and lived!). Still riding mostly mountain bikes and loving high speeds, he has completed the grueling Leadville Trail 100, a one-hundred-mile bike race across extreme terrain of the Colorado Rockies, all above 10,000 feet.

SANG-EUN LEE lives in Los Angeles. She grew up in Korea and studied English and French language and literature in Seoul before coming to Southern California to study transportation design. Her creativity and desire for a sustainable world led her to come up with the idea of the origami manufacturing process for transportation design. She worked as a design intern at BMW Designworks in California and Renault Samsung in Korea. She recently graduated from Art Center with a degree in transportation design. She wants to instill a soul into the cars of the future in order to help buyers identify themselves with the car and, at the same time, for the car to be harmonious with

CONTRIBUTORS

the environment. She has a 2001 Ford Taurus that has been her bed, cafe, truck, and best friend during her time at Art Center.

STEVE MAZOR, audiophile and Trekkie, is the chief automotive engineer at the Automobile Club of Southern California. He has served as manager of the Club's Automotive Research Center (ARC) in Diamond Bar, California, since 1985. The ARC is a state-of-the-art automotive emissions/fuel economy/performance laboratory producing research on subjects including fuel economy, emissions, cost of operation, vehicle technology, safety, maintenance/repair, air quality, and aftermarket products. Mazor was test engineer on the electric and hybrid vehicle project and the U.S. Army's methanol fuel project at the Jet Propulsion Laboratory from 1980 to 1986, as well as the fuel system development engineer for Ford in Michigan from 1978 to 1980. Mazor received a bachelor of science degree in automotive engineering from the University of California at Los Angeles in 1978, where he led a team that designed, built, demonstrated, and campaigned several hydrogen-fueled passenger cars. He served a year as chairman of the Southern California Section of the Society of Automotive Engineers.

SHANNON SANDERS MCDONALD is a practicing licensed architect and assistant professor in architecture at Southern Illinois University, in Carbondale, Illinois, who is exploring the future of mobility, sustainability, and design. Her book *The Parking Garage: Design and Evolution of a Modern Urban Form*, published by the Urban Land Institute, was the basis for an exhibit at the National Building Museum titled "House of Cars." She is a frequent speaker on architecture, parking, transportation, sustainability, and community issues, including for the

Library of Congress, the American Planning Association, and the American Institute of Architects. McDonald is a 1992 graduate of the Yale School of Architecture, and worked with Carol Ross Barney in designing the award-winning Little Village Academy, in Chicago. She has also worked on many other community and transportation-related projects. Being in motion to understand our world is her top priority.

ERIC NOBLE is the founder and president of The CARLAB, an advanced automotive consulting firm that helps manufacturers and suppliers plan and design new vehicles. Founded in 1999, it remains the most influential automotive development consultancy in North America. The CARLAB's clients include General Motors, Honda, Subaru, Toyota, and Hyundai/KIA, among others. Noble has a BS in business economics from California State University Fullerton and accreditation in automotive technology from Saddleback College. He is a faculty member of the transportation design program at the Art Center College of Design in Pasadena, California, one of the most influential and internationally respected programs in vehicle design.

MONICA NOUWENS'S extensive print photography work and films can be found in various collections worldwide, including Stedelijk Museum, Amsterdam; Salvatore Ferragamo, Florence; Levi's, London; Prada USA Corp., New York; Imaginary Forces, Los Angeles; OMA, Rotterdam; Michael Maltzan Architecture, Los Angeles; Jon Jerde Partnership, Venice; Bartle Bogle Hegarty, London. Nouwens's solo exhibition "Rubbernecking" was displayed at the Stedelijk Museum Bureau Amsterdam. She has also had recent exhibition at the Netherlands Photography Museum

Rotterdam, the Netherlands Architecture Institute, Stedelijk Museum Helmond, Gallery Paul Andriesse in Amsterdam, and Trafalgar Square, London, for World AIDS Day. Nouwens was a lecturer at the Southern California Institute of Architecture (SCI-Arc). Her career has included publication in a number of magazines such as *Icon*, *Volume*, *Re-Magazine*, *Blueprint*, *Archis*, *Surface*, and many others. Nouwens completed a postgraduate fellowship in Art Media Studies at the Rijksakademie in Amsterdam and attended the California Institute of the Arts exchange program for film and photography, where she developed a fascination with California's urban landscapes. Nouwens has a car. Her website is www.paradox.nl/lookatme.

SIMON PASTUCHA lives in Los Angeles without a car. He leads the Urban Design Studio of the Los Angeles Department of City Planning. He began a 20-year career after graduating from California State Polytechnic University, Pomona with a degree in landscape architecture with an emphasis on ecosystematic design. He was part of the core team that developed the first context-sensitive street solutions in the city. Pastucha implemented new design details in the City Engineer's Street Standard plans and now works on creating simplified processes for the adaptation of roadways, flexible development standards for new construction, and a community-based vision for the city. He teaches, lectures, and writes on the subject of urban design and the adaptation of cities.

MOHAMMAD POORSARTEP is project manager at the Connected Vehicle Proving Center (CVPC) at the University of Michigan–Dearborn, where he leads and oversees transportation-oriented projects with emphasis on autonomous and connected vehicle technology. Poorsartep's typical day in the office includes business development, industry outreach, training, and research, just to name a few. He has a penchant for advanced technologies, especially when he gets the chance to look at them from a strategy point of view. He has worked on a variety of projects: forecasting future technologies for autonomous vehicles, autonomous driving solutions for vehicle testing/evaluation/verification, performing market research analysis and formulating market entry strategies, providing strategic roadmaps for automotive suppliers, and so on. He received his BS in civil engineering in 2004, with an emphasis on transportation, and in 2008 received his MBA. He received a second master's degree, in industrial engineering, from the Rackham School of Graduate Studies, University of Michigan–Dearborn, in 2010.

KATI RUBINYI is project director of the Car Future Group and the founder of the non-profit Civic Projects Foundation. Civic Projects initiates and develops creative public benefit projects, experimenting with new approaches that combine planning and design. Rubinyi did innovative work for The Planning Center, a consulting firm in Orange County, California, and previously was an instructor in architectural history and design studio. This followed years with architecture firms, working mostly on institutional buildings. Originally from Montreal, Canada, Rubinyi has a B.A. in philosophy and a B.Arch. degree in professional architecture. She received architectural registration in 1998 before moving to Southern California to pursue an MFA from the Art Center College of Design's graduate fine art program. She looks forward to the day that texting while driving is legal.

CONTRIBUTORS

THOMAS SMILEY is an industrial design graduate student at the Art Center College of Design in Pasadena, CA. He previously interned at the consulting firm The CARLAB in Orange, California. At The CARLAB he worked on advanced planning projects for major original equipment manufacturers (OEM), helping them to predict the future of automobiles. While working at The CARLAB, Smiley worked on a research project involving alternative fuel vehicles with a focus on hybrid cars. His research took thirteen years of hybrid vehicle sales and tied them to vehicle attributes and market forces, creating a predictive formula that can accurately predict the sales potential of a hybrid automobile. At Art Center, he is focusing his studies on automotive product planning and how design influences the automotive experience.

JOHN STUTSMAN, who grew up in Indianapolis within earshot of the Indy 500 and later sold newspapers on race day during the glory years of the Offy Roadsters and the inimitable supercharged V-8 Novi race cars, at one point considered attending the General Motors Institute. Instead, he pursued mechanical engineering at Purdue University. Discovering that his interests were more in the area of fluid mechanics and heat transfer, he had a brief stint in aerospace engineering, working on both launch and re-entry vehicles. Recognizing that this was important work for the nation, but not for him, he returned to school to pursue urban and regional planning at the University of Southern California. Though an auto enthusiast, his professional career has focused on urban transit projects that provide a viable alternative to our auto-dominated, increasingly gridlocked, and fragmented communities. Stutsman is a principal at the transportation planning firm Fehr & Peers.

DOUG SUISMAN, FAIA, is an internationally recognized, award-winning urban designer and architect. He founded Suisman Urban Design in 1990 to build city places through an innovative process combining architecture, research, planning, landscape design, filmmaking, and graphic design. His projects include transit systems, downtowns, cultural districts, civic and community centers, plazas, parks, and streetscapes. In partnership with RAND Corporation, Suisman designed The Arc, an acclaimed plan for a new Palestinian state which won the top master plan prize and the Future Project of the Year award at the 2010 World Architecture Festival in Barcelona. His current iQuilt cultural district plan for downtown Hartford has won an AIA Honor Award and two major grants from the National Endowment for the Arts.

A former London bus driver (routes 43 and 134), **JOHN THACKARA** is a writer, educator, and design producer. He is the author of *In the Bubble: Designing in a Complex World* (MIT Press) and of a widely read blog at designobserver.com. As director of Doors of Perception, Thackara organizes festivals around the world in which communities imagine sustainable futures, and take practical steps to realize them. The most recent Doors, in Delhi, was about food systems and design. It brought together paradigm-changing designers, technology innovators, and grassroots innovators. Thackara—a Brit who now lives in southern France—studied philosophy and trained as a journalist, before working for ten years as a book and magazine editor. He was the first director (1993–99) of the Netherlands Design Institute in Amsterdam and was program director of Designs of the Time (Dott 07), a new social innovation biennial in England. Thackara is a fellow of The Young Foundation, the United

Kingdom's social enterprise incubator, and sits on the advisory boards of the Pixelache Festival in Helsinki and the Pecha Kucha Foundation in Tokyo. He is also a member of the United Kingdom Parliament's Standing Commission on Design.

BILL TRIMBLE grew up in Lakewood, California, an early post-WWII suburb where he could go almost everywhere on his bicycle. He has worked for more than twenty years as a land use planner with the city of Pasadena, California. In the twenty-two years between Lakewood and Pasadena, he learned to walk at the University of California, Berkeley, and then in cities from Albuquerque to New Haven. He continues to learn. Pasadena's specific place in the Los Angeles region gives him plenty of opportunities to consider how people get from one place to another. In Pasadena, he gives much of his attention to the connections—historical and future—between the city and the rest of Southern California.

After a successful global career as a car designer and now as a transportation design educator, **GEOFFREY WARDLE** is passionate about bringing visionary design and systems thinking to future transportation solutions. He believes designers should lead the facilitation of the many disciplines required to create smart, sustainable and fulfilling mobility. He is particularly interested in the research and development of autonomous road vehicles, which he believes could be the silver bullet for the automobile industry and for sustainable personal mobility. Wardle is Executive Director, Graduate Transportation Design at the renowned Art Center College of Design in Pasadena, California. This new major is the result of extensive research that Geoff has done in the past few years as Director of Advanced Mobility within the

Graduate Industrial Design department. He is cofounder of OnGoing Transportation and consults with select vehicle manufacturers on design and innovative product development strategies. Having enjoyed his time as a car designer, Wardle is now repenting for his sins by focusing his energies on solving the issues that automobiles bring to the world as well as their pleasures.

In spite of a nineteen-year student career studying architecture in a program that was supposed to take but five years, **MICHAEL WEBB** nevertheless participated in the "Visionary Architecture" exhibition at the Museum of Modern Art, New York, in 1961. In 1963 he became an FT Visionary (a pretentious term with its overtones of mysticism, but what else will do!) in the newly formed Archigram Group. The group's output concerned the making of a new architecture that could stand alongside the space hardware and the explosion of new media and fashion then transforming British society. Since then he has produced the Drive-in House project, a study of the relationship between our cars and the buildings we use daily, and a study of perspective projection and infinity, using as a test-bed site the Henley Regatta.

ACKNOWLEDGMENTS

The editor and contributors are extremely grateful to Art Center College of Design in Pasadena, California for its generous financial contribution to this project. But our project owes more to Art Center than just the financial support that helped make it possible. Several contributors are alumni or faculty members of the college and, not coincidentally, this project embodies the blend of art, design, and professional practice that is unique to Art Center.

PARTIAL FINANCIAL SUPPORT

Art Center College of Design
The Auto Club of Southern California
Fehr & Peers
The Planning Center|DC&E
Sally Kaled

THANKS TO

Phyllis Alzamora, Tim Ballard, Matt Barthes, Megan Belanger-Powrie, Juliette Bellocq, Ewan Branda, Anne Burdick, Mark Butala, Ken Chafin, Kimberly S. Clark, Nicki Dennis, David DeRosa, India Dunnington, Arwen Duffy, Tim Durfee, Fred Fehlau, Todd Gagnon, Robin Gilliam, Heather Glick, Marshall Glick, Jered Gold, Randy Jackson, Brian Judd, Sally Kaled, Jay Kim, Tony Lopez, Stuart Macey, Anna Macaulay, Geoffrey Mak, John McCord, Emily McMahon, Pat Morton, Kristina Newhouse, Anita Pace, Michael Pinto, Kim Parker, Richard Parkhurst of Motorsport Productions, Steve PonTell, Stuart Reed, Iris Regn, Wendy Shattuck, Paulette Singley, Melani Smith, Stanley So, Stephen Villavaso, Michael Warner, Valerie Watson, John Welchman, and Jon Yoder.

Image on p.63 by Mr. Artistic Precision (Adam Porrino).

Image on p.273 by Dolly Crespo.

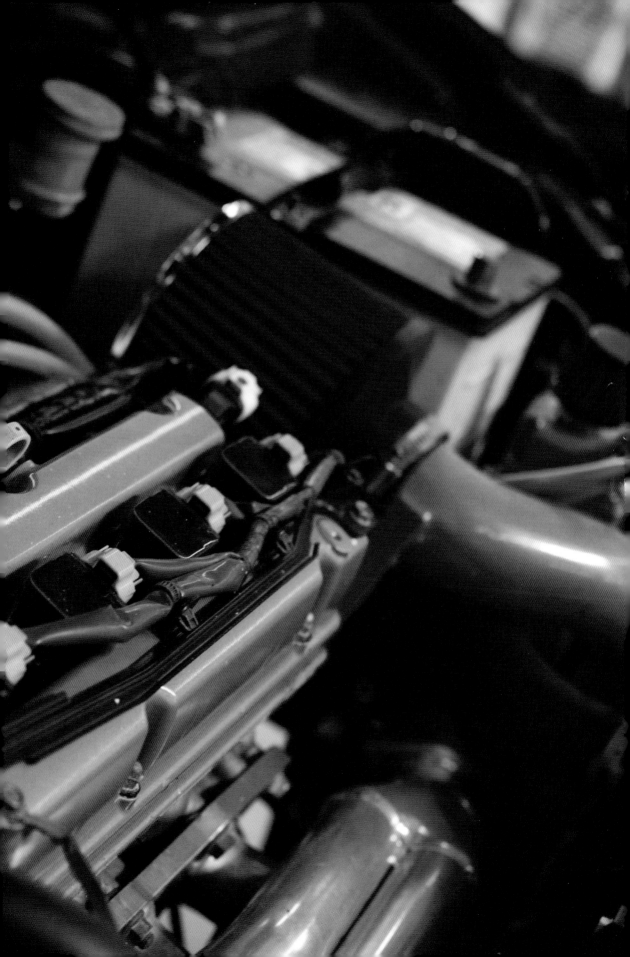

WILL HONDA G35 SNOWED IN DREAMCARS XTERRA LOWRIDER MUSTANG ROLLIN ON TRUES VOGEES
WWW TOPLOWRIDER 2007 MUSTANG WWW OGOGOG COM TRUCK XTREME IMAGE RIDE BIG MY 2ND BA
HIT SWITCHES PUTTIN THE BAGS ON BLUEBERRY HILL REACHING THE PEAK TO SUCCESS SITTING LOW
GLODEN MI OTRA S10 MY BF RID3 DIS R MY GIRLS 66 CHEVY N 04 TOYOTA TACOMA DIS R MY GIRLS LEC
CAPRICE WAGON HYDRAULICS 3 WHEEL PUMPS DAYTONS TV CHROME DV LOW SIEMPRE FIRME NISSA
CHEVY CAPRICE AIR RIDE SHAVED 1991 CAPRICE CLASSIC AFTER THE CAR WASH MOTO LOWRIDER BL
SKITTLES SKITTLES CAR MI DONK W 22 S 94 CHEVY JUICED ME AND MY 95 LOVEINIT LA MEXICAN MAFIA
THE BOSS 516 SUPERMARIO OLDS CUTLASS SUPREME 13X7 LOWRIDER OLDS CUTLASS SUPREME LOW
LOW 1963 LOW RIDER MY NISSAN SKYLINE ESPANOLA NM MY 94 CHEVY ON 22 WILL HONDA G35 SNOV
WORKING HARD LOWRIDER BIKE LOWRIDER BIKE PART LOWRIDER BIKE FROM WWW TOPLOWRIDER 2C
CHEVY MERCEDES BENZ NEXT INTERIOR PICS YOU LIKE MY CHOICE READY TO HIT SWITCHES PUTTIN TH
SO FRESH AND SO CLEAN CLEAN BIANCA WARE CAR 13 BANK SCARFACE 100 GLODEN MI OTRA S10 MY
CARS HONDAS 2007 300 22 THE CUTLASS WELO SUCH A SHOW OFF CHEVY CAPRICE WAGON HYDRAULIC
ME BACK DIS IS MY GATOR CHEVY IMPALA HER NAME IS TJ N A GATOR CHEVY CAPRICE AIR RIDE SHA
AWESOME CAR TURBO BUICK REGAL HOMICIDE AND JAZMAINE CAMION SKITTLES SKITTLES CAR MI D
JOHANA HIS RANFLA 1963 IMPALA MY CAR MY ART WORK MY LIL LOW LOW THE BOSS 516 SUPERMARIO C
INTERIOR 1963 IMPALA 4 DOOR HARDTOP BONESBLACKYUKON MY LOW LOW 1963 LOW RIDER MY NISS
MUSTANG ROLLIN ON TRUES VOGEES MY RIDE HJJ STEFAN LAMBERT WORKING HARD LOWRIDER BIKE
XTREME IMAGE RIDE BIG MY 2ND BABY MY BABY MY 1ST BABY HEAVY CHEVY MERCEDES BENZ NEXT IN
THE PEAK TO SUCCESS SITTING LOW BOMB DIGGLE WIGGLE KIDO HAH SO FRESH AND SO CLEAN CLEA
TOYOTA TACOMA DIS R MY GIRLS LEGENDARY TIME TO GO CARS TRUCKS CARS HONDAS 2007 300 22 THE
DV LOW SIEMPRE FIRME NISSAN 370Z TROY FACET PHOTOGRAPHY HIT ME BACK DIS IS MY GATOR CHEV
WASH MOTO LOWRIDER BLUE MOTO BLUE CHOPPER THIS IS AN AWESOME CAR TURBO BUICK REGAL
LOVEINIT LA MEXICAN MAFIA HATERS WHAT 63 IMPALA LOWRIDER JOHANA HIS RANFLA 1963 IMPALA
OLDS CUTLASS SUPREME LOWRIDER 13X7 CHEVY CHEVROLET INTAKE INTERIOR 1963 IMPALA 4 DOOR
ON 22 WILL HONDA G35 SNOWED IN DREAMCARS XTERRA LOWRIDER MUSTANG ROLLIN ON TRUES VC
FROM WWW TOPLOWRIDER 2007 MUSTANG WWW OGOGOG COM TRUCK XTREME IMAGE RIDE BIG MY 2NI
TO HIT SWITCHES PUTTIN THE BAGS ON BLUEBERRY HILL REACHING THE PEAK TO SUCCESS SITTING L
100 GLODEN MI OTRA S10 MY BF RID3 DIS R MY GIRLS 66 CHEVY N 04 TOYOTA TACOMA DIS R MY GIRLS L
CAPRICE WAGON HYDRAULICS 3 WHEEL PUMPS DAYTONS TV CHROME DV LOW SIEMPRE FIRME NISSA
CHEVY CAPRICE AIR RIDE SHAVED 1991 CAPRICE CLASSIC AFTER THE CAR WASH MOTO LOWRIDER BL
SKITTLES SKITTLES CAR MI DONK W 22 S 94 CHEVY JUICED ME AND MY 95 LOVEINIT LA MEXICAN MAFIA
THE BOSS 516 SUPERMARIO OLDS CUTLASS SUPREME 13X7 LOWRIDER OLDS CUTLASS SUPREME LOW
LOW 1963 LOW RIDER MY NISSAN SKYLINE ESPANOLA NM MY 94 CHEVY ON 22 WILL HONDA G35 SNOV
WORKING HARD LOWRIDER BIKE LOWRIDER BIKE PART LOWRIDER BIKE FROM WWW TOPLOWRIDER 2C
CHEVY MERCEDES BENZ NEXT INTERIOR PICS YOU LIKE MY CHOICE READY TO HIT SWITCHES PUTTIN
SO FRESH AND SO CLEAN CLEAN BIANCA WARE CAR 13 BANK SCARFACE 100 GLODEN MI OTRA S10 MY
CARS HONDAS 2007 300 22 THE CUTLASS WELO SUCH A SHOW OFF CHEVY CAPRICE WAGON HYDRAULIC
ME BACK DIS IS MY GATOR CHEVY IMPALA HER NAME IS TJ Ń A GATOR CHEVY CAPRICE AIR RIDE SHA
AWESOME CAR TURBO BUICK REGAL HOMICIDE AND JAZMAINE CAMION SKITTLES SKITTLES CAR MI DC
JOHANA HIS RANFLA 1963 IMPALA MY CAR MY ART WORK MY LIL LOW LOW THE BOSS 516 SUPERMARIO C
INTERIOR 1963 IMPALA 4 DOOR HARDTOP BONESBLACKYUKON MY LOW LOW 1963 LOW RIDER MY NISS
MUSTANG ROLLIN ON TRUES VOGEES MY RIDE HJJ STEFAN LAMBERT WORKING HARD LOWRIDER BIKE
XTREME IMAGE RIDE BIG MY 2ND BABY MY BABY MY 1ST BABY HEAVY CHEVY MERCEDES BENZ NEXT IN
THE PEAK TO SUCCESS SITTING LOW BOMB DIGGLE WIGGLE KIDO HAH SO FRESH AND SO CLEAN CLEA
TOYOTA TACOMA DIS R MY GIRLS LEGENDARY TIME TO GO CARS TRUCKS CARS HONDAS 2007 300 22 THE
DV LOW SIEMPRE FIRME NISSAN 370Z TROY FACET PHOTOGRAPHY HIT ME BACK DIS IS MY GATOR CHEV
WASH MOTO LOWRIDER BLUE MOTO BLUE CHOPPER THIS IS AN AWESOME CAR TURBO BUICK REGAL
LOVEINIT LA MEXICAN MAFIA HATERS WHAT 63 IMPALA LOWRIDER JOHANA HIS RANFLA 1963 IMPALA
OLDS CUTLASS SUPREME LOWRIDER 13X7 CHEVY CHEVROLET INTAKE INTERIOR 1963 IMPALA 4 DOOR
ON 22 WILL HONDA G35 SNOWED IN DREAMCARS XTERRA LOWRIDER MUSTANG ROLLIN ON TRUES VO
FROM WWW TOPLOWRIDER 2007 MUSTANG WWW OGOGOG COM TRUCK XTREME IMAGE RIDE BIG MY 2ND
TO HIT SWITCHES PUTTIN THE BAGS ON BLUEBERRY HILL REACHING THE PEAK TO SUCCESS SITTING L
100 GLODEN MI OTRA S10 MY BF RID3 DIS R MY GIRLS 66 CHEVY N 04 TOYOTA TACOMA DIS R MY GIRLS LE
CAPRICE WAGON HYDRAULICS   LOW SIEMPRE FIRME NISSA
CHEVY CAPRICE AIR RIDE SHA   R WASH MOTO LOWRIDER BL
SKITTLES SKITTLES CAR MI DC   LOVEINIT LA MEXICAN MAFIA
THE BOSS 516 SUPERMARIO O   DS CUTLASS SUPREME LOW
LOW 1963 LOW RIDER MY NISSAN SKYLINE ESPANOLA NM MY 94 CHEVY ON 22 WILL HONDA G35 SNOV